I DID IT

From Iraq To Freedom: A True Story

MARK MARDIROSSIAN

I DID IT

From Iraq To Freedom: A True Story

MARK MARDIROSSIAN

CITI OF
BOOKS

CITIOFBOOKS, INC.

3736 Eubank NE Suite A1

Albuquerque, NM 87111-3579

www.citiofbooks.com

Hotline: 1 (877) 389-2759

Fax: 1 (505) 930-7244

Ordering Information:

Quantity sales. Special discounts are available on quantity purchases by corporations, associations, and others. For details, contact the publisher at the address above.

Printed in the United States of America.

ISBN-13:   Softcover   979-8-89391-391-0

                    Ebook   979-8-89391-392-7

Library of Congress Control Number: 2024921330

Table of Contents

Dedication

This book is dedicated to my parents, my grandmother and my beloved younger brother, all who have departed this world before this book was published. My parents gave me the same love about books and writing, which inspired me to write this true story about my family and the harsh truth and unforeseen circumstances which moved us to another stage in life. Thanks to the sacrifices of my parents and to some of our relatives for their financial and emotional support in helping us flee Iraq.

It is to my father that I owe this success

Acknowledgements

I wish to thank all of you who have purchased my book, "I Did It! From Iraq to Freedom". I would like to thank both of my sons for their unlimited support. To my dear wife, I can only express my love and deepest gratitude for the tireless hours spent and for her utmost dedication to help edit and bring this book to light, which is very commendable.

I want to extend a sincere thank you to my neighbor, Mrs. Celia Michel-Garcia, for encouraging me to write this true-life story.

Stating God's name is essential for me to acknowledge Him for the success of this book. His love, guidance, and protection have been my inspiration throughout my entire life. He has filled my heart and mind with His wisdom and the passion to learn loving others.

Disclaimer

All names and characters in this book are fictitious. Original names and characters have not been used to protect the individuals, their identity, and their privacy.

All other names in the "Overview of Governments and Regime Changes in Iraq" section are real from actual events and actual historical facts.

This book is a true story of the author, and it has been written to address important events in his life, which may be educational in its form, and could benefit all who want to know and learn from someone's life experiences and apply them for their own common good, or to serve humanity in general. This true story is not intended to represent or offend any individual, group, organization, family member, law enforcement agency, or friend.

The author does not intend to misrepresent or deduce in stating or making any religious or political statements to discriminate, denounce or ignore any minority groups, countries, nations, establishments or other political and non-political parties in that manner.

Introduction

Historically, Iraq is well known as the beginning of all civilization. The Garden of Eden, as it was told before our time, was located on this land. Noah's ark was built on this land, and Iraq was where God gave everyone a new and different language to speak with while they were building the tower of Babel (located today in the southwest region of the city of Baghdad) as well as trying to reach the almighty himself. In addition, kingdoms and lots of other important events throughout the history of civilization had taken place on its soil. Nevertheless, Iraq, after the Baath regime which had ruled its land, had not been bright enough to run its own affairs or to secure a better future for its own people. This land should have been proud of what it accomplished throughout its history and should have been free of evil and from wrongdoing against all humanity. But, nevertheless, during this brutal regime which took over the fate of this historic land, it proved to itself only the opposite. It's very sad for me to realize all this about a country I was born in. In theory, for anyone who is born on any soil in this world, that soil is a place called home. Unfortunately, it was not the same for me. I didn't get the same feeling being born there and living among them.

I want to leave the detail of every regime's governing events to the historians to tell since this is not what my book is about; however, these events affected my life throughout the years, and I believed in having an assurance to grow up with confidence and security. There was no guidance or role model to follow in that society other than your own family, and no just or fair treatment was practiced by the rulers toward you as an individual or society in general. The reality was the discrimination aspects which existed toward minorities by the religious clerics. The individual Iraqi couldn't plan for his/her future with certainties. All these were based on circumstances and not by the individual's planned objectives. In other words, uncertainties of planning were the dominating factors in life due to the corrupted Iraqi governing system.

My parents were able to complete elementary education only. They both loved books and reading, especially my father. He was a poet and a writer. My mother had always encouraged us to finish our education at any cost. The harsh events of their lives in Iraq had brought untold problems and specific events to their family life, which, without their sacrifices and dedication toward us, it was not possible for me to write this book.

CHAPTER

1

My Parents and Grandparents

It was a very nice, sunny spring day in April of 1953, and you could see the sunset starting to set in the golden Arabian desert in the eastern part of Iraq. A large station wagon was rolling toward an oil field petroleum station in a village called K3. My father Mike and his friend Joe were invited to another friend's house whose name was Paul and who lived in this K3 village. Hours of driving in the desert does not get you tired as much as the excitement and the purpose of the trip for Mike. He was going to visit his friend Paul, and in two days they were going to travel north to a city called Kirkuk where some of the Iraqi oil fields and refineries were located in that part of the country. Paul knew of a family in this region who had a beautiful, dark-haired and white-skinned daughter named Elisa. The time had come for her to start a family of her own and leave her father's nest behind at the age of twenty-three. It was the same situation for Mike in the year 1953 at the age of twenty-four. Paul knew that Elisa's family was in search of a well- raised, honest, family-minded, and young Christian Armenian man to marry their daughter. In addition, Paul knew that his friend Mike wouldn't fall short of their expectations. He was handsome, honest and a hardworking individual. Mike was a member of the Iraqi track and field team, which was a group of athletes who were all competing against each other to win the national championship position in order to represent Iraq in the upcoming world Olympic competitions. Iraq, at that time, was ruled by King Faisal II. Paul knew all these facts about Mike who was a qualified young man in his mind. Elisa's family was very strict and conservative, as it was with most families around the '50s in that region of the world. In the past, and especially in conservative and protective communities in the Middle East, arranged marriages was believed in and was a must. That was the way it was back then; especially with Christian Armenian families living among a Muslim society like Iraq, or it could have been the same thinking into marriage lines with other non-Christian family groups.

Paul was going to be the middle man (in this case, middle man means someone close to the family whom they trust and who would introduce the other party to them). The middle man who would cause all this to happen must be a married person in most cases. No single man can play the role of middle man. The belief was that single men were not wise or mature enough yet and, in some cases, could not be trusted. The middle man is called first, and he should be qualified to solve disagreements that happen between couples. He is to interfere to resolve some of the disputes among a newlywed couple to the best of his ability and to prevent separation of a couple because divorce was not an option at that time with Christian families, but there were some exceptions to that rule as well dictated by the local Christian church priest.

In observing today's life standards, it might seem very strange. As I'm writing this story, I see my adult boys who are sitting across the kitchen table from me. Both were born in the West; ages twenty-eight and twenty-one. They're shaking their heads and are amused at what I'm saying in writing regarding their grandparents' lives. It's hard to believe the facts.

After a long drive that day, Mike and Joe arrived at 7:00 p.m. at the gated community in the K3 village camp. Before they reached the gate, Joe stopped his car at a distance from the gate and asked Mike to jump into the back seat of his station wagon. He told him to hide underneath the bags of fruits and vegetables. Joe had bought them earlier from a vendor on the side of the road to deliver it to his uncle's house. He told Mike that he forgot to call the camp security office earlier to get a temporary security pass for him (this process would take all night if they found out that Mike didn't have a pass). "We will come back tomorrow and take care of the pass issue, or I can do it myself for you without your presence," said Joe. Mike, not knowing the region's rules, had agreed. Mike went to the back and hid himself under bags of onions, potatoes, lots of parsley, and topping it with a blanket. Joe proceeded to the gate. The soldier who was guarding the gate knew him and his uncle. This was going to ease things up a bit. Joe pulled a brand-new pack of British- made and a well-known brand of cigarettes from his pocket and handed them to the guard. The passage was finally cleared to go into the village town. Since this village was a government petroleum camp, guarding it with heavy security was a must.

Around 8:00 p.m., Paul, along with his wife and children, received Mike. Joe had to go and stay with his uncle for a few days until both Paul and Mike would return from their visit to Kirkuk and then Joe was to pick up Mike for a journey back to Baghdad. The dinner was ready as most Armenian wives always take pride in their work in the kitchen. I know this because my wife, Rosemary, is one of them, and then some.

The evening was pleasant and full of laughter. Mike had purchased some gifts from the big city (Baghdad) to give to Paul's children. The kids were very happy to receive them after they had finished their dinner. There were other gifts for Paul and his wife as well. They all had some tea after dinner. Iraq is mostly a tea-drinking country. They all went to sleep. The children slept with Paul and his wife in the master bedroom, while Mike was given the children's room as their guest.

As tired as Mike was, he had to lie down on a not so comfortable short bed. He decided to move and sleep on the floor as it was more comfortable for him to do so. Mike had to keep in mind that he had to wake up in the morning before Paul's family woke up to sleep on the bed again so that Paul didn't feel bad for Mike's arrangement. Mike knew, as well, that this was the best Paul could offer to him as an accommodation. Paul knocked on Mike's door in the morning and greeted him saying, "Hello, Mr. Groom. Wake up, wake up. You are not married yet."

When Mike woke up, he was lying on the top of the children's bed. He opened the bedroom door, and they both started laughing. Mike picked up his towel and was going to the outhouse (a bathroom set up outside the house with a floor pit toilet and cold-water faucet connected to a short hose) to wash up with fresh water and soap.

They all had breakfast together, and Paul's wife had ironed their guest's shirt and handed it to her husband, Paul, to take it to him. Her husband and Mike would be heading north; a drive of several hours on well-maintained asphalt paved roads going to the city of Kirkuk to meet with Elisa's parents. Paul's wife decided to stay behind and not take the journey with her husband because the younger child was sick.

Paul made a phone call to Elisa's home. When someone else answered the phone, Paul was shocked and confused. You see in Iraq at that time in the '50s, you cannot own any tele- phone device. The lines and the equipment belonged to the phone company, and the phone company was part of the communications department, which belonged to the government.

"The first switch had been established in Iraq and Middle East in 1920 with a capacity of three hundred lines, and also another manual switch had been established in Baghdad with a capacity of five hundred lines and telephone service expanded as a result of increase of people so the post, telegraph and telephone office was ready to prepare projects and plans to cover these increases and from technical and administrative needs, motivated to extend its work and after that became the foundation of post, telegraph and telephone." (History of Telecommunications and Post in Iraq, 2009)

Do you know why Paul was confused? I will explain this, so you can get an idea. In Iraq if you have a phone number that you use, this number is registered under your name at your resident address with the communication department which belongs to the government. If you move or sell your home, that phone number will no longer be yours and it'll stay registered at that address. You will not be able to take it to your new address site to use it once more. If you want to have a new number, you should be able to know how to bribe someone higher up in the management in the communications department. However, Paul learned that Elisa's family had moved and didn't live at that address any more. He learned this from the new owner when he called Elisa's phone number. Elisa's family happened to move because Issak's (Elisa's father) work had been transferred to Paul's village town, which is called station K3. They had moved several months ago, but they gave their new phone number to Ahmed who was the new owner of their residence, just in case someone asked about them later.

Paul didn't tell Mike about this and right away called the new number and talked to Issak. When Issak answered the phone, Paul told him that Mike is visiting him now since they had agreed about this issue a month ago. Paul was to arrange a meeting between Mike and Issak, and the subject was Issak's daughter. In the old days you couldn't just go to anyone's house and say I want to marry your daughter. The father of the bride must meet with the potential groom elsewhere first, and if he likes the groom, then he can be invited to see the whole family including and briefly with the bride. These were the rules with Elisa's family, and it didn't necessarily apply to other families in that region. After the phone call with Elisa's father Issak, Paul turned and told Mike that he has very good news for him. He told Mike, "Listen, we don't have to travel far for your bride after all." Mike was puzzled in the beginning. Paul was the only one who could explain everything to Mike as to what occurred so far. He had advised Mike about what to say and how to react because Elisa's dad, as Paul instructed Mike, was very strict in nature. He belonged to a peaceful, cultural organization where they were involved in preserving the Armenian culture from fading or dissolving its importance, existence, and the Christian religion in Muslim dominated countries for the next generation. After Mike heard all of this from his friend, he told Paul, "Say no more my friend because my own father Mark was also one of those people in our region in Baghdad who was serving the needs of the Christian people for the same reason and cause. Since my father's passing in 1945 due to leukemia, his friends have passed the torch to me to be one of them and serve my own people in my region as well." He told Paul, "Don't worry. I can blend in with Issak very well, and thanks for telling me about it."

That afternoon when Issak met Mike at Paul's house, their conversation was not about Elisa. It was about their own community and people in general. But at Mike's surprise, after a meaningful conversation with Issak, Issak told Mike that his deceased father named Mark was his own best friend for years. Elisa's subject came up next. Issak didn't respond at first with an answer, but he called his wife, Anna, from Paul's home and told her that he is going to invite Paul and his family along with Mike, the son of his deceased friend, Mark, to their home for dinner.

At Anna's surprise, she responded, "Wow, I didn't know Mark had a grown son." That evening Mike, along with Paul's family, went to Issak's residence, which was located on the other side of the village town of K3.

They all arrived at Issak's that evening, and, as impatient as Mike was, he rushed to knock on the door. When the door opened, there was a young woman, four foot eleven inches in height, welcoming him. She said, "Hello. I am Veronica, Elisa's younger sister." Then everyone went into Issak's house. Sitting left to right was Paul's wife, Paul's children, Paul and Mike. In the middle of the room was Issak, and at his side was his wife, Anna. Veronica ran inside after she opened the door for the guests to inform Elisa about the arrival of their guests. You have to know that a gated community like K3 is located approximately five hours driving distance from the capital city of Baghdad, and guests are a rare thing to hap-pen. Occasionally, everyone travels from the village to the big city to see their friends and relatives, unless their friends or relatives were a part of the working force in K3's petroleum station. In other words, this was a big, happy occasion for everyone to be a part of.

All of this was happening at Elisa's house, and Elisa was not informed about the purpose of the visiting guests. She came out of the kitchen with a big tray in her hand full of tea and biscuits to serve them with no clue as to what was going on. Mike's heart dropped to the floor, and from his nervousness he picked up the teacup and the plate but forgot to pick up the teaspoon. Everyone was almost halfway drinking their tea while Mike was so shy to ask for a spoon. Elisa noticed that earlier, and she wanted to take advantage of looking into Mike's eyes one more time. She bravely came out of the kitchen and told Mike that he forgot his spoon on the tray. They all laughed, and Elisa ran back to the kitchen.

The evening was very positive and pleasant. Mike fell in love at first sight, but no time was lost because Mike came from Baghdad and was prepared. He reached into his pocket and pulled out what is called a promise ring to put it on Elisa's finger. Issak called Elisa back to the living room, and the ring was put on her finger. Everyone started to cheer for them. In those days, a girl didn't have any say in what she wants or what she thinks. Unfortunately, the decisions were not hers to make. Her fate to marry was decided by her parents regardless how their daughter felt about it. Believe me if I tell you that their marriage, fortunately and luckily, was made in heaven, as they say. God does make wonders because my parents were really meant to be for each other.

Paul told Mike, "I knew that you would like her because she is a very good woman from a very good Christian family." Mike responded that he couldn't wait to go back to Baghdad and tell his mom and his sisters about the happy developments. The next morning, Joe called Mike that he was cutting his trip short and would be returning to Baghdad. He had heard that some unrest had been developing in the capital, and he wanted to be with his family just in case. At no surprise to anyone, Mike said he would love to go back early, and we all know why. Don't we?

Mike and Joe returned to Baghdad. Earlier that morning Mike thanked his friend Paul and his wife for everything they had done for him. He told Paul that he was a true friend. They waved goodbye to each other, and Joe drove away. Both travelers arrived in Baghdad around 7:30 p.m. That evening Mike noticed on his way home that the streets were not as busy as usual. This got them worried so they both rushed into their homes early to avoid any external conflicts that might happen. Mike's mother, Knar, welcomed her son home. Then

Mike happily told his mom about all what had happened, and he told her that he was ready to arrange for the wedding soon.

I want to share a bit of history about my lovely grandmother Knar (Mike's mom). Knar was an employee at the central hospital in Baghdad. She was hired as a washer of bed sheets. And, in 1945 when my grandfather Mark passed away due to a battle with leukemia, my grandmother found this job at the hospital, so she could raise her six children as a single mother. There were no washing machines in the hospitals in the country in those days. Everything was washed by hand. Knar's mother, Kishmo (my great-grandmother), was also helping her daughter financially to pay for her husband's medical costs before he had passed away. Kishmo spent all her reserved gold coins on her son-in-law trying to save him from his illness, but with no success. He died anyway leaving behind a widow and six children including my father Mike. But with Knar's hard work, she managed to raise her six children by herself.

Let me give you a little important background about my great-grandmother, Kishmo, as well. She was born in 1871. Her husband was a successful businessman, and he was promoted to be the mayor in some sub-region of the village of Van. Van is located today in the occupied Armenian lands of Turkey. During the Armenian massacre, which took place in 1915, an ethnic cleansing was going on by the Turks of the Ottoman Empire against the Armenians. The war crimes that were committed by the Ottoman Empire had encouraged the local government to kill and destroy most Armenians and their villages around the entire region of Van. Deportation of everyone from their homes by force was taking place. Kishmo had witnessed her husband being shot and killed, then thrown from the rooftop of their residence down to the first floor. Two of her brothers were shot to death because they were accused of treason against the local government, which was Turkey. After being looted by the local soldiers and after seeing all these unfortunate miseries done to her own family members with her own eyes, Kishmo didn't waste any time staying around. She picked up her belongings and whatever was left along with her only daughter (my grandmother Knar), to run away, but she failed in her mission only to be captured by the Turkish soldiers and to put them with the rest of the villagers in one place in order to march them into the desert the next morning. Kishmo was a very brave and wise woman. Before they were directed to march across the desert by the Turks the next day, she managed somehow to shave her daughter's head by nightfall that evening to make her look like a boy at the age of nine to avoid her daughter's kidnap and rape. These horrible acts were being done by the Turkish soldiers against the villagers only to kill them later and leave their dead bodies behind to rot under the desert sun. She had explained all these facts to me, which she had witnessed, when I was at the age of eleven in Baghdad and before her death at the age of ninety-four in the year 1965. She also managed to smuggle some of her husband's fortune of some gold coins where later she had to spend it all on her son-in-law in order to save him from his fate of dying of cancer at the age of forty-two.

Please be aware that the Armenian genocide is a historic fact and event. It has been in denial until today by some of the world governments, including Turkey, due to unspecified agendas.

I, personally, don't hate any race or any nation, but I strongly disagree with any wrong-doing to another human being, and, no matter if you're a person, a government or a nation committing the crime, then a price must be paid for these actions. I teach my own children not to hate anyone, but I also make them aware of the real facts about being Armenian and what we had to sacrifice to keep our identity as Christians to survive as a nation among other nations. I do this out of respect to my ancestors whose blood shouldn't have been shed in vain and until a government like Turkey will admit their wrongdoing against humanity around the years of 1915 to 1917. I'm so glad that I live in this country, the United States of America. One of the privileges of being an American citizen is freedom of speech, which was not a choice where I came from.

Now we're back to the story. Kishmo, my great-grandmother, managed to smuggle her daughter and some gold coins of her own with her. I believe that God works wonders because everyone's destiny is written. Kishmo, with her strong Christian faith, survived the horrors of the 1915 war crimes. I wanted to remember them in my book because they both had a big influence on my way of respecting people's rights and helping the needy, as well as the courage to fight my own life battles, more than what my own parents had taught me about these values. By now, Kishmo spent all her gold on her son-in-law's illness (my grandfather, Mark) without any hesitation or regrets, but there was no hope for his survival. He passed away on May 25, 1945 in the city of Baghdad.

Aha! The wedding of my parents. It was scheduled to take place in Baghdad in the month of October, on the tenth day of the year 1954. Everyone was getting ready weeks before. Elisa, Elisa's family, her parents, her sister (Veronica), and her three brothers were all present. And, from Mike's side of the family, his mother Knar, most of his relatives and all five sisters (Noyem, Hrepsime, Victoria, Sofina, and Sonia, some of whom were married, and some were not), and Mike's best friend, Paul, with his family who started it all for Mike. All were present, except for Elisa's belated sister, Sara.

Elisa had some fears in her mind of getting married. Her father, who she was influenced by very much, had encouraged his daughter constantly to marry this young man who had dignity and honor. He had been saying to Elisa that they were very proud of her, and she should really marry Mike without any hesitation. Elisa's fear was not the wedding itself as much as what had happened in the past to one of her sisters, Sara. Her parents gave Sara the same advice which Elisa got, but Sara's marriage was a disaster. Her husband turned out to be so insecure and jealous. He was an abusive alcoholic person. In the past, there was no point of turning back for a woman once she was married. The woman belonged to the husband, and he was free to do whatever he pleased with her like a piece of owned goods. This is exactly what happened to Sara (my aunt, who I never had the chance to meet).

One day from his constant jealousy, her abusive husband gets up and separates the children from their mother and locks them in their bedroom. Then he takes his wife to the kitchen and, to her surprise, the husband takes a tank of gasoline and he pours it on her and lights her on fire, letting her to die. The screaming was very loud which caused the neighbors to call the police, but by the time the police arrived, it was too late. When the husband was investigated later, he testified that the kerosene lantern in the kitchen accidentally exploded, and his wife caught on fire. The fire was so high that he couldn't put it out himself. During the police investigation the children were placed at Elisa's house with their grandparents by the city authorities. Before he let the children go to their grandparent's house, the abusive father instructed them that the lantern was the cause of death of their mother, and nothing else. Later, the police talked to the children in order to find out what had happened and to establish the facts of the case, but the children, out of their fear, told the police what they were instructed to say by their father. Even this tragedy had gone unpunished. We all know the truth lies somewhere, and that somewhere was with the downstairs neighbors. My relatives had told me the downstairs neighbors had heard what happened and when. All along, they had been witnessing all the fights and the abuse, but due to their fear of knowing the methods of abusive investigations and the prison system in a Muslim country like Iraq, no one dared to speak the truth or to step forward, so justice could be served. This was the way it was back then. The case was closed with no witnesses coming forward to expose the truth. Today, Sara's children, a son and a daughter who are my cousins, are living somewhere in Europe. I don't know how to contact them, and I wouldn't know what I could change to ease their pain, if I ever had a chance to meet them. But life must go on for all of us eventually with God's will.

All these past events regarding Sara were still bothering Elisa's mind, but then she heard the celebration outside the room. They were getting her ready at her relative's home in Baghdad, a short walking distance from the groom's house. The area that the groom was living in was called Gilliani Camp. It's an area of approximately forty to sixty acres of land full of mud and brick homes in the middle of the city of Baghdad and was populated mostly by Armenian and Assyrian families. Right after the genocide period, they were fleeing from Turkey as survivors crossing Syrian and Iraqi borders as refugees. They were welcomed by the Arabs. One family pulled another to follow them to this area, and it was like a refugee camp for all until years later it got more modern compared to the way it was ten to twenty years earlier. The name "camp" was a label that got stuck to the area and to the residents.

Elisa is ready now to go out of her room. It took several hours as a tradition to make her ready, yet she hears the cars honking their horns, making a loud noise in the street, and alerting that the drivers were ready to go to the church. The groom would be waiting in the church with his best man as tradition calls for it, and then both sides of the families would show up later.

The old Armenian tradition calls for that the groom shouldn't see the bride that very same day until the wedding takes place in the church; the same tradition applies as well for her wedding dress. Supposedly, this will bring bad luck to the couple if the groom sees the dress before the wedding day. Wow, it's an unbelievable thought, but an interesting one.

After entering the church, Elisa paused and told herself, "I am here" while she looked down the aisle at the church alter in the old St. Mary's Armenian Church in Baghdad. She had some relief in her mind after remembering what Mike had told her previously regarding this church's location, and that is Mike had attended his elementary classes at this school, which was located behind this church as a big Christian community complex. Then at some distance from the church, there was the famous Tigris river of Baghdad, which was running south non-stop. I believe it was Elisa's childhood dreams and wishes of getting married in that church, which just came true. That very day, the entire city was also under a curfew due to some civil unrest. You were allowed only to be out of your residence at a certain time of day until the government announces a change to lift the curfew later. The average citizen had no choice in the matter, and I mean all citizens must follow the rules. No exceptions.

It was October 10, 1954. When the church bells started to ring, Elisa got back to reality and walked down the aisle in her white wedding dress. She was looking right into Mike's eyes freely, and he was doing the same. Both of their minds were alike for a moment, and their actions were speaking louder than words. Elisa's father gave his daughter away to Mike at the altar and the ceremony began. They both faced the alter, and the Best Man stood behind the couple and also faced the alter while carrying a golden cross in his hand that belonged to the church, which was held high above the couples' heads as our wedding tradition calls for. The prayers were going on, but half-way into the ceremony there was a lot of rallying-like noise in the street outside the church. It was the Islamic student movement rally. They were preparing for a demonstration against the ruler of the country, King Faisal II. Unfortunately, the priest had to speed up the wedding ceremony so that every-one could rush out and go back to their homes without endangering anyone. The wedding was cut short, and everyone went back quietly to Mike's parents' house, which also was the newlywed's new residence. The reception started quietly and was also short. And due to a lack of finances, the affordability of traveling to a honeymoon destination didn't exist. The couple spent their honeymoon inside their master bedroom while everyone else was still outside in the living room celebrating and having a good time, supposedly.

A month had gone by, and life had started for Elisa and Mike. He was working as a clerk for the Department of Water and Power (DWP). This was a government paid job, or you could call it a federal position thanks to Mike's friend, Azad, who directed and helped Mike to get this position. Azad was a federal employee and an inside man who helped Mike to be hired at the DWP. You see, in Iraq, who knows who was important at that time, and this understanding still exists today all over the world. If you were a Christian or a Jew, it was not easy for you to be employed with this kind of position, big or small, unless you knew someone within that organization. Working in a position with DWP, your duty was a sensitive one in nature. The hired individual was to collect funds from the public, meaning actual cash money. And, by the way, the Iraqi public financial system mostly dealt with cash funds. Checks were not a form of financial transaction within the public sector, but it was with businesses. The idea of a banking system was not in effect for the standard citizen. The banking system was available mostly for merchants, big businesses and the rich. Government agencies were watching everyone like a hawk. Most people learned to save and hide money and gold at their residence with many different methods and means because they knew that every three to five years the ruling government was being pushed out and replaced by a new revolution. There was no security in depositing money in the government-controlled banks and banking system. Iraqi people always lived mistrusting their government and the system, especially to deposit their own hard-earned money in any bank.   In Iraq, there was no knowing about the fate of your funds, especially when you wake up the next morning and look outside your window to see a military tank rolled out and parked on your street during the night while you were sleeping, not knowing that a revolution had taken place the night before. Can you picture that in your mind? And, do you see what I mean?

The cash funds that were collected from the public would go entirely to the government. The payment process for DWP was that the public would come to DWP's office windows, daily and at random, to pay their electric utility bill. Mike would collect the money and give them a receipt every time they paid their bills. The field office that Mike worked from was too small, possibly 10 × 15 in size, and they were run by three people. One of them was unskilled and worked as a gofer and servant. The other was an armed policeman who waited all day at the front window like a security guard. In this event, this would leave Mike to act as the only working clerk. At times, and at certain locations, the servant or the employee with the lower paying rank was a government informant, hired to spy on the regular clerk as to what he was doing. If you made friends with them, they treated you well. Nevertheless, some of them hated their positions doing what they had to do, but they did it because they had no choice in the matter for being an informant in a country like this. They had to make a living to feed their families, especially when they were unskilled and uneducated. The new Baath regime had twice developed this kind of human spying system to control its population, unfortunately; once in the late sixties, and second, in the late seventies because they were in power twice.

As you can see, life was not easy for any young individual like Mike and others to raise a family. He had just become a newlywed and had just gotten started to raise a family of his own. Life was conditioning my father with the wrong messages; things like living in fear constantly, without the freedom of speech, or expressing their thoughts freely. This had caused some severe strain on Mike's mind and restrained him from learning to work or do anything else in life but be a robot and work only in one position for the DWP all his life. Yet, a federal employee like Mike was to be trusted 100 percent in order to be given a position like that with the department. The penalty for stealing government funds in Iraq with the new regime was prison and torture, and, in some cases, hanging, if I'm not mistaken.

Mike's daily field office routine was to finish his usual workday by collecting the funds that he was supposed to collect. The servant would then start to clean the office floor and the counter, which had a huge and locked cash register machine on top of it. Then all three employees would have to leave the place all together. The servant would go home, and Mike and the armed police must catch a cab in order to go to the main office and hand over the funds. After that, they were both freed and released from their duties for that day. The average working hours per day for a federal job was six hours (8:00 a.m. to 2:00 p.m.). The entire city was working five and a half days a week. The work week in Iraq would art on Saturdays and end at noon on Thursdays, and everyone was off on Fridays, which is thste so-called weekend (in Muslim countries like Iraq, weekends are Thursdays and Fridays, resembling Saturdays and Sundays in the western countries).

Parents, like my father Mike and my mother Elisa, were very honest, extremely kind to others and generous in helping the needy, and they were respected for that by all their friends and their families, including their own sisters and brothers and their families. Often, this resulted in lots of envying from others, which created some unpleasant outcomes between my parents by other people's actions. However, the respect and love that Mike and Elisa had for each other overcame many, many obstacles and issues throughout their marriage.

Elisa was an excellent homemaker. It was a struggle and a battle to keep her house clean, dinner cooked on time, clothes washed, and always taking care of all of us including my grandmother (my father's mom), my uncle and his wife, and one unmarried sister of my father's named Sofina. All were living with her in the same household. So much for privacy! Yet, she managed to do everything, and she had a very polite and understanding attitude toward everyone's needs. In return, everyone was getting along just fine with her as well. But in reality, and as a new bride in the family, this was not much of a life for her other than being a servant and a compromiser for accepting fewer things in life than what her true mind was telling her to be and to have. She was a "like father like daughter" type of person. Her father was not a materialistic person, and he raised Elisa to be just like him.

Mike's mother's house was not very big; only three bedrooms including the master. The two windows to one of the bedrooms faced the front of the house. There was no privacy at all because outside of their bedroom windows and across the other side of the street there was this daily public marketplace where the noise and the summer flies and other insects were escaping the marketplace daily and entering their home. Also, Mike's uncle, who was self-employed and running a meat grinding business at one point, had a stainless-steel table with a manual meat grinder hooked at one end to do the work. This table was set up outside the house on the street where Elisa's bedroom window was located. In other words, everyone that needed ground beef must visit Mike's uncle's business. Often, there were long lines and public noise during the day to allow conducting this meat grinding operation. Due to excessive foot traffic outside the home and for security reasons, everyone inside the house always kept the main entry door locked to keep intruders or thieves out. It was not a secure place or a clean environment for everyone to live there, but that's all there was to accept at the time.

Another challenge for Elisa was having one old-fashioned bathroom without running hot water for six to seven people. The process of boiling hot water for bathing took between forty-five minutes to one and a half hours per person. This also put a lot of strain on her as well.

This was the house where Elisa lived to raise a family that was not her own, but she had to live there after her marriage. Life was not easy for Elisa being a homemaker. Nevertheless, she didn't complain, and she was an "up to the task" sort of woman. In the old days in Iraq, most women were homemakers. They didn't work outside their homes. Often, there was some sort of discrimination against them in a Muslim country like Iraq, and especially against Christian women because their face and body were always exposed. They didn't have to wear black veils and cover their face like Muslim women did. If we have a debate about this discriminatory issue, not everyone will agree with what I'm saying. The public was in fear to expose such matters which still exist until today, but no one wants to talk about them. In those days in the early fifties, equalization or the word equal between a man and a woman as far as being 50-50 was not an option, and it didn't exist in the Iraqi lifestyle. Possibly, the rest of the world was the same at that time. Men were always right, and woman came second in terms of her authority and opinions. Also, some of the Iraqi laws were written specifically and according to these beliefs in discriminating against females. If a father of a family passes away for any reason and without a written will, the Iraqi court will divide the inheritance to two-thirds of the wealth going to all the male in that family, and the remaining one-third to be shared amongst the females, including the wife, regardless of the number of females in that family. It's unfortunate, but that's the way the system was set up. That's the way society had handled themselves. But we had to respect their ways of life, right or wrong. That was their business. Some Muslim-ruled countries have changed since the fifties to the better, but they will never be like the west or Europe no matter how much they try because regarding women as second-class citizens is not just a cultural issue, but it also has to do with their religious beliefs.

In relation to what I'm saying about knowing which women are decent and which are not since most Muslim women didn't cover their face, here's a true example. One evening as I stopped one of the taxicabs to go home after basketball practice with the sports club which I was a member of and located in mid-town Baghdad, I witnessed a woman sitting in the front seat all covered up with a black veil and outfit. As she opened the door to exit out, I saw the taxicab driver pulling this woman passenger forcefully back into his cab. The driver tried to kiss her while one of his hands was on her breasts, and the woman was resisting him with her one hand. Then she turned around and told the driver in Arabic that she had done her job and if he wanted more, he should have paid for more. I realized right then and there that night that she was a whore, and all this had happened in the thirty seconds as I opened the taxi door to get in. I waited until this drama had ended so I could get into the cab. I got in, and I didn't know what to say and how to react. I had no choice because it was late at night and the chances of calling or stopping another cab was very slim. Then I changed my mind and asked the cab driver not to proceed. I got out and decided to take the bus instead because I didn't trust the taxicab driver after what I had just witnessed because he smelled like liquor, and he was drunk. I reached half way home by bus because that particular bus line was not going to take me to my destination, and I had to walk home the other half late at night. I was hoping during my walk that I wouldn't encounter and be attacked by stray dogs or get kidnapped because I was walking through unfamiliar neighbor-hoods to get home. In those days, there were not enough police cars to protect the public, or most of the police were lazing around at their stations. Oh, I hope I didn't get carried away too much. I was just trying to give you an idea how the city of Baghdad in some areas were like during late nights; unattended and unprotected.

I had mentioned my mother's (Elisa's) home before by describing it and how it was designed room-by-room, but I forgot to tell you about the kitchen. Oh baby, nothing like you know or have seen in today's lifestyle with modern home kitchens. There were two long counters, a sink on one side, and a stove and two long shelves on the other side. Everyone was using the counters at any time of day and at random. There was no rhyme or reason to this so- called organized kitchen. What goes where and why was left for Elisa to organize and keep it all together because it was the new bride's responsibility to do all that, just like Cinderella's story that we know. Wipe the floors, keep everything clean, cook, etc.

Elisa's life was not short of new surprises, and before you knew it, she was a few months pregnant with her first son. They were going to name him after her father Issak at first, but life has good and bad surprises. It often happens for a reason. When Elisa was three months pregnant, she and her husband Mike were invited as a newlywed couple to a wedding reception taking place at the home of one of their relatives. It was a winter month and Elisa and Mike arrived at the reception. Both had stepped out from the taxicab and walked to the residence where the reception was taking place. Before they reached the doorbell, Elisa's foot slipped over a puddle of water at curbside and she fell on her back with her legs spread wide open. This was not good news. She was rushed to the doctor's office (doctor offices, including a small clinic, used to be located at the doctor's residence and were used to respond to house calls and emergencies). After a careful examination by the doctor, he decided to perform minor surgery. While the surgery was going on inside the doctor's residence office, Mike was waiting outside impatiently and was worried. He didn't know what was going on until the doctor was done with his work to save Elisa's life. After an hour of operation, the doctor came out of his clinic and told Mike the bad news. Elisa had lost her baby. At first, Mike didn't know how to handle this and what to do because he was not accustomed or disciplined to be told the truth in one shot. I was told about his habits later in life. You see, my grandmother, Mike's mom named Knar, and Mike's five sisters were over protective of their only son and brother. They didn't tell him any bad news directly to his face because they were afraid that bad news would harm Mike emotionally and would cause him lots of pain. This is because he was the only male in the house who was the bread winner. Most of the time, Mike's family's method of telling the truth to him was to illustrate it and was not the whole truth, or they made the entire picture a rosy lie or a colorful truth. The doctor didn't know all this, and he flatly told Mike about the loss of the baby. At one point, Mike started to walk away and was walking back and forth confused, angry and looking for answers as to how to face his wife and which way he should comfort her. All these thoughts didn't leave his mind, but as we know, no man is made of stone. Mike, like everyone else, was raised, as best as I can justify it based on being the product of love and care, by normal and decent parents. As a rule of thumb, they say a man is a reflection of his own father or mother. In Mike's case, he didn't have much of a father and son relation and guidance to learn from because his father died when he was a young teenager. This left him with his mother and five sisters to grow up with and to learn. Thinking philosophically, life is like a drama on a stage, and we all have a part to play. The stage of life is not the same for everyone. Every one of us are directed to play his/her part in life in a different fashion with God's control. We all have to face the truth and learn the good from the bad. And one day when the curtain of our life as a stage is down, then your number is up. God needs you to be next to him regardless of who you are; good or bad, or rich or poor because you will have completed your journey on earth. Mike had not seen his father's death. As a teenager, he was sent away to his relative's home, so he didn't have to face the truth and the pain of his father's death. We need to understand life, or the way that society was accustomed to think in the Middle Eastern Muslim countries. Most families were very proud to have their first child be a boy instead of a girl. Fathers had felt that they were less respected among men back in the fifties if the firstborn was a girl. It sounds crazy, but that's the way it was back then in that region of the world.

Now, can you can imagine how Mike faced his own unexpected loss? He felt the curtains of his life stage were closing in on him. As thoughts were crossing his mind, his heart started to beat fast, and fear created some anxiety in him. He left the doctor's office from the front doors and started to walk fast and reached the end of the street. All the street lights in that town were halfway lit. Then suddenly, an old man with a white beard and a white cane in his hand came out of the shadows and was visible under the street lights. The old man told Mike in a very soft voice, "Listen, my son, I know what is going on in your mind, but someone has better things planned for you for the future." As confused as Mike was and with his mind going one hundred miles an hour, he turned back to ask the man, "What things?" And, before he knew it, there was no one behind him. This created some courage and motive in him to run back to the doctor's office and take his wife home. All the way home Mike's mind was occupied by the voice he had heard and what he had been told. This was not an unusual event for Mike and his family because most of Mike's great-grandfathers were priests centuries before his birth. Mike and his family were blessed, and they encountered events like this in the past every time any one of them was in a life-threatening or bad situation or danger. For Mike and his family, this was another phenomenal vision which had solved the problem one more time. My grandmother, Knar (Mike's mother), had told me this when I was eight years old, and that our entire family was protected by angels.

The next morning, Mike's family woke up and everyone heard the news and was comforting Elisa; first for her courage, and second for her handling of their brother Mike, and his fears as well. Life went on. Nevertheless, this negative experience of losing their firstborn child didn't let the couple down, but they went on and decided to try again and have their next child. On the afternoon of December 8, 1955, God blessed Mike and Elisa with a son. They named him Mark after Mike's father. Mark was the joy of the whole family where everyone's attention was circulating around him when he was young. Mike's sisters were all spoiling him without limits. The whole house was full of joy because he was named after their deceased father. And, just by calling the name of Mark alone, everyone felt that their father was alive and well among them. They couldn't wait until Mark grew up so that they could all have another responsible man in the household around them, so he can handle things for everyone (wow, lucky me). Between 1955 and 1961, Elisa gave birth to two more sons.

My father Mike was very talented, and he had many hobbies like writing poems and acting, and he was a member of Baghdad's Armenian Cultural Association's (ACA) theatrical group. For Mike, school was a priority for his children. He didn't want to see history repeat itself because Mike couldn't finish his school and education in general. First, due to the dependency of his family after his father's death, and, secondly, he wanted to be a professional athlete practicing the sport of running or track and field. He also wanted to learn only two languages: Armenian and English. This was a bit of a problem for Mike's mother, Knar, because living in Iraq, which is an Arabic-speaking country, the country's school system was dictating a requirement without any exceptions that all students must learn the Arabic language, which is the native language of the land along with all the other required lessons (Math, Chemistry, Geography, History, etc.). Mike refused to follow the rules, and he didn't want to learn the Arabic language. He dropped out of school and his education at once. He continued to practice the one hundred-meter freestyle run. Luckily, he managed making a name for himself as the fastest runner by competing through some local city competitions. In 1947, Mike had earned first place in this sport and his majesty, King Faisal II of Iraq, had awarded Mike with a trophy and medal. He was picked by others to join the Iraqi National Track and Field Team where they were preparing to participate in the 1948 Summer Olympic Games which were going to be held in London. Mike's running record was 10.9 seconds at the time for the one hundred-meter freestyle run, but circumstances and some prejudiced judges didn't allow Mike to succeed in his life's goal because he was a Christian. Suddenly, a month later the judges' ruling was overturned, and in order to choose a final list of runners, Mike was allowed to participate in the final run before departing for the Olympics. But on April 1, 1948, while the race was on, a spectator, supposedly and by accident, had thrown an object in the air where it landed on Mike's right cheek while competing and prevented him from winning the race. Mike reached the finish line and came in second. He didn't make it onto the Olympic list. (After the race, the spectator was nowhere to be found. Hmm, so much for being just.

Following sports for Mike was like a religion, and, because of it, he gave up school education limiting himself to paid private home lessons of the English and Armenian languages. Throughout his life, Mike realized that the impact of not being educated enough was causing him not to advance in his workplace and that created a concern in his mind and drove him to encourage his own children not to follow in his footsteps. He decided they must have education. Nevertheless, as they were growing up, he enrolled them in a private school named the Baghdad Armenian Elementary School. The school was accredited by the Iraqi Ministry of Education. This private school was in existence for a long time and for many generations before me. It was the only non-Muslim Christian Armenian school that accepted a mix of male and female students.

The year was 1959 and the president of Iraq who was in power was General Abdul Karim Kassem. Iraqi diplomatic relations were restored with the USSR making him more adaptable toward his people. He was more involved in his people's affairs than being a politician as everyone had described him to me later in life and that he was a very good but poor president. He loved his country Iraq dearly, and he believed in a resolution that no government should take from the needy due to greed. He planned to split the countryside of Baghdad into residential buildable lot sites and to give it to his people so that they could build their dream homes. He never took anything for himself from his people in return. He protected the needy and the labor unions as well as the country's industries. Creating jobs was a priority for him. He loved his people, and he loved Iraq. One night, as all of us at home were watching a big concert on television honoring his birthday as a broadcasting program, and in the middle of the party, the president stood up and announced, "I'm declaring tomorrow (which was a Monday) a paid holiday for all." Everyone was cheering to have a day off which was paid for by the government. Well, his government was a socialist one, but not a tyranny.

The country, as I was told and as little as I can remember, was on the right direction to inspiration. He always kept his promises toward his people. He found some large lands in the suburban part of the capital, Baghdad, and he wanted to sub-divide them and distribute them to the Department of Water and Power's labor union employees. This action had made all government employees, including my father Mike, afford to purchase lands from the union at a fraction of the cost in order to start building and owning their own homes. This was very good news for Elisa and Mike. A dream came true to build their own home and to raise their children in an environmentally better place and in a better location. Also, it was going to be a more spacious and healthier place for all to live and share together.

Mike's confidence in himself to own his own home and to go through the pain and worry of constructing a new home was not at its best. It was almost impossible in his mind to achieve doing so. My mother Elisa was not raised like Mike. She was strong, and she came from an independent thinking and risk-taking family. She was like her father Issak. She decided to encourage Mike every day and to remind him about their way of survival in an environment which was not healthy at all for the children due to past failed kidnapping attempts of one of their children. In addition, there were other health related issues with the trash piled in the streets from the public marketplace since they were living within walking distance from there. The attempted kidnapping happened during one afternoon in 1957, and while daily life was in motion. A Muslim Arab lady, who was a thief, walked in from the street through the front door of Mike's residence because Mike's uncle, while he was running the meat grinding business outside the home, had left the front door open by accident. He went inside the house to get his new grinder blades sharpened, which he stored in the kitchen located at the back of the house. This gave an opportunity to the lady who was dressed and covered in a black veil (hijab) and an Arabian abaya (long, black dress) to enter freely into the residence. She went inside the house and went directly to the master bedroom where she picked me (the firstborn child) up from my crib (my grandmother told me about this when I was older). Then this Arab lady hid me under her abaya to smuggle me out. She went one step further in her theft to collect some of the gold items from Elisa's jewelry box as well. Elisa heard the noise from the kitchen and rushed to her bedroom to investigate only to see this veiled lady trying to rush out. The crying of Elisa's firstborn from under her abaya was loud. Elisa blocked this lady's passage by standing in the doorway of her bedroom and started yelling for help from her mother-in-law. After a short physical fight between the thief and the two women from my household, they managed to take the law into their own hands and beat the lady up and put her down on the ground. Then my grandmother managed to save me from this lady's grip. This process saved my life from being lost forever that day. My granny called the police, and this woman was handed to the authorities a brief time later. Now, when my mom reminded Mike about this incident, he told her that he will consider the land purchasing matter tomorrow.

In 1961, God blessed Mike and Elisa for the third time with another baby boy. They named him Van, named after a village called Van in the occupied Armenian lands in Turkey where my grandmother was born. Our family started growing, and the space of our house in the old neighborhood started getting tight. Mike decided to surprise everyone and joined the hundreds of employees at the Department of Water and Power and purchased from the union a piece of land to build their dream house on it. A year later at the end of 1962, the construction of Mike's dream home was completed. In February of 1963, Mike's immediate family went to live in the newly-built home. This change discouraged some of Mike's other family members who were living in the old house with Mike from moving with him into his new home. They decided to live elsewhere. They didn't want to follow Mike and his family to live in this new section of the city. Mike's uncle and his wife moved to live with their daughter in the southern province of Iraq in the city of Basra. Mike's mother and his grandmother, who were both genocide survivors and who we all had lots of respect for and for their wisdom, along with Mike's sister, Sofina, all moved with us to this new home; to a new life in a new place altogether.

My father's sister, Sofina, married not long after she lived with us in this new place. She got married to a man that she was introduced to by relatives. He was rich and was running his own family winery business. He had two kids from his first marriage; a daughter who was twelve years old and a son who was eleven years old. Sofina promised Mike, like any other sister who cares and loves their only brother dearly, to help him in the future if he ever needed any financial help to support his family and his new home. By stepping into this marriage, Sofina didn't know what kind of challenges she was going to face. Although her husband was a kind and generous man, the rest of his family was against this marriage because Sofina came from a poorer class of society; poor, but very honest and hardworking. She took care of her husband's children and loved them more than they could expect from a stepmother by adding more value to their lives and teaching them respect toward each other and equality to others. Folks, people often say the rich should marry the rich and the poor should marry the poor. But things are often the opposite, and this is how the world has been running for ages.

CHAPTER

2

Growing Up in Iraq, and My Childhood

It was Thursday, December 8, 1955, when Elisa had her labor pains. She was rushed to the Al Mejedia Hospital in Baghdad with her mother-in-law, Knar, at her side in a taxicab. The taxi station was three blocks away from their home in the heart of Gilliani Camp where Mike's parents' house was located (the old home). All were living together in one household; Mike's mom, Knar; his grandmother, Kishmo; his uncle and his wife, as well as one unmarried sister, Sofina.

In 1955, Al Mejedia Hospital was not like the hospitals that we all have seen and experienced today. It was set up more like a World War II military style hospital. All the beds were placed next to each other and were about three to four feet apart in a rectangular shaped hall. Between each bed was a chair that was placed for one visitor, and there were a few big windows with iron bars just like prison windows. Oh, before I forget, these windows were the only air flowing in and the only available ventilation source for the patients along with free- standing circulating fans which were not available for everyone. There were no private rooms or special rooms for maternity. All the patients were lined up next to each other. What separated the patients from each other was some curtain-type material on metal aluminum rods on rollers. The curtains covered three sides of the hospital bed only as a privacy measure, and these curtains were getting rolled to each patient's bedside during doctor visits.

The hospital conditions were horrible due to it being a public hospital. It was free and paid for by the government. At night time you needed to have someone next to you to watch over you. There were only some who were called nurses who were uneducated and unkind working at that location. You would be lucky to call and find them in times of need. Most, but not all, were unavailable and because they were sleeping throughout the night, bribery was the only way to get help and attention. Also, you had to manage feeding yourself or feeding the baby.

My grandmother, Mike's mom Knar, was a guardian angel, if I may call her that. She watched and took care of Elisa after she gave birth. Knar knew some people at the hospital because she had worked there before in her earlier years as a washer of hospital bed sheets, which was a low-ranking job, but she had to work and make a living to take care of her children. She lived a hard life raising her children while working at the hospital. During her working days, there were no washing machines to utilize at that time. She, along with others that had worked the same job, had no choice but to wash all the hospital sheets by hand, and they used toxic chemicals to hand wash the bed sheets due to their lack of education and knowledge. In other words, they didn't know any better and there were no safety precautions or guidance by the hospital to follow at that time subjecting their skin to harm. Knar didn't care about her pride or reputation or making a name for herself as she was very humble. This was one of the reasons why I call her a superb person. She will always have a very high mark in my book.

Knar managed to take care of my mom Elisa at her bedside at nights with the help of her nurse friends. Oh, and before I forget again, I must tell you about the other danger that existed at this hospital, which was stealing or switching babies. At night, some of the nurses stole babies from their mother's bedside while the mothers were asleep, or, at times, switching them with Muslim babies after birth. These facts were based according to my grandmother's testimony. She shared her stories with me one night while sitting at her bedside when I was ten years old. These were little known fear factors that existed at this government-owned hospital in 1955. But I believe these were possibly some isolated events in 1955 that had nothing to do with the managing and running of this hospital by the Iraqi government.

My father Mike was notified about this happy occasion, and he had to leave work immediately to meet his family at the hospital that afternoon. God blessed Mike and Elisa with their first baby boy, and they were so happy. They were walking on cloud nine from their excitement, if you know what I mean. Elisa's self-confidence was restored after she had had a miscarriage a year before and learned that her loss was a baby boy. Mike felt the whole world just began for him once more. His pride, as well as a father to a son, was restored. Mike decided to move Elisa and his newborn son back to their residence after a two night's stay at the hospital. The next morning the joy was for all. They couldn't wait for the baby to wake up. The family members all lined up, and each one took turns to have a look. They took care of Elisa while she was in bed for two weeks until she could get her strength back and start moving around and could take care of her daily chores. The time had come to name their firstborn. There were two options. The first option was to be named after Elisa's father, Issak. Issak was alive at the time, and he, too, was proud of his newborn grandson. Option number two was Mike's father's name, which was Mark, but the latter choice was the prevailing one in the process. Mike's father and my grandfather, Mark, was deceased at that time. I never met him. He was a good friend of Issak, Elisa's dad. At this point, Issak didn't mind it at all when he had learned the outcome of the chosen name. As a matter of fact, he suggested the idea for them to move forward with naming the baby Mark due to great respect for his good friend. The baby was named Mark (short for the Armenian name of Markar, which comes from the name Markareh, which means prophet from the word prophecy).

The Christening of the newborn baby, Mark, had taken place after several months at the Armenian Diocese Church of Baghdad, Iraq, which is still in existence until today. It belongs to the Eastern side of the Armenian churches of the Holy Mother of all churches called Etchmiadzin. Armenia's churches got divided because of Communism during the Soviet Armenia era in the 1900's. You either followed Etchmiadzin's Eastern ceremony where the original church was located at the edge of the capitol city of Yerevan in Soviet Armenia, or the Western ceremony of the holy church of Cilicia (Giligia) located in Beirut, Lebanon. Both are of the same Christian faith, but a bit different in singing the Divine Liturgy. Etchmiadzin, the Holy Mother of all churches, is in Yerevan, the capital of Armenia, which was one of the Soviet bloc countries in the past era but is now in the independent Republic of Armenia. The Republic of Armenia got its independence after the Soviet regime collapsed and ended in the early nineties.

After the church ceremony, everyone was invited to Mike's residence for a small celebration and gathering, and, as usual, everyone came with a gift for the newborn. My childhood years were full of love and care and lots of attention was given to me at the time as I was told this by most of the families and friends who used to visit my parents regularly. I was a very special child for the whole family on Mike's side as was stated and especially for my grandmother Knar, Mike's mom. Her memories of her belated husband were renewed. She was thirty-eight years old when her husband died leaving behind six children (five girls and one boy) for his wife, Knar, to take care of and raise. Knar was not selfish in nature, and she didn't want to marry anyone after her husband's death. Some of you who are reading this now will ask who would want to marry a widow with six kids. But there were at least two men who asked her to marry them. I asked my grandmother the same question that we would have in our minds today in relation to her baggage of six children and marriage as to why she turned them down. She said it was out of her love and dedication for her first husband. She was committed to him with all her life, and, folks, this is the old-fashioned love and dedication which, in today's world, is short of. But, of course, I understand each situation is different for us as individuals, depending on our cultural and intellectual preferences.

My grandmother Knar found some comfort every time my name was called, and she had the motive and the will to take care of me as her grandson who carried her hus-band's name. She told me about this years later when I had grown up. My aunt Sofina, who was living with us as a single young lady at the time, was not short of love and care for me because of the same reasons. Being the first born of her only brother, I was special. Sofina was her father's favorite daughter as she once told me, and she loved her father dearly. This type of love and care toward me was equally the same from my mother's side of the family where her only sister, Veronica, was doing the same as Sofina. She was caring and loving toward me being the newborn.

Since we are mentioning Sofina in this book, I would like to share her story based on true facts related to her devoted love to her father that was told to me in 2008 as a grown up. I managed to ask Sofina about this once I had a hint of such a happening to understand about this experience, so I could include her in my story because it was a very interesting phenomenon. Those who believe as I do about Christ and the heavens, please read on. Sofina shared with me her very interesting, out-of-body experience type of story that had happened to her in the past, which starts like this.

When Sofina was a young girl at age eight, her father passed away. None of her siblings were next to their father's bed when he died. Sofina had this out-of-body experience when she was very sick. She had a high fever and had passed out. Everyone thought she would never make it because she slept for three days without waking up, as if in a coma. This is not a made-up fairy tale or a fantasy; it's the real thing. She said she does not remember what happened. While she was passed out, she suddenly dreamt that she was looking at this man standing next to her bed with a beautiful long bright white robe asking her why she was crying. She replied that she wanted to go see her father because she missed him very much. This man told her, "I will take you to him, but you have to promise me one thing. You will not ask me any questions about what you are about to see or whatever passes by. Is that understood, Sofina?" She agreed.

Then they both walked on this long white trail. She said that she saw a woman who was sitting on the floor and baking lots of bread. She was working so fast and so hard to do them and using some type of stove. This woman was sweating so hard doing the work, and her mouth was watering. She wanted to eat some of the bread herself, but she couldn't for some reason. Her tongue was always rotating in circles to moisten her lips. Sofina said she broke her promise as a child and asked the man in the white robe about what was happening. Then the man asked her, "Didn't we agree not to ask me any questions? But, yes, I will answer you, my child."

The man told her, "You see, Sofina, this woman was very rich all her life, yet she declined to help or give anyone anything in her past life or even offer help to anyone. At this place she will have to bake all her life to feed others, but she cannot eat the bread that she bakes." Then Sofina said that they walked again, and she saw this big tree and all the branches had babies sleeping on them. Some were sleeping, and some were hanging from it. It was a big cherry tree, and the babies were from fetuses, to premature, to grown babies. I asked my aunt Sofina how she knew that they were premature babies when she was only eight years old. She said, "The man in the white robe told me this as he was explaining and before I had a chance to ask him my next question regarding these babies. It was as if he was reading what was on my mind. Then he explained to me that these were the babies who didn't live long, died and didn't consume their mother's milk. Here we're taking care of them, and they're going to eat the cherries that grow on this tree all their life and live eternally." Sofina continued telling me her story shortly after she wiped her tears and said that not too far off when she and the man in the white robe both had to stop at the front of a tall brick wall that had a red apple tree along the side of it, Sofina said the man with the long white robe picked a very dark red apple and told her that he was going to see if her father Mark is staying behind this wall. She told me she was puzzled. When she asked him how they would know this when they can't see the other side of the wall, the man in the white robe told her that he was going to throw the red apple across over the wall, and if the apple was half eaten and thrown back to them, then they would know that her father is there because her father likes dark red apples. Sure enough, he did what he said he would do. Then when they saw the half-eaten apple was thrown back to them, her father appeared. Her father Mark asked her how she was doing. Then she said the man in the white robe kissed her on her forehead and left her with her father.

Sofina ran toward her father, and she couldn't believe her eyes. She hugged her father. She said, "I didn't want to let go. My father was sitting on a horse, and he made me ride with him. He took me all over this place as I'm riding on the back of the horse holding on to my dad."

Sofina's father said to her, "My girl, Sofina, this is heaven, and the man who brought you here was Jesus Christ himself who is taking care of us all." Her dad said he was very comfortable there and very happy. He was looking for everybody in his family to have a safe life and to have glory on earth until all could come there to live and unite with him in the future. My father went to a tree and cut a small branch that had three little white flowers on it. He told me I should give it to my brother Mike, his only son, and to tell him that both he and his wife Elisa will be blessed with three boys in their lifetime. Then she said she got back on the horse again as her father told her to do so. Mark told her, "Now, my girl, I have to take you back to your mom, and when we reach there, you must promise me one thing." She asked, "What?" Her father said, "You have to wake up from your sleep, Sofina." Sofina said to me, "I promised him that I would do that. My father took me back and told me, 'wake up, Sofina, wake up, you're home'. I haven't seen him since then. I woke up and started to tell everyone what happened, but no one believed me. They were happy that I could wake up after three days of endless sleep". I admired my aunt for her courage and the faith she had. She was like her mother; kind and wise enough to guide everyone. (God bless her soul. She passed away on October 19, 2011, at the age of seventy- eight).

I was surrounded with kind and loving people around me as I was growing up. Even though the class in my neighborhood was poor, people always cared about each other, shared things amongst themselves, and they were protective of each other's families. Crime was a rare happening. My family was very well respected among all the other Muslim families living around us thanks to my grandfather Mark. In his young days, he was young and restless, sincere, kind to others, and respected the properties of others, as well as being brave enough to defend people's rights at any cost. He loved fairness. If he saw anyone needing food or shelter, he took them to his house, gave them money on the spot, or sheltered them for that day to solve their needs. It was a rare thing and a wonderful habit of his. We all know how the world is neither fair nor unselfish. These were qualities that were inbred in him. I was often resembled to him since everyone who knew him and who also saw me said this boy will be replacing his grandfather. They used to say to my parents that they were glad that I was named Mark after him.

Time had passed, and it was 1961. I was six years old at the time and ready to go to Kindergarten at Baghdad's private Armenian School, which was built next to the Armenian Church where my parents had gotten married many years earlier. The Kindergarten was located on the back side of this church, and on the other side was the Armenian Cemetery of Baghdad. Next to the cemetery and along one side of it there was the elementary section of this school as part of the entire complex. After you graduated from Kindergarten, and if you wanted to con- tinue going to the same school, you could transfer to the elementary section of the school building where later Junior and Senior High Schools were added to the whole complex. The Baghdad Armenian Private School was in the heart of the capital city of Baghdad. The Gilliani Camp where I was a resident of was also located along the far side of this area and across the street from it where most of the minority group families were residing at that time.

I remember some of my Kindergarten days. I was very active, and I had friends that were active as well. We used to cut holes in the paper lunch bags and wear them on our heads to scare the young girls during the recess periods. We got punished for it, and our parents were notified. It was not too pleasant to have your parents know about these things because it was very embarrassing. I can't wait until my sons have children, so I can spoil them. After all, you're only young once in your life. When a year passes, then it's a year gone from your life, so I believe to let go and enjoy life to the fullest.

The uniforms in my Kindergarten class were checkered blue and white in color. They were made of cotton fabric, and you wore them just like the surgeon doctors wore their robes. It had strings that would tie in the back, and it was long and was reaching my knees. Occasionally, I would wait for my father to pick me up after school. I loved my father very much. I was also assigned and trusted to be picked up by my father's uncle. His name was Martin. He was a contractor like his brother and my grandfather, Mark, and he lived in the same neighborhood where the school was located a few blocks away. He used to pick me up after school and take me to his home along with his two older daughters. You see, in Baghdad you can't trust having your daughters wander around or walk alone without a man along their side, so he was killing two birds with one stone by picking all of us up at the same time.

When I was at their home, they were very kind and generous to me. They used to feed me and, at times, bathe me until my father got off from work and came to pick me up. This happened for many years, and I'm grateful to all of them for all their help and caring. They were, and still are, very special people in my heart, and I can't forget them, ever.

Poems and singing were my favorite subjects. My scores in school for the Armenian subjects were, believe it or not, 100 percent. I took after my dad who was a poet and a story writer until his passing on July 9, 2012. Also, I loved stage performances. On my graduation day from Kindergarten, I was on the stage in front of a microphone, and I said my poem before an audience of five hundred people. No video cameras existed in those days to tape the event so that I could remember my childhood. Being from an over protective and conservative family, the fear of making mistakes or failing was constantly bugging me in life until my high school years. I would jump in fire for others and save people, but when the time came to save myself, I was defenseless and could care less about myself because I felt there were always others more important than me. That's the way I was raised back then, but things have changed a little in the later years.

Two years have passed, and it's 1963, and I had already graduated from Kindergarten and had already gotten enrolled in the Elementary section of the school. All my friends had moved up with me to the first grade. And before I forget, the Baghdad Armenian School was self-funded as no government grant or help was issued to it. This was a private school, and the students were charged a tuition fee to keep the school going financially. Textbooks were purchased from the school because the school was purchasing all the Armenian related texts and books from out of the country from Lebanon. The Lebanese community, to a certain point, had freedom of speech more than our Iraqi community. We were living in a Muslim dominated country and freedom of speech was not granted for all equally. The school tuition was paid by my father, and it was a heavy burden on him financially. Thank God, we didn't have to wear the surgical-like robes in elementary school. It was all casual uniform of dark blue shorts, solid white shirts, and, of course, an added expense on my father's list.

I had my share of experiences throughout the four years of my elementary school days. There were some mean and some kind teachers mentoring us through all kinds of subject matters as a curriculum. In addition to the country's required subjects, we learned three more different subjects which were not available from the state. These subjects were the Armenian language, Armenian history, and the Christian religion. All were written in the Armenian language. The latter subject, the Christian religion, was as important as the other two were for me and my parents living in a Muslim country. One must know his/her own religion and history and to preserve one's language as part of one's culture. These were the wishes of my elderly as well as my teachers who were instructing us. They said we should learn the native language, which was Arabic, and the history, which was in Arabic, but we should never ever forget our own. Our teachers' advice was about articulating the reason for being able to transfer all what we had learned as subjects to our next generation of Armenians.

I had a very good habit of listening to my mentors at school while they were teaching, and I respected them as much as I respected my parents. I was very good in my own language as far as grammar and poems. Needless to say, and this is not bragging, but I was one of the top students in my class in these subjects. Also, I want to mention something here about my English teacher. I loved the English language, and I was as good in English as I was with the rest of the subjects. My scores were always B+ and A's. But what got me there was the roughness and the meanness of the teacher. Most kids get turned off when a teacher is mean and very demanding. Even though we were all afraid to talk to him or look him in the eye, it was a challenge for me at a young age to try to understand why my English teacher was mad all the time. On certain occasions, he was abusive with his actions in class, as well as with his words. If you cheated in his class, you would get a big hit on your head with his famous big gold ring. He had it on his index finger on the right hand. He would hit you like no yesterday, and some of us had complained about him to the Administration Office through our parents, of course. Specifically, one time I saw my friend's head start to bleed after he hit him on top of his head with his gold ring. It wasn't funny. To be honest, I didn't like what he was doing, yet we had no choice and no court or legal authorities to complain to other than the school administration itself. The parents tried to avoid escalating matters because the authorities were looking for any incident that might happen inside our school, so they could interfere and take over some of the management positions and possibly the school itself to gain advantage to close it down or convert it from private to a regular public school. Then, again, the school solved everything or every problem within the parent/teacher board. We were all minorities in the city, and we didn't want any interference from the outside. All problems were manageable relating to behavioral issues only and not criminal ones, which didn't exist anyway. Yet, on the bright side and opposite from the English teacher's character, there was my grammar teacher. We were all waiting for her to teach us. She was so sweet and beautiful to us young boys, and we all had a crush on her. But she got engaged and then married later. Oh well, too bad.

The year is still 1963. My family moved to a new neighborhood, and my dad got his first brand new home which had just gotten built. It was quite far from the Armenian school we were attending, and elements like time pressure and the financial burdens were all tremendous on my father's list to do every day. He got up very early every morning and took a cab in order to take me to school. After dropping me off at school, my dad caught a bus to work and came back in the same afternoon to take me back home. Then, in the meantime, I was staying, as I had mentioned before, at my father's uncle's home in our old neighborhood.

My dad was evaluating an idea when he learned that there was a young man living in our new neighborhood who was already stopping every morning by our school to drive a female student back and forth daily. She was in junior high school. It was a good idea to ask this young man who was in his twenties if he would do him this favor for a fee, and that is to take his children back and forth to school each day as well along with his already existing passenger. This young man owned an army jeep, like a Willy's brand. The man agreed to do this, and my father was happy that this problem was somewhat solved for him for now, and we were not going to lose the opportunity to attend this private school. One Saturday when school had started, (in

Iraq the weekends were a half a day on Thursdays and a whole day on Fridays; their Saturdays are like our Mondays, and normally the weekdays will start on a Saturday). As a child, I was very excited about traveling with this young man on the first day of school. He stopped at our house and honked the horn, and I ran to sit in the back of the Jeep. My mom came out to say goodbye to me. I sat on the inside seat and not along the outside because this jeep didn't have any outside rails as a barrier to avoid falling off the jeep while it was being driven.

There were no seat belts, so I had to hold on and hold on tight to anything. Then the driver went and picked up this beautiful girl from our neighborhood. She was also a Christian, and I had never seen her before. She was to sit in the front seat as the driver had asked her to do so. Girls shouldn't mix with boys in this city. It was not a common thing that you would see every day on the city streets; especially, for a single woman. They were always home unless the family went out and took their daughters along with them. This young man was extremely happy, and it was unusual for me to see a man this happy because he was doing nothing more than a delivery service. I didn't catch it or understand it in the beginning. This went on for several months. One day halfway home, the jeep stopped, and the driver told me to get off at the side of the road and said he would be back with the girl in five minutes to pick me up later. I couldn't argue. I was a little boy at the time, and I was somewhat scared being left out on the side of the road waiting for him. Twenty minutes later, they came back to pick me up, and they were laughing and happy together all the way home.

I got home. My mom was worried about me. She asked, "What is going on? Why are you coming home late?"

When I told her what had happened, she smiled and didn't say anything to me. The next thing we knew, she told my dad. Oh boy! My dad went and told the girl's parents. Then the next thing we learned was that we all lost our ride service to school not knowing the facts. The driver had fallen in love with this girl, and he had done something against the principals of all families. He flirted with her in a shameful fashion while we were waiting to be picked up by him that day.

As adults, my parents knew what was taking place in life. When they were talking to the girl's parents, I overheard them say that the driver had kissed their daughter several times and touched her inappropriately. Now some of you will say big deal, so what! Well, let me tell you this. In a Muslim country like Iraq, at that time, or when living among an obsolete conservative society, an individual's freedom of expression was not allowed. The young generation was not as free like any other type of western society, and it was a very big deal and almost a sin to touch and kiss and fondle a female without her parents' consent. Luckily, she was a Christian girl with Christian parents where forgive and forget plays a role in their discipline. If she was a Muslim female, she would have been killed by her own parents to wash the shame off their family's name because image was everything for the family, regardless. Then you had to lose a beautiful young life for nonsense reasons. But that's how it was with their beliefs. This is the way the society was treating women or a religion that had identified women as second-class citizens (we are talking around the sixties in a country like Iraq). But, nevertheless, life had to go on. My dad had already canceled out this jeep riding business, and he was stuck taking me to school again for several months and on a daily basis.

Three years later on April 13, 1966, Abdul Salam Mohammed Arif, the President of Iraq, was killed in a helicopter crash and his brother, General Abdul Rahman Arif, was named as his successor as the President of Iraq. At my young age, I could only see and hear for the second time that people were cheering again for another downfall of another so- called bad man. I was ten and a half years old then. People were happy that this happened because I could see it from their cheering. They were running in the streets and calling out a phrase in Arabic that translates like this, "He flew like a meat and landed like a charcoal," meaning the president just got killed in a presidential plane crash. Being young and not knowing what the words of the people meant, I started yelling with the same phrases in Arabic about the president. This was before my mom realized the danger of the words that might cause us harm by living among the Muslim population in this new neighborhood of the Baghdad suburbs. She ran out and slapped my face so hard that I was not aware of what had happened. I was punished that day. No playing soccer with friends and other fun things like playing card games. That was bad.

The television sets started again to broadcast the site where the crash happened, and the mosque started to announce the prayers throughout the whole town where there were many mosques. When they all prayed together, it sounded like the sirens of war. We were listening to prayers several times a day regularly anyway, but now it was more serious and there was no stopping. They were horrible and scary moments for me to see the burned remains of the crew and the President on national television, uncensored and unedited.

As I mentioned before, the President's brother, General Abdul Rahman Arif, was appointed to take his brother's place, and, unlike his brother, he was not much into fanaticism about his religion of Islam, so to speak. He was more into looking at what was undone by the past government, so he could rebuild or lead the country toward a different direction. Sometimes, you could say he was closer in thinking with the West. But and this is a big but, no president like him would last too long without any other revolution to overthrow him. Today, I believe that the west or the western governments were always involved in those processes with possibly other Arab countries to instigate a revolution to change powers in that region because of the mutual interest in the region's oil products as a vital natural energy resource, which the entire world was heavily dependent on to run their industries.

Going back to my schooling. My father Mike came up with a clever idea which was to transfer me from my private school where I was attending the local public school located in our neighborhood. This transfer was to first eliminate the cost of paying for private school, which got to be a challenging task for my father to fulfill and handle monthly. Second, having me go to a school where the location was minutes away and not hours away from my residence so that I could walk rather than ride a cab to get to school, also just in case any other national emergency or other crises like a revolution or civil unrest should occur in the near future. Taking these steps helped me to be home in minutes and be safe. The Iraqi government's daily fate was not short of sudden events like revolution or strikes. My dad was the only family member who was working away from home, and taking these steps loosened the burden of worrying about me, plus it helped him to make better financial decisions since he was the only bread winner in the family.

In order to accomplish the transfer from a private school to a public school, there were certain rules that were a must to be abided by, which were strictly discriminatory against all private schools. You see, most private schools were non-Muslim and non- public. The educational ministry rule said that any time a student requests a transfer from a private school, the student should be demoted one grade if he or she wants to attend a public school. In other words, if you were in third grade and in a private school and you wanted to be transferred to a public school, you would be losing one full year of your education, and you would be placed back into the second grade according to this example. This was a big obstacle for me because I was an A student, and I loved education. I couldn't wait to proceed to the next level. I needed to graduate soon and get my goals in life accomplished. I wanted to work and to help my father by standing next to him as a man, so everyone could be proud of me for helping my dad. This was one of my objectives, but I was not the one who was making decisions for me. My young mind was always planning for the future for all of us to have better lives and a comfortable one. And, in order to accomplish them, I would have to graduate first.

My father built our first home on a piece of land in the suburbs of Baghdad, the capital of Iraq. He won this land through a raffle award at his workplace, which was the Iraqi Department of Water and Power (DWP). We had moved and settled in an area which was populated mostly by Muslim families. Very few Christian families had lived there. Some of the families in the area were kind towards us. Some were honest people, and others were not so friendly or not so happy seeing Christians moving into their neighbor-hood. Our next-door neighbors were Muslims and very generous people. Their eldest son and two of the older daughters were teachers in various public schools around the city of Baghdad.

One summer evening, my father invited our next-door neighbors to our house for dinner to get to know them better and be friends as we were going to share life living next to them. My father was not short of opening the subject of the school system, and they talked amongst themselves around different matters as well. My father learned how he could bypass this nonsense educational ministry rule from talking to our neighbor's son, a teacher. My father was getting bothered a lot about this school rule. No one wanted to lose a whole year of hard work and sacrifice just because they had to follow a rule. It was discriminatory to start with anyway.

You see, at that time in Iraq you could break every rule, only if you knew how and whom you should approach, and sometimes, unfortunately, with some bribes to accomplish doing so, or doing favors to others in exchange for services.

Well, sure enough, our neighbor's oldest son, Adnan, came up with an idea. He told my father that he would be talking to the principal of his school to fix some paperwork through his school administration board which would confirm that I had been registered with their institution as an attendee at his school during the past year. This paperwork from his public school was to be filed immediately with our local school district in the immediate neighborhood. This was to avoid raising any doubts. This process was going to maintain my grade levels as the same without any changes or demotions. I believe the dinner invitation was well planned by my dad. The plan was on, and on the very next day, I went and registered with a new public school in the Nahda area in the middle of the city of Baghdad with the help of our neighbor's son and teacher, Mr. Adnan.

Today, students here in the US, and like my own children, are all talking about peer pressure in their schools, but that's nothing compared to the peer pressure in the school that I enrolled in and attended. I was speaking the Arabic language with an accent, and the whole school knew I was Christian. There were no other Christians at this school, and we were outnumbered. Also, the school was teaching the Holy Quran to the Muslim students as a religion that was mandated by the Department of Education for all public schools. We were not accustomed to this one subject being included in our schedule compared to our previous private school. Non-Muslims, including Christians and Jews, were specified as sinners in their religious books. Luckily, in public schools there was a rule that protected us non-Muslims. The rule said if you are not Muslim, you cannot attend this class. I am not being disrespectful to other religions here, but as a young child, it was a new experience for me to observe and learn new habits and rules, which were, at times, causing me a great deal of discomfort and confusion. Our religion was not discriminatory at all as Christians, but it was teaching us to respect what God created; a man and a woman. And, in God's eyes, we are all loved equally regardless of diversity or religion. It was very uneasy for me to attend this school. The reason being was I had to stay out of this class for that period. Then I witnessed some of the students who were exiting their Quran class and going into the recess period were pumped up with their religious beliefs where you could see the hatred towards us in their eyes. It was obvious. The students hated to see us mixed in with them, and, at times, during recess we were spat on several times, and this lasted for a good several weeks. But it was an experience for me to see what I had stepped into by switching to this public school. I'm not saying that all Iraqi public schools were doing the same, but these were the facts and experiences that I had encountered with this school. My only safeguard was Mr. Adnan, our neighbor's son and teacher. I complained to him at times because I had a fear of going out during recess. Mr. Adnan was very fair, and he understood the situation. He told me not to worry and not to talk about being a Christian too much and said whatever happens to come and tell him first and not to engage in any sort of fights. I nodded my head and agreed with him and his advice even though fear was always on my mind and that I could be harmed one day.

The good education and discipline which I had received in private school paid off. I was scoring very high marks and grades in the weeks I attended this school. English As a Second Language was the icing on the cake for me. I associated with and changed the attitude of one of the rough Muslim students who constantly hated me by helping him with his homework. He became my best friend and protected me during recess periods from getting hurt by others or by being abused by others who were spitting on me. This protection was in exchange for me to do his English homework for him. He hated the English language, and, oh boy, I had a hold on him on this one. This had gone on for a good several weeks, and, thank God, the time had come for me to move on. I was done with this jungle. In the same semester I got transferred to our neighborhood elementary school where things were a bit less troubling. Of course, a million thanks to Mr. Adnan, our teacher and our neighbor's son, and all his efforts. The funny or not so funny part of this experience was when I told my parents about what was happening, they laughed along with Mr. Adnan and told me this was a big test and that they knew this was going to happen. But this had created some discomfort in me and mistrust for a while toward my own parents since they knew all this was going to happen and they didn't say anything about it. For me, it was not funny at all.

My parents were good and helpful individuals toward our Muslim neighbors next door. For example, my parents were helping them when they couldn't pay their electric bill. I remember my dad had to extend a long electrical wire into their house through one of our windows for them to have electricity, and sometimes for a period of months. Also, he helped them with some food or money for groceries as a loan at times. All these were done by my father out of the goodness of his heart. Our neighbors used to exchange the favors with other things in return. For instance, they built a type of stove in their backyard where they baked fresh Arabic bread daily from scratch. This stove was mostly made from clay, and it looked like a big diagonal cylinder which is called "tanoor" in Arabic. Some were freestanding, and others were built below ground level. They put wood logs to burn in the middle of it as a source of heat and fire. Then the wood would burn to a maximum degree just like the wood pit oven concept in restaurants. Every mid-day around noontime when our neighbor, Mr. Adnan's mom, made fresh bread to serve her family, she would give some of her baked bread away to her neighbors as well as to us. She was trying to pay us back for the things we had done for her family by returning the favor instead. Again, let's not forget these were our good Muslim neighbors, yet my father always advised us not to trust everyone in the neighborhood too much. They were very careful, and I don't blame them for it because they were right.

Time flew by, and the new school was not too difficult to adapt to at all, or, perhaps, I saw it that way. When we were out of the classrooms during recess, I could see my home located a short distance from the school. This was creating some comfort in me, and I felt safe. There were other Christian students among us as well in our neighbor-hood schools. We were all backing up each other and sticking together just in case unwanted events like discrimination should take place against any of us. We had a geography teacher at this school who was a member of the Muslim Brotherhood organization. His name was Mr. Salam. He passionately hated us. He did not dislike, but hated Christians. I was told this by my neighbor's older son, Mr. Adnan, who was a math teacher himself. Somehow, he knew Mr. Salam, our geography teacher, and remembered him from being with him in prison at one time serving a sentence in the past. Mr. Adnan was taken to prison previously and was tortured by mistake because the regime thought that he was a communist and working against the government. Then Mr. Adnan also added that Mr. Salam was a violent person and knew him from the past because he was his cell mate.

Every time we had a test for geography, Mr. Salam looked to find any mistake done by us Christians, the Sunni Muslims, and the Kurdish students so he would have a rea-son to beat us up. He used a short tree branch or a short water hose and used it as a whipping tool to punish his students with. He would ask you to open your hand to see your palm, and he would strike an unkindly whip as hard as he could on to it, and the pain was unbearable. You had to use a lot of ice for at least two days to overcome the pain. It was horror for us students. Sometimes, he was the teacher who was assigned around the recess periods to watch over the students in the school field as well. He used to play games to spread fear among us. Usually, he would catch one of the students, meaning one of his own people, during the recess period and would charge him with disturbance. He would make that student stand in front of the whole school in the field, and then he would start beating this young kid up with whatever means he had and made others watch his actions just to plant fear in everyone's mind in order to fear him. We were only ten to thirteen years old at the time. I didn't accept this kind of abuse to any student, regardless if they were Muslim or non-Muslim. During one recess period, I jumped in the front of the crowd and yelled at him in Arabic while he was in action beating this kid and told him a man that believes in God cannot abuse what God created. I told him that he was a teacher and that he was nothing but a human being like us. There was a sudden silence in the school field. The principal was rushed out to investigate what was going on that day, and, as angry as I was, I turned to the principle and told him what was going on not only on the school field during recess but inside the classrooms as well. Mr. Salam couldn't believe his ears as to what I was saying about him to the principal of the school, who was his boss, regarding his brutal abuse towards the students. Mr. Salam gave me a very bad look. When the beaten up student got loose from his grips and was set free, the principal asked the geography teacher, Mr. Salam, to follow him to his office. Then everyone started cheering and yelling.

Two of my good friends and I pretended that we had to go to the teachers sitting quarters because we had questions about various subjects before we had to go to our next class. In doing so, we were following the principal and Mr. Salam as they were going to the principal's office. The teachers' sitting quarters was next to the principal's office with one wall separating the two offices. Three of us walked to the teachers' sitting room, and I let both my friends ask questions to one of the teachers, pretending I had the same questions to ask while I was listening with one ear to the principal's voice from the other side of the wall yelling at the top of his lungs at Mr. Salam and warning him about his actions and methods of dealing with the students. Then I heard the principal tell him he is suspended for a week, and if he didn't change his methods, he was going to be transferred to another school outside the city. The principal was going to type a written recommendation to the Board of Education for his transfer if he didn't clean up his act. I smiled very happily. We finished getting our answers and we left the teachers' sitting quarters. We went to our next class, and I went to tell everyone the good news.

A week passed, and Mr. Salam, like a bad hurricane, came back and classes started again. In the meantime, we had a substitute teacher teaching us geography for a week. The first thing Mr. Salam said when he took over the class was, "Close your books, and all of you pull out a sheet of paper. We are going to have a test."

I stood up with a big fear on my face this time and told him that we are not ready to take the test until next week when the finals are due. I said, "This is what the substitute teacher told us yesterday."

Mr. Salam smiled and told me to kindly please sit down. But I felt something was about to happen, and this teacher had not changed his attitude yet. We did what he ordered us to do. We took the test, and I scored 84 percent. But I let my guard down when I celebrated too soon, only to attract his attention. He said I was making too much noise in the class and asked me to come to him and stand in front of the classroom next to the board. I got up and walked like a sheep to the blackboard and stood there while the teacher went out and came back with a tree branch to punish whoever failed his test and for the so-called disturbance of making too much noise. This was his plan to get revenge on me. The pain in my palms was not pleasant. He struck unkindly, whipping my palms with the tree branch. And, as he was striking his whip, I looked at his face and understood that this was his revenge for what had happened a week ago. Luckily that day, that was the last class before we went home. I waited until my father got home, and then my mom showed him what had happened to my hands. This blew his top, and he said he was going to the police to report this. I told him why not consult our neighbor about this? I said Mr. Adnan had told me previously that he knew Mr. Salam from his prison days. My father was a good dad. He always listened to us. He decided to meet Mr. Adnan. Mr. Adnan told my dad that Mr. Salam wanted to build a new mosque in our neighborhood, and he wanted all the parents to donate to towards this mosque. He added that Mr. Salam knew that his son is a Christian, and he wouldn't help his project come to light because of his belief. He also said if we leave the choice to Mr. Salam, he would turn Baghdad into a mosque; culturally, so to speak. He would have one built on every corner and every block. He is a fanatic person, and you should watch out for him. He also advised us not to go to the police because this might harm us later because members of his organization are everywhere in every trade and workplace.

When my father heard this, he said he would go to my school and meet with Mr. Salam the next day. My dad came home early and came to my school to meet Mr. Salam. He walked to my school and asked for me and Mr. Salam, and we were both called to the teachers' sitting quarters. He asked my teacher to meet with him after hours on the site where this mosque was to be built in order to discuss the needs and the plans that were drawn to accomplish this project. My teacher was surprised, and he agreed. My dad told the teacher that he didn't raise disturbing, foolish kids and explained to Mr. Salam what kind of Christian people we were. He told my teacher that he doesn't have any right to abuse children, and the way he was handling things. My father said that he will forgive what he had done at this time. Then he left my school to go home. I was in fear after that moment to go back to my class, thinking what will happen to me after my dad leaves the school and until the end of the school day that day.

The time was 3:40 p.m. that afternoon, and the last bell rang. It was a big relief for me to rush out and go home. Later that evening, my father and I met Mr. Salam on the site of the mosque project. I was very surprised by the way Mr. Salam was looking at us. He was very welcoming and kind for a change. He took his time to explain to my father how this project was important to him, and being a son of a Muslim religious leader, he must accomplish building this mosque. His father was going to be the preacher and the top holy man of this mosque. Then I saw my dad reach into his pocket and pull out some large Iraqi paper currency called dinar. He handed Mr. Salam a chunk of cash as a donation to start building his project, and he told him to contact him if he needs anything further or any other help. My father mentioned to him that just because we are Christians, that doesn't mean we hate Muslims, and that we are all God's children, including him; referring to Mr. Salam. My father told my teacher that he shouldn't hear any complaints from his children about any abuse or harm from him. Mr. Salam agreed with my dad that he was right, and there will be no harm coming to me from him since he understood us better now. I didn't trust his words, even though he agreed with everything my dad told him. Thank you, Mr. Cash (money talks, and you know what walks).

In the following weeks, Mr. Salam's style of dealing with us Christians, and especially with me, had changed. We didn't believe what we saw or heard; he was polite and kind. But it didn't seem much of a change because he was not normal to me. He was a fanatic and things could change again regardless of his promises. Well, I got by and finished elementary school throughout the following years. And, while I was in the sixth grade, Mr. Salam handed in his resignation to the school. He was going to help his father at the new mosque that had just gotten built and was located about four hundred yards from our residence.

I said to myself, "Oh, that's just great!" I came to the realization that I was a citizen of a Muslim country, and that's the way it was; take it or leave it. You can't complain about having a new mosque being built; otherwise, you would be thrown into prison for the rest of your life without any trail. Who knows if you would be lucky enough to live long and unharmed in the Iraqi prisons in those days? You might have a chance at survival and of getting out alive.

It was July 17, 1968, and, sure enough, it happened once more. General Arif's government was overthrown this time, and "Major General Ahmed Hassan Al Baker" was appointed head of the revolutionary command council of the Baath party governing Iraq. It was called the white revolution because there was no bloodshed this time. When the old government was thrown out, all Iraqi's were cheering again and again. I remember leaving my school early to run home and climb over the school's perimeter walls during recess (the walls were built of concrete blocks six feet in height). I was trying to avoid exiting from the school's main entrance while all the students and the teacher's administrative body were preparing to rally in the streets for a new celebration. I didn't want to be a part of it. My elementary school was in our neighborhood a half a block from my house in Baghdad. In the panic and confusion, I left all my text books in the classroom that day when I had to run out of the classroom along with others, as we were asked to do so by the school administration.

Fear was an undivided and constant visitor one more time in my life at the age of thirteen. Suddenly, I felt a strange feeling in my heart that life was going to change again, and it wouldn't be the same anymore. Maybe it was just a sense of different feelings. I don't know. Or, was it a call from the heavens, which could be a warning sign for me that this revolution was a bad deal. Then it was proven to me that I was right about it later in life. I didn't know it at the time when I was thirteen years of age. I will explain why and how in the next chapter.

Months later, my elementary days were over, and junior high school was next for me to continue. Luckily, the junior high school was located in our neighborhood as well within walking distance on the other side of this newly built mosque. I had to pass by it every morning and every afternoon. I wanted to see how Mr. Salam was doing his preaching to brainwash others like himself with false information that had nothing to do with the Islam religion or faith. Well, it didn't bother me very much as long as it had nothing to do with me anymore as a student.

Junior high school was pleasant. I found new friends; one was Jewish, and his name was Hassan. (He said it was changed from Haskell to Hassan. I didn't know why at the time.) My other friend was a Kurd and a Sunni Muslim whose name was Moostafa, and some other Christian friends from my neighborhood. The school system had somewhat changed as to how to hire teachers. I saw more new Christian teachers had been placed as a good mix to teach in our neighborhood schools in all subjects except religion. I was happy that there was some balance, at least, so we could learn and not to get mixed up with nonsense things and issues.

One more important thing that was going on was that Mr. Adnan's younger sister, Hudda (a girl's name in Arabic), was my age and in the same grade as well, but, of course, in a different school because Baghdad public schools are not mixed. Boys attend school with boys and girls attend with girls; but colleges were mixed.

Hudda's skin color was tan. She was a bright and ambitious girl. She was not your typical, average Muslim girl. She understood that other people's rights must be respected, and respecting others was a priority for her. She told me once that it was the key to the future generation to be free from being partial in any way. We were talking about these kinds of subjects and issues when we were growing up as neighbors. See, I mentioned boys and girls didn't mix in Iraqi's lifestyle very well but because of the trust that was built among us being neighbors, her mother didn't mind having her daughter associate with me. As a boy, I knew how to respect and care about other peoples' rights as well. Hudda and I became good friends. We were competing against each other every year in the sense that we could pass our finals and advance to the next class without going to summer school. This meant we both had to be so prepared and ready to face and attack the finals without any hesitation. At the end, we both finished junior high and off we went to the next level for senior high.

CHAPTER

3

The Senior High School Years, and Our Haunted New Home

June 13, 1969 was the year I enrolled in senior high school, which was far from home. I took a bus ride via the Iraqi public transportation system which lasted a half an hour. My new high school was called Al-Ressala High (the word "Al-Ressala" in Arabic means the message). Al-Ressala High School was located in an area called Maydan near the Department of Water and Power building (DWP). The DWP was located centrally in the Maydan area. My father worked for the DWP at one of their branch offices, which was also located near the area of Maydan City. In other words, my new high school, the DWP, and my dad's workplace were all in one area convenient enough for me to move around in. After closing the branch office that he worked at and at the end of each day, my father had to make a trip to the DWP main building to deposit the funds he collected from its custom- ers, or the public, which was done on a daily basis. On occasions, I used to see him, and we used to wave to each other from a distance when I took my bus ride home from the bus station, which was across from the DWP building. On days when I had to leave my school early, I used to walk to my dad's branch office and help him log all the entries in the books just to speed up the process, so he could close down and go home early. We used to walk together to the DWP building. I had to wait outside the building because I was not allowed to go in as I was not an employee there. My father would go in and finish his work. Then he would come out and, on some days after a short walk to the bus station, we would take a bus home together.

One afternoon I walked to my father's branch office of the DWP where I noticed a young man was hired to help him with his work at the office. His last name was Moondery. This young man was well educated, and he was sharp with his answers. Whenever I needed help, he would help me with some of my high school subjects like physics and algebra. Months after I got to know him, my dad told me that we were going to have Mr. Moondery move in with us for a few short days. I was puzzled. With all the fuss made by my father in the past about not trusting any strangers, we were having a stranger move in and live with us in the same household. When I asked my dad what was going on, he said not to worry and said they are looking to arrest this young man because he had said some bad words and disagreed with some of the authorities regarding ethnic issues. We were doing him a favor. I asked, "How so?" My dad replied, "We are not going to be involved with what he believes in or what he follows, son. I have nothing to do with what he has done. All I know is he didn't harm anyone by telling the truth, as he explained to me." My dad added that he just didn't want him to be harmed as Moondery had told my father earlier that day that he would be killed if he was captured. He is well raised and is an honest young man, and he had done a lot of good to Christians and other non-Muslim ethnic groups. I asked my dad to assure me that there was no danger to us in doing this. He assured me not to worry. Then he said because in a few days' time this young man will be traveling out of the country anyway. Moondery had relayed this information to my father, and my father, out of the goodness of his heart, was willing to help spare his life, ignoring the fact that he could be a target along with all of us. Furthermore, my dad said that Moondery's friends, who he didn't know and had never met before, were going to pick him up and help him get out of the country. Then he advised me not to speak of this information and arrangements to anyone in the family. I told him it's done. All what was planned happened exactly as my father had explained to me. A few days later, Moondery was contacted one evening by three people and was picked up outside our house with a station wagon. We never saw him after he left us; at least for a long while. You see, my dad was kind and somewhat naive at the same time, but anyhow.

A year passed by, and as I was attending my high school in the Maydan area, I witnessed soldiers were stopping students in the streets and searching them at random. All students were to have their ID cards with them, and everyone was to keep short groomed hair along with their sideburns. No long sideburns like Elvis was allowed. They didn't want us to look like westerners as this was the new rule for all the students throughout the city from the new Baath regime. In the beginning, I ignored the warnings and kept my hair long along with my sideburns. I didn't care much what they said since I was attending high school. I thought I could live differently and be freer since I was older. The crowd I mixed with after- hours was my own Armenian community. I was an athlete in the Armenian Athletic Club (AAC) of Baghdad. The reason that I had kept my hair long was what if I am to meet a girl? Then my short hair and sideburns wouldn't be very appealing at this club in the sixties. I was playing basketball, and I was also in the Boy Scouts group at the same time. I cared less what everyone was doing with their hair. I was going to keep mine long as I liked it. I got away with it for several months because I changed my route taking the bus and always had a boy scouts beret hat on my head to hide my long hair after leaving school.

One afternoon, I had just left school and was not looking around when I took the normal route to catch the bus. I was surprised when a soldier approached me and asked for my student

ID card. As I leaned to pull it out of my bag, my hat fell off my head and he saw my long hair. Right away I was arrested by him and taken away to ride in an army truck that was parked next to the Department of Water and Power building where my dad went every afternoon to deposit the public utilities collected funds.

I sat down in the truck with a big fear on my face next to the other students who were all arrested earlier that afternoon. All of us were talking about what was going to happen to us next and as to what kind of a regime this was that they had nothing better to do than to try to control people as to how we should groom ourselves and how we should get dressed. It was very strange and annoying. And, as for the female students, they had other disciplinary rules, which was that no female student should wear any short skirts above their knees. This kind of fear spread all over the city when the Baath regime took power in order to control people and their minds through fear. These kinds of incidences were one of many different kinds of methods that were being used when this nonsense and brutal regime took power and ruled Iraq.

We all learned this by seeing it on the TV screen weeks after this government took charge in the country and what could happen to you if you didn't obey them. They forced you to have your hair kept short. If you didn't obey their wishes, then you would be taken into a room and they would shave your head like a big plus sign while the TV cameras were rolling, and that evening you would be broadcasted on the air all over the city just to make an example of you to others.

Now all of us arrested students were sitting in the army truck and were chatting about these subjects. Coincidently, I saw my father passing next to the army truck and yelled for his help. The soldier guarding the truck turned around and ordered me to sit down, but I was not going to do so until I got my dad's attention. My father saw me, and I witnessed the color of his face turn yellow all of a sudden due to his shock and fear of seeing me in that army truck. He managed to control himself and to communicate with me with his eyes. This was like sign language between us. By pointing to my head and pulling on my hair, he understood what was going on because a week earlier at home and at the dinner table I had opened up this subject to him, so he would know what was going on in the streets regarding us students. Then, for a moment, my dad forgot that he had a job to do that day, which was that he needed to deposit funds at the DWP building. But he approached the truck first and spoke softly to the soldier, who was guarding the truck, and I could hear what he said to the soldier; that I was his son and that he works for the Department of Water and Power. He showed his ID issued by the local government to the soldier. If you were a federal employee in Iraq at that time, you carried some weight, and you were considered a trustworthy person. I saw him looking and winking at me while the soldier was about to pull me off the truck. As I went down and off the truck, both my arms were held behind my back by the soldier like a criminal. I saw my dad was getting ready to slap my face, and he did. He started yelling in my face in the presence of the soldier by asking me how many times he had told me to have my hair cut. Then he said how he was going to take me right away to a barbershop and get my hair cut according to the new rules. I saw both soldiers who were guarding the truck were happy at what my dad did and said. To my shock, I was released free that afternoon. It was a miracle.

My dad asked me to stay put outside the DWP building until he comes out. He went in and deposited the funds, and then we both took a taxicab home and not a bus that day. My dad knew the driver was a trustworthy individual, so we knew we could chat in his cab. This regime had designed other methods to control people as well, and that was by planting informers amongst us in the form of cab drivers and inside public buses. All the way home, I was really pounded by harsh advice from my dad in terms of how times were changing to the worse so we all had to be careful how we conducted our daily lives. I agreed with him totally because he saved my life, especially since I had a place to go that evening. I guess I took after some of my parents' habits; the good ones, of course. I took after my mom for being very loving toward her family, kind to everyone and always patient, and she liked to see everyone happy. Also, she suffered when she saw human tragedy. I took after my dad in being a good athlete and sports loving individual as well as culturally oriented and talented in dance, drama, poem writing, and story writings. I took after my grandfather for his courage, fairness and helping the needy. I am not saying that I am perfect. Like everyone else, I have some shortcomings as well. I had to follow the rules and have a haircut; short enough to pass by the guards. I then went on to see my friends that afternoon to tell them what had happened.

While I was attending high school, I was involved in playing basketball with the school team and the AAC. I was also enrolled in the Boy Scouts in both the high school and the AAC. With this being said, I was taking everything seriously and performing to the best of my abilities with each group. One evening while I was at Boy Scout practice at the AAC, I was introduced to a cultural dance instructor who was teaching Armenian cultural dances for boys and girls. He was the main dance instructor for the Iraqi Folkloric Dance Group of Baghdad. I was honored to join them and be a part of this joyful cultural pride and of learning new things and challenges. Not much later, every one of my relatives knew I was part of the dance group, and every time my relatives had gatherings, my family was invited. They used to put the music on, and I was called in to show them some dance steps and to dance with their daughters and so on. It was pleasant for me to do so equally with the sports activities. The word got around in our neighborhood that I was part of the AAC. It was a private club that allowed boys and girls to mix in all sports activities. The club was a well-respected and talented club in the sport and cultural arena. All other regular youth clubs in Baghdad were trying very hard to schedule sport events like basketball, volleyball, soccer and other games to compete against this club. When any of them won any games against us, they bragged about it and made it sound like they won the world championship. That's how good we played for the AAC Club. Very often, I was invited to join a local soccer team in our neighborhood. The game of soccer was one of my favorite games. Some of my high school friends also lived in our neighborhood. We used to go back and forth to school together by bus, and they were also soccer fans and good players. I was asked by my friends to join our neighborhood soccer team at one point. I started to play with the team and practice with them on the weekends only, not knowing that I was dragging myself deeper into the field of sports, and I was not paying very much attention to my school subjects and homework. My neighbor's daughter, Hudda, was proceeding fast. Remember, as I had mentioned before, there was this big educational competition between us. During one of the school years, I had no choice but to go to summer school in order for me to pass my classes and move to the next level due to failing some of the subjects on my finals. Hudda and I made a promise that neither one of us should go to summer school and must pass our classes in one shot. No exceptions. I couldn't keep that promise that year, but I did pass my class by attending summer school. Now, the promise was broken between us regarding school finals, and this had shaken up our friendship a bit.

My goal in life was to pass my classes every year. In Iraq, the regime made life difficult for the male students. If you didn't pass your classes yearly to the next level, you had to face the consequence and inconvenience of joining the Iraqi army. Joining the army was not by choice, but by force. The rule said if you fail to pass your classes for two consecutive years, meaning if you repeat the same grade twice in a row, then you would be drafted into the armed forces.

In a way, this was not so bad because during my years of attending high school, it created a big motive and energy in me that encouraged me to succeed and not to fail my class. But things got much worse in the later years around the year 1972 for all students and young people. The school rules changed every now and then by the regime without any notice and practically sometimes overnight. Due to the regime being a dictatorship, they had the control to change any rule at any given time. The idea was to get as many of the young students to join the armed forces with such a maneuver in the education system. The government's intention was to draft those students who failed their class into the army, all with the possibility of preparing for war.

Let's go back to playing soccer for now, which was my favorite thing to do in our neighborhood. One afternoon, my Christian friend Mazan and I were called outside our homes to play soccer with our neighborhood kids and our regular crowd. We were to play in this big, empty field, which was located directly behind our house. The neighborhood kids gathered, and we started to play soccer. In the middle of the game and as I was running, I saw Mazan getting hit by one of the players. I thought to myself that it's part of the game, and he should know better and run fast. But after a while, the hitting didn't stop until Mazan was on the ground; he was defenseless. So, from the far side of the field I ran to investigate only to hear that this kid was yelling at Mazan while tripping him down to the ground and calling him a dirty Christian. I said to myself, "Here we go again", and that was enough for me to start a fight with this young boy that was hitting Mazan so hard on the ground. I jumped in and I hit this boy in his face with any means I could to get him to stop. Then I saw that most of the other opponent players started to gang up against both of us. Here's where boys got to do what boys got to do, and that was to fight and not give in. I was hitting whoever was hitting me first, and, in the meantime, I was trying to protect Mazan who was still on the ground and in pain. I don't know how, but I saw our neighbor's son and his parents run out along with my dad to calm the situation down. I was not going to say anything, but one of the other kids started shouting, "You dirty Christians." Then my neighbor's mom reached out and slapped this kid on his mouth and told him, "Don't you dare call them dirty. They are much better and cleaner children than all of you." Being a Muslim herself, she knew everyone's mother in our neighborhood, and she said she was going to visit all their parents just to ask them what kind of unhealthy minded children they have been raising lately. Afterwards, everyone went on their way home. Mazan and I thanked our neighbors for their efforts in doing what they had to do.

The years of our youth were passing by very quickly. After we built our new home in 1963, my mom's sister, Veronica, and her husband, George, who were both very kindhearted and hardworking people who also worked for the Department of Water and Power at the time, wanted to move and live with us in our new home. Veronica and George met each other at the workplace, fell in love and got married. For them to start a family and have children, they needed someone to look after their children's welfare, and since my mom Elisa and her sister were very close from their childhood days, my mom was a good help to Veronica in looking after her kids while she was at work. Somehow, Veronica and her husband decided to move in with us and rent a bedroom from our newly built home. My parents didn't mind the change since we had a two-story home, and the upstairs bedroom was not used at all. The upstairs bedroom led to the flat roof of the house, and, in the summer, that's where the entire neighborhood placed their beds on their rooftops to sleep in the cold breeze of Baghdad's Arabian nights along with the desert shiny moonlight, which was glowing at nights. I had not yet seen anything like it anywhere in this world.

All homes were built basically with the same design. The perimeters of the rooftops had solid walls made of bricks and were four feet in height to protect anyone from falling off. Baghdad has a beautiful summer sky full of stars, and the moon gets so bright it's unbelievable. I remember one night in the sixties as we were listening to the shortwave and FM radio (which was given to us as a gift by people from Lebanon who visited our home a year earlier) to a station called, "The Sound of America". I was listening mostly to American music and some news. One night, the station announced that one of the American space rockets were orbiting around the world. I believe it was announced as Gemini 1 on the FM radio, which would be passing over the Middle Eastern skies. I got very excited because I loved space and astronomy. Every night I waited to see if I could find and spot the rocket movement while it was passing high in the sky by using a small telescope, which was given to me as a Christmas gift. Sure enough, two nights later and around one a.m. while I was looking at the sky and everyone was asleep, I yelled with a very loud and excited voice, "I can see it, I can see it!"

Everyone woke up in fear wanting to see what was happening, including several neighbors who were close by. They were also sleeping on the rooftop like us at nights to catch the cool summer breeze. We all got excited to see the American space rocket orbiting far in the sky, which was as small as the size of a star.

The next morning, some of the neighbors still didn't want to believe what they saw in the sky the night before. Knowingly, no one dared to talk about it, especially if it had to do with an American subject. We had this shortwave radio including the FM frequency channels that were being broadcast through an unknown station or satellite and possibly all over the Middle East. This kind of radio equipment was also a forbidden item in Iraq, and it was a dangerous tool to have. You couldn't let anyone know that you had a shortwave/FM frequency radio in your possession at any time because the government didn't want anyone to know what was going on in the outside world. This was their way of forcing their false ideas to control your fate and mind. Most of the police car radios at that time in Iraq were using FM frequency reception, and it was possible for anyone that had an FM radio to receive the police car reception as well. This was a big no-no, and it could have landed you in prison.

The year was 1964, and the summer season was over. We moved back down to the interior of the house to sleep at nights due to the winter season approaching. Living in our new home was scary at times. This was true because our home was haunted by a ghost, and my parents knew about this when they built the house. My parents slept in the master bedroom downstairs, my aunt Veronica and my uncle George, her husband, lived in the upstairs bedroom, and my grandmother Knar and my other siblings and I used to sleep in the family room, which was located at the end of the main hallway to the master bathroom towards the entrance of our house. On the other side of the master bathroom was the main kitchen, which led to the side of the house into the backyard. One night, my cousin Pete visited us to for a sleepover. As usual, the mattress was set on the floor tiles in the family room. There was this free-standing lamp with a single bulb next to our feet along one side of the mattress, which served as a night light for us. Suddenly, while Pete and I were up talking about school and games and everyone else had fallen asleep, the night light, which was standing on the floor next to my head, got knocked down and the bulb broke. Unfortunately, my grandmother was gone that night as she was staying at her daughter's house, which made us uncomfortable not having her there. Then suddenly, we were both in an unkind darkness on the floor in the middle of the family room. I told Pete not to move because I was going to the kitchen to get a new bulb from the cabinet using my small flashlight. I got the bulb, and we helped each other clean the broken glass and replace the bulb in the lamp. Then we decided to move the lamp away from our mattress about two to three feet because we thought one of us accidently knocked it down as we were laying and talking in bed and moving our arms freely in the air as any kid our age would do.

We moved the lamp away from us, and it was standing free again on the floor lined with our pillows. As we were talking, I noticed from the corner of my eye that the lamp moved slowly toward our feet again. This time around, we couldn't wait, and both of us got up in fear and ran to my parents' bedroom, knocking on the door for help or an explanation. My parents comforted us and said they will sit up with us in the family room until we slept. They said it was nothing but our imagination. My cousin Pete and I looked at each other in disbelief as to what my parents said. We knew what we saw, but we couldn't prove it. When we went back with my parents to the family room, I couldn't believe my eyes! The lamp was back in its original place! This made us look like fools. Well, we went back to bed, but none of us could sleep. I saw my mom was the only one who was watching over us since my dad went back to bed as soon as we had gone back to the family room. My mom said not to worry and said good night. She went to her room, but both of us couldn't sleep. Our eyes and minds were focused on the lamp. Oh boy, not again! This time not only was the lamp moving, but the mattress started to shake just like an earthquake. We both got up and ran again, but this time my parents were kind enough to take us into their bedroom, and we slept that night without any other mystery. We spoke about this the next day to my entire family on the breakfast table, but none of my family members took us seriously.

The year was 1965. The winter season had gone by fast and summer had started again. All the beds had to go up again and be set up on the rooftop to sleep at night. One summer night, it was hot and without any cool breeze blowing through. One of us boys had to go downstairs to get a cold pitcher of water with some cups for everyone, and, naturally, it was me. I went to get the water from the kitchen, so I turned all the downstairs lights on. My family was on the rooftop resting and sleeping, and no one was present downstairs in the house. I opened the door that separates the rooftop from the interior of our house to go downstairs. I heard a noise like someone was breathing on my neck, and I turned around, but there was no one there so I continued to go down. But I could hear something as if someone was following me down the stairs. At the same time, I knew what it was, but I didn't want to make it known that I was aware of its presence. I took the pitcher and the cups from the kitchen and slowly went back up the stairs, but I left all the lights in the kitchen on. I didn't tell anyone anything that night, and I went and closed the rooftop gate door shut and slept in my bed. But one of my eyes was watching the door for some time before I completely went to sleep just in case it would open so that I could alarm everyone.

In the morning when everyone got up, I explained to them what went on last night and both my parents decided to get a priest from the Armenian Church to bless our home since this was customary for some of us to do when you move to a new place, but we had not done this yet for this new home. It was not blessed as usual yet. During Easter week, the priest and his helper walked to our home one afternoon and blessed our new home per my dad's request. But this still didn't stop what was going on. Every now and then someone was surprised with another strange event. One day when we were talking to our neighbors, they said that most of the entire surrounding areas in our neighborhood including the land we had built our house on next to their property had been a killing field decades ago when there was civil unrest in the city. They had killed people and prisoners and buried them all over these areas. Everyone had been building their new homes here, but no one had encountered any graves or bodies to be found anywhere. My neighbors had also seen the same ghost walking in their backyard as well as in their living room, and even they couldn't understand how and with what they could get rid of this unwanted and unrested soul.

I remember another event with this ghost. One weekend, my parents had left me a note on the main entry door. Of course, no cell phones or pagers existed then in the sixties; all we had to communicate with were paper notes and house landline phones. I got home that afternoon from school and saw a note written in my own language by my parents and placed on the entry door to the house. The note said they were not home. They had gone to my mom's cousin's house where we were all going to gather that evening for dinner. My parents' advice to me was go in, do my homework, shower, and put some clean clothes on, then ride my bike and come over. My mom's cousin's house was not too far; only half a mile away. That last summer, I had gotten a new bike from my dad for passing my grades with high scores and passing onto the next level. I could use it to go anywhere with it, but not too far away as instructions were given to me by both of my parents just like in the old days when parents would advise their kids not to play and go far away from their sight. This was their style of being protective. I got excited because my mom's cousin had three daughters that wanted to socialize and that I could spend time with to chat. Also, I could dance with them whenever there was music playing and when I was asked to do so as it had happened on previous visits. This was going to be an exciting evening I told myself, if, and only if, I enter my lovely home, start getting ready and follow instructions as it was given to me by my mother. The very first thing I did, and thank God I did that first, I pulled my bike out and parked it in the backyard with my backpack which was still hanging from it. I was not worried about thieves or intruders stealing my bike, and the backpack was safe at tet time. The reason for doing so was because I decided to exit from the kitchen door when I was done, which was located at the back side of my house. Later, as I was getting ready to go into the shower, I heard some noises, and one of the windows upstairs was slamming back and forth. I put my towel around my waist to go and shut it for good. I got up the stairs, and there was only one window that I could see open. Aha! It's happening again! Then I said to myself, "It's nothing! So, what? Was this the ghost again?" As I was thinking about it, I started yelling in a loud voice, "Hey ghost! I'm not afraid of you! Go away!" But, folks, this was very strange. I had never experienced it before. It was just like someone wanted to communicate with me, and with a loud, cat-like noise just like someone was yelling back at me.

Let's stop right here for a moment and let me ask you this. What do you think happened, folks? Can you guess? Please don't. I believe if there were any Olympic referees at my house that day, and without any doubts, I would have been the winner of the one hundred-meter freestyle running sports event. That's right! You guessed it! I ran from the bathroom to my mom's bedroom and to my dresser, since I didn't have a bedroom of my own, and pulled all the cloths that I could get, like my underwear. Of course, there was no towel sitting on my hips anymore, so I managed to run out naked to the backyard, and, luckily, no one was outside. I had to put my clothes on fast and then grab my bike. My backpack was still hanging from it with all my school books and homework. Then, very fearfully, I went back to the kitchen door and slammed it shut, and then I was on my way to my mom's cousin's house. Folks, who cares that my clothing colors didn't match? Especially since, in my hurry, I grabbed my dad's shirt, his socks and my pants. Thank God, my mom stored her stuff in a separate place from the boys. I hope you get the picture of what I'm trying to say, meaning that I didn't accidentally grab any of my mom's clothing to wear in a hurry and in the confusion.

Some of you who are reading my story now are saying why did he, or why did they, have to put up with such a house. Well, folks, I'll tell you why. You must understand that this was the Middle East and Iraq and owning a home, especially a new one that just got built, doesn't happen often or every day to regular citizens. It was like a dream come true. Most of the labor force that had built a new home for themselves usually lived their entire life in the same home. And, on occasion, they died in the same house. My father was a federal employee, and he was defined as part of the labor force. The society classified him as an average income individual and not as a rich person. The rich could build their own home on any given day. Not all can afford to move around like we do in the U.S. Most real estate agents in the U.S. would starve if they had to deal with only a few selling and buying of homes, so most agents had other jobs next to their real estate business in order to survive.

Everyone was buried very much in this big habit, which is called routine, but life was not boring at all. People got to meet each other often to socialize. My life never stopped being challenging throughout, and this kept me going pretty much. But, again, I really needed to live a normal, free young boy's life without much fear, so that I could enjoy my childhood or teenage years for that matter. I believe whatever was going on in my life then was all God's will, and He was directing me accordingly. I was learning courage and control and these last two elements paid me off in life every step of the way, step-by-step. I was always ahead of others in thinking of a solution for specific events or matters at times because I could speak my mind faster than others to the best of my ability through experience. For all the tough decisions in life and situations that I or others faced, I was always there first to meet the challenges, if those challenges were intended for me to learn from it, or if intended to be for my friends. I faced them head on and without any hesitation. With this being said, our ghost had to live, and we had to live there with the ghost without any choice. It was not pleasant, but it was somewhat manageable.

It was very funny. I loved sports all my life, and it was a big challenge and hard work for me to win the hearts and minds of my high school peers because I had won the championship for my high school in track and field. It started like this. I was involved with playing basketball and soccer for my high school, Al Ressala High. My Physical Education teacher's name was Mr. Hesham. He was from the northern part of Iraq from a city called Mosul, and he was a Christian individual. I have reason to state it this way, and no offense to any-one in this case. There is a reason why I am saying he is a Christian and not a Muslim. Mr. Hesham knew I was playing basketball for the AAC in Baghdad. Also, some of my classmates had previously told the teacher that I played soccer well with them, representing our neighborhood team, so this raised some interest with the teacher personally, and I was called during one recess period to meet with him in his office. He asked me to join the high school team to play soccer. It was a dream for every student to compete and win a spot on the high school team, but mine was an offer that I couldn't refuse. That's because all my friends were part of the school soccer team and not the basketball team. I was not a bad basketball player, and, as a matter of fact, I was chosen to play basketball with the high school team as well by Mr. Hesham because of my high jumping abilities and dunking with my short height. My height was only five feet five inches at the time. I used to control the ball by stealing it fast from the air and so on. This was mentioned to me by the coaches and that I had a rare quality that they didn't see happening in the other players. Although, I must admit, there were other far better players than me in this game. But, nevertheless, I was one of the first five players to play in the startup of any basketball game. But my love for soccer was without borders because it runs in the family. My mom's younger brother, Uncle Sam, was a professional soccer player and played with one of Iraq's most famous soccer clubs. He was drafted to play with the Iraqi national team in the sixties, and, obviously, soccer runs in my blood as well. One day as I was watching the track and field games of the world Olympics on the black and white TV screen that we had, and due to the love of the sport and the passion to be a champion, my attention was directed toward the high jump competition that caught my eye and got me very interested as a young student. Right away, my mind started to drift towards it. I wanted to drop all the other team sports at the school and just do high jumping instead. But how could I do this to get there, and when? I figured it out by asking myself the following question: how? I had to win my high school competition.

In order to be in the track and field events for the city of Baghdad high school competitions, I needed to hire a trainer. I knew that my father couldn't afford to pay for any private trainer or teacher to teach me this sport and its tricks.

It meant I would have to give up my place on one of the team sports at the high school in order to join the track and field. This meant I wouldn't be able to play all three games at once; otherwise, I would fall more behind in my studies, and I couldn't allow myself to be in such a failing situation. But the hardest part was to decide. Then I told myself when there's a will, there's a way, and God, so far, had been very kind and helpful towards me as I always consulted him in private regarding my problems. Now, after thinking a long time and considering my position with the school teams, the time had come for me to ask my sports teacher, Mr. Hesham, about my new decision to quit and leave the basketball team and to join the track and field team instead. So far, so good. I went to his office during one of the recess periods and asked him about it. I tried at least three times verbally and once in writing to allow me to do this, but he always declined my requests. This didn't stop me from trying with other alternatives and creative ways to win a spot on the track and field team, and especially since I was persistent about it. Most of the time, this was part of my nature. I wouldn't take no for an answer if I knew in my heart that I was 100 percent right about an issue. So, I started to learn the sport by watching it on television, also by reading about it in the sports books and finally practicing it on a mattress in my aunt Sofina's backyard away from home because I didn't want to attract my parents' attention yet. I practiced by placing an old mattress on the lawn using her living room lamp poles and a rope, which was long enough to reach from one pole to the other, so I could jump over it. I asked my step cousin Jack, Sofina's stepson, to get all these items from his house so I could set the whole thing down in their enclosed front yard. My step cousin Jack didn't care about damages anyway, and he would do anything just to get attention to himself. He didn't care much about his home furniture. I always respected him and cared for him regardless of his way of thinking.

God had given Jack a gift. He was a free-hand artist. He could sit down and draw your face on a piece of paper or canvas like a portrait picture just as a professional artist does or draw any subject in this manner and turn it into an art piece. He won first place in art in his high school competition for the entire city of Baghdad. Let me drift away and tell you a little bit more about him since it was a heartfelt event that makes me very angry every time I remember what happened to him back home. Then we can come back and learn more about my track and field issues.

Jack's father was a rich man. His family owned a wine factory for over two generations, and he always wanted to send his son to the west, so he could live free, settle down, get ahead in life and advance with proper education in the field of art, which his son liked very much. Iraq didn't have any opportunities for him at the time. Jack's father, through his connections, managed to bribe some officials in Iraq to get his son to travel out and then to the United States back in the late '70s. Jack made it. He arrived in the states in 1977 and lived in New York City with his aunt (his father's sister). She was one of the top people in her field, but not so well known in the dress making and pattern design industry in the US. I heard from my uncle's family that Jack's aunt was a dress fitter for a lady who had connections with the Kennedy family. I believe it may have been Jacqueline Kennedy, who was the first lady and wife of the late President John F. Kennedy. God bless both of their souls. Jack's father trusted his sister in New York City to take care of his son as soon as he arrived there. I was not aware of any of these connections and people's positions. I never had a chance to meet Jack's aunt.

After Jack lived with his aunt in New York for a short while, he didn't like it at all; especially his aunt's husband. He said he couldn't get along with him, so Jack wanted to move to the West. He said that New York was a madhouse, and it was not for him. I was living in the states at that time on the west coast. I told him he was welcome to come here to live, but he would have to have his own place and attend school. I had to remind him that his visa was a student visa, and he couldn't stop going to school; otherwise, he would face deportation. I also told him that I would help him find a school and an apartment. Time passed, and Jack moved to the west coast and lived in a studio apartment near his college which he was going to attend. Jack managed to learn his art subjects as the years passed and finally got his college diploma.

The college which Jack was attending during those years was also a home for many, many Arab and Muslim students. Most of them were from Iraq and other Arab countries combined, as he had mentioned to me on one occasion. They were attending the same classes as he was. The years passed by and Jack started missing his parents and his family. The phone calls to his family back home were not enough to fill his heart in terms of emotional fulfillment. This was a great emotional dilemma and distance for him, especially since he had never lived alone anywhere before in his entire life. I was trying to help him change his mind by asking him not to return to Iraq, and I advised him to pay a visit to a US immigration lawyer in order to change his visa status legally with whatever other legal means the law would allow where his status would change so he could stay and work here. I knew through the news that a war was just about to break out between Iran and Iraq, as I mentioned in a previous chapter where I said, "The black chapter for humanity is just about to begin in Iraq with this regime." Ruling Iraq at the time was not an actual army general as he claimed himself to be but was the Iraqi president, General Saddam Hussein, who was appointed as President of Iraq in 1979. During the same year, Jack had just finished a two-year degree program at the college.

I started to see a gradual change in my step cousin's behavior, and day-by-day he was getting worse. I asked him what was going on with him and why he was angry all the time because whenever we talked about any issues, he talked to me as a brainwashed young man already. He started to label me a traitor and that I had forgotten my country, Iraq, by sticking with the West. I slapped his face several times one day and told him to wake up and snap out of it. I told him not to let those students affect him and warned him not go back to Iraq. I told him what they were doing was collecting an army of students for Saddam Hussein to use them in a war against the Iranians. I told him all this, but he didn't listen to me. I managed to find out how they were doing this at the school so that I could relay to him an example, so he could understand right from wrong.

I said, "Listen, Jack, they're using your family and the love of your country as an emotional tool to provoke you to go back, and all the good memories that you left behind is being used against you." They were telling the students that they should go back and defend their country's fate against Western aggression. At certain times, they were inviting students to their personal homes and showing them some movies that had to do with people's lifestyles and how the westerners were taking advantage of them and driving them to live bad lives in all aspects, presumably. In other words, they were using the media to get to their objectives.

Islam and the East was the answer for all, which was what they were telling their peers; especially, if you have been away from home for so long. For sure you could fall into this kind of talk by others, if your faith was not a strong driving force for you to stay and maintain the course for your life and intended goals. Not everyone was getting affected by their methods of doing what I call brainwashing with some nonsense ideas. But my cousin's faith in himself and his self-esteem was very low and weak. Arab students from Iraq and Palestine managed to get to him and made Jack believe their unfounded agendas. They had given him a free, two-way airfare ticket to fly to Baghdad. I don't know who had paid for these tickets. He was told he could go back to visit his folks and return to the US again, but he must surrender his Iraqi passport to them (them, meaning possibly a student body). I never had a chance to know them or meet them in person with the hopes that I could have changed things, not only for Jack but for all those innocent students who were falling victim to this kind of scam and conning operation. I met one of Jack's friends from the college and asked him what had been going on (he was the one who told me about what had been happening). He said they had approached him as well, but he had turned them down and didn't want to listen to them. I asked if he could do something about this at the school. He said he had already asked his teacher, and the teacher had responded that he would take care of it and not to worry. Well, I had to trust his word because he was Jack's best friend at the college. Years later and by accident, I met with one of the students who was attending the same college at one of the shopping malls, and I remembered him being with Jack and going to the movies. I recognized him when I attended Jack's graduation. He explained to me what was going on at the college, but it was after the fact, and it was too late. Many years later, I learned from others that this particular student who explained everything to me was nowhere to be found.

Jack didn't listen to me and did what they wanted him to do. He surrendered him- self and his passport to them and went back to Iraq in 1980. When he landed at Baghdad airport, the Iraqi authorities welcomed them home, but they never again returned the passports back to the students (I was told this by my aunt sometime later).

In 1980, Jack, along with a lot of innocent young and untrained men, was drafted into the Iraqi army. Luckily, because of Jack's handicapped status he had with his left leg, they put him on non-active duty in the kitchen to peel potatoes. But after Jack woke up from all of this, it was too late. He ran away from the army only to be busted soon after. The punishment for this by Saddam's regime was death by hanging. Jack's father had turned poor by now since Saddam's regime put a lock on his business (which was making wine) and forbidding him to produce any more wine years earlier. Jack's father was well educated with several diplomas from England in the field of business and languages. He managed to contact his connections before his death in 1986, and he managed to save his son life. At that time, brutality was a daily and common thing with the regime. They didn't hang him, but they took him to a hospital room and gave him several severe electrical shocks to his brain. Today, it has been more than thirty-nine years since Jack's brain has had permanent damage done to it. He has been residing at Baghdad's psychiatric mental hospital and taking his pills daily to survive. But he has never forgotten the gift that God gave him, which was drawing pictures, the art that he mastered. I heard from others that he has been doing what he knows best at the hospital with what he had mastered, which has kept him alive and away from suicide as others had done. His artistic skills were working well for him. I am hoping that one day it won't be too late for me to see him again and to remind him about the mattress and the lamp poles he used to set up for me to practice so I could win the high school championship. I miss him very much.

Sometimes, I wonder if we should think twice or change our immigration laws as to who we should accept as a foreign student in this country and from which country they should be allowed to come here. But I don't know if that is right or possible according to the rules of the free world or according to the constitution!

Folks, so much for Jack. Let's go back and learn about my high school track and field team, which I was trying to join.

After several months of high jump practices, I learned some of the tricks of the trade. I was trying to assure myself that I could take this challenging sport to the next level and win, but I never knew the time would come for me to perform in public and compete against others. One day during school recess, I heard a lot of noise coming from the school field and students were cheering, so my friends and I went to investigate. We saw our recent high school champ jumping over a bar and landing on a set of sponge mattresses. They were set on the concrete floor on the school field. Our school champ was wearing the full sports gear that was needed to do the job that day. We watched him carefully as to what was happening from a distance from the second-floor balcony of the school. I went down to be near the event where all the students were watching and cheering for him. My classmates, Mazan and Emmad, followed me as I was going down. As we were watching, both my friends asked me if I could challenge the school champ knowing that I was capable of taking on the challenge since I was keeping them informed about my practices. Mazan, my friend who was walking behind me as we were going downstairs, said, "Mark, it's now or never because in three month's time all of Baghdad's high school track and field competitions will start," He added that if I win the event, I would be representing our high school for the high jump. Wow! This was a reality now, and I got very motivated and my veins got filled with tremendous energy to compete against our high school champ. The motive to stand and take the challenge in the presence of 750 students was tempting. I walked to the trainer and asked him if I could challenge the school champ by jumping over the same bar to compete against him. The trainer looked at me and laughed. He said that I should have some sports gear or shoes on me first in order to compete. I got concerned, and I couldn't answer the trainer back because he was right. I asked myself how, in the name of sports, am I going to jump with my long bell bottom pants and leather shoes. The school administration had hired this trainer to train this student and make him the champion of the school. The trainer had spent six months to train this athlete. I asked the trainer if the champ ever competed against anyone at our school to get to this position, which was granted only to him recently. The trainer got mad because I questioned him about his work. I don't know why, but I was only curious to know, that's all. Then he turned around, looked at me and started yelling at me in Arabic saying, "You son of a bitch! Don't ask me any questions! Go away!" His yelling was heard by our student body president in the crowd, and that was unacceptable because when Saddam's regime came into power, they created a student body where they used them to recruit students to join the government's Baath party or the regime, just like it was happening in the communist countries. They had created this system in every high school, and the government had managed to control certain events at those schools. For example, this student body could tell anyone or any authorities at any school what to do, when to do it and without any questions asked. Our student body recruiter had asked me several times in the past to join their cause, but I always turned them down because I never agreed with their idealism. The same person who had asked me in the past to join them was the same person who overheard the trainer using bad language at me and asking me to go away. To my surprise, he helped me change the trainer's decision by talking to the trainer on the side and asking him to let me participate to challenge the school champ. At this time the trainer didn't have any say, and he couldn't object. He had no choice in the matter other than to agree. I personally didn't know what was going on inside the student body's president's mind, but I didn't care. I wanted to jump and show the rest of my school peers that I could do this and that I'm capable. I shook hands with the champ, and they set up the bar for me to jump over it. The competition started, and the bar climbed from three feet to five feet gradually by raising it a few inches at a time. I was jumping and passing over the bar every time and with only one jump, while the champ of the school had to jump twice in order to pass to the next level of any height set. We reached four feet eleven inches. I was already tired because this was not the actual track or the right field, especially with bell bottom pants and leather shoes where it was slippery to run on the school's hard concrete field. I could definitely injure myself badly due to unavailability of the correct sports gear on me. I managed to pass over the height of four feet eleven inches, and so did the champ. The bar was elevated to five feet. For the high jump competition, the rule is you should be able to jump over any given height that is set for you, and you could do this with a maximum of three jumps before you would be disqualified. The school champ didn't pass the height of five feet on the first two jumps, and neither did I. There was one jump left, and my turn was right after the school champ, meaning he was jumping first at the new elevated height before I could try it, which was somehow an advantage for me. It was my final attempt to try to pass the last height of five feet. Right at this important jump, and as I was going up in the air, I saw one of the students go to the area were the sponge mattresses were set on the concrete floor right at the landing spot. As if someone had given him the instruction to do so, I saw him move the position of one of the mattresses. He had no right to do so. The next thing I knew when I landed on the one mattress, the impact of my body slammed against the concrete floor. My body landed positioning itself half on the single mattress and half on the concrete floor. Wow! Falling on the concrete from the air at five to six feet free fall was not pleasant. It hurt the right side of my body like hell. I believe it was a setup and was done on purpose so that I couldn't win. My right side got hurt badly. I got up, but I was walking in pain, and I saw the look of sorrow in everyone's eyes for me. But, nevertheless, the blood was still running in my veins and no matter what happened to me, I had to win this game. I was just not going to give up and quit. Soon enough, I forgot my pain while everyone was watching carefully to see what my next move would be, even though one side of my body was semi-numb. I was granted another chance to jump my third and final jump again. This was the last jump for the champ before I would be up next, and this gave me a few moments to rest and rub my painful side. The event was stopped to fix the mattresses. They put back the mattress that was moved, and all were back stacked up together as it was originally. Then I noticed the school champ was looking in my direction and breathing hard, and he was nervous when he took his third and final jump. Folks, he didn't make it, and he lost his last chance. A big booing went on as if everyone was waiting for me to make it. I asked my friends to help me out and stand next to the mattresses while I would be doing my jump and not let anyone touch them. They agreed. I positioned myself carefully. I went back twice the distance from my running point, and I ran and ran hard. I picked up speed, and the next thing I knew I was in the air over the bar two inches higher than the height of five feet, and I passed over it successfully.

At this point, the whole school and some of the teachers who were watching this event during their lunch period were cheering for me after seeing what happened. Then, the main sports teacher came out to see what was going on. He looked at me and asked, "You again? What did I tell you before?" He then asked me to follow him to his office. Everyone headed back to their classrooms because the school bell had rung, and lunch break was over. The show was over. I went and sat down in pain outside the sports teacher's office. The trainer and the sports teacher went inside the office, and they started arguing. I didn't know what it was all about or what they were arguing about. I told myself it must be about me. I saw the trainer walk out of the office angry. Mr. Hesham, the sports teacher, asked me to come and sit closer to his desk, and then he went and shut the doors and the curtains to his office.

He said, "Do you know what we were discussing, or what our argument was about between the trainer and I"?

I responded by asking, "Was it about me?"

He nodded his head and said, "Somewhat," and added, "Do you know why I always refused you doing the high jump?"

I was puzzled!

He said, "Look at both of us. What do you see?" I was more puzzled!

He replied, "We are both Christians and the school administration had told me before if there are any games that require individual competition like track and field, and not a team game, that position should be awarded to a Muslim student because this year the newly formed student body by the regime has been dictating and enforcing new rules to follow on the school administration. This is totally discriminatory for our school's sports programs, meaning first, they didn't want any Christian in any individual games to represent our school; and second, the last names of Christian students should be altered and typed as initials in the program book. The Christians were to play in team games where their names wouldn't be so noticeable or paid attention to." My teacher then added that this decision was not from the Ministry of Education, but it was this school's principal's decision alone.

Mr. Hesham said that he saw the competition that had gone on outside through his office window. He told me he was sorry that I got hurt, and he knew what had happened and where it came from. Then he added by saying the student body's president had told one of his followers to get that mattress pulled so you wouldn't win since you had refused to join the student governmental Baath party. Nevertheless, and to my surprise, my sports teacher, Mr. Hesham, lowered his voice this time and said, "I don't know how to hug you and thank you for what you've done. You are a true athlete, and you should be proud of your accomplishment." He said that when he was studying to be a sports teacher, his instructions towards winning any game was that the best team or athlete must be given a chance to compete and may the best athlete win without any consideration to their religion, race, or background, and everyone was eligible. That's the right thing to do, but he said we are not living in fair and just times at this school with such an administrative body. He said he wanted me to know that he agreed with my efforts. Mr. Hesham added that a fair competition is the only right thing to do in sports, and our school should be represented only by those who can do their best and win the challenge for that spot. Then he shook his head disagreeing with the present situation by stating, "It's true that the old days are gone and in the twenty some years that I have been teaching sports, I haven't seen these kinds of biased and discriminatory people. But the day will come when everything will go back to normal again." He asked me to keep everything that he discussed with me a secret and every word should stay within his office walls and not to mention his position about sports to anyone, including my best friends at school because if any information leaked out, it could be cause for his dismissal. I promised that I would keep his conversation with me a secret. I didn't want anyone to harm him or get him fired. Mr. Hesham was a very fair teacher. He loved everyone and cared about every student regardless of their religious beliefs or nationality. I had been doing the same as a student. I didn't see any difference in Muslim or Christian friends, but the regime was not fair and they started gradually creating divisions among their own population; specifically, if the Muslim Brotherhood was in the mix.

After our conversation, I asked Mr. Hesham what my next move was in this new development. What will happen? Especially now that everyone knows who the new school champ is. He looked at me with a joyful facial expression, and, like someone who had just learned how to breathe again on his own, he said, "This time, I'll put my job on the line, kid, because I'm tired of being pushed around and having the student body control my decisions in my own profession." This was taking away and changing the quality of life and, most importantly, his teaching skills, which was part of mentoring through sports to build self-confidence in his students and to improve their achievement skills. Sports competitions are the key to those two elements in life. As to what was next for me, he replied that he would call a special emergency meeting that afternoon with all the teachers and the administration and would let them vote on this issue. Then he asked me this particular question, "Kid, if I could get you to be declared the school champ, which team sport would you be dropping?"

Right away and without any hesitation I said, "Basketball, sir."

He agreed and said, "You can go back to your classroom now, son."

The teachers and the administrative body got together that afternoon for an emergency meeting regarding this issue, and it took several hours to come to their decision. The outcome was in my favor. And, if you ask me how they had done this or how they could bend the regime rules, I am neither an expert to answer it, nor do I know what happened that afternoon behind closed doors. But it was a joyful day for me especially knowing how prejudiced the school had gotten to be lately. I'm sure that Mr. Hesham had been fighting for my position that afternoon. Who knows? But he had some weight as a teacher at that school for being a very fair-minded individual throughout the years.

This unpleasant event had made me gain more motive and courage to go on and continue. I loved my high school, and I have great respect for anyone that can stand up and defend the rights of others and for being fair. This kind of mentality or thinking was occasional in Iraq because most everyone was frightened for their lives, and for their family's lives. God bless everyone who helped me to be the winner. Now I had a big responsibility and a heavy burden that was being placed on my shoulders to place my school on the winner's list. My high school was going to benefit the most from all of this; that is, only if I could win the high jump title for my school in the upcoming track and field competitions against all the Baghdad high school champs.

The next day I saw my school's previous champ walking in the school's field and being a good sport, I went to him and shook his hand. Then I thanked him for yesterday's com-petition and encouraged him by telling him what a great athlete he was and that it was an honor for me to compete against him. He thanked me and said he would help me by passing on some of the training lessons and materials which he had obtained and learned from the trainer, just in case I needed them. He handed me some training materials to study and to be ready for the upcoming competitions, which really made me happy to see him accepting me as a friend. The road was rough for me as usual, but I could see the light at the end of the tunnel, as they say. There were a lot of miles to go yet before I could reach the top, so I made up my mind to go all the way by pushing myself with self-training as hard as I could. The school administration had decided to hand me the keys to the school's main gate through Mr. Hesham including his office key where the training equipment was stored. I made a schedule to train myself in track and field every Monday and Wednesday afternoon, and every Tuesday and Thursday evenings I practiced basketball with the beginner's team at the AAC (Armenian Athletic Club).

I practiced the high jump on Mondays and Wednesdays after school inside one of Baghdad's famous stadiums called Al Keshafa Soccer Stadium where a lot of international as well as local soccer and track and field competitions were held from the 1940's and on to the early 1970's when I had to be part of its history competing on its field. Also, I learned later that my father Mike had used the same stadium in his younger days in the 1940's to compete where he won first place in the one hundred-meter freestyle running competition in 1947. He received the first-place trophy at the age of seventeen by King Faisal II when Iraq was a kingdom during my father's younger days. Now the Keshafa stadium was located some distance from my high school, and I had to ride a bus back and forth to my school to get there. The reason I couldn't practice at my school field after hours was due to some opposition by the school sports trainer. He didn't let me do the practices at the school field. He had developed many reasons of his own and for his own personal vendetta against me. He still couldn't get over the teacher's and administrative body's decisions regarding my winning and my nomination. I kept my distance from him in terms of communication. I had a feeling that the school trainer was going to make it very difficult for me to reach my goals. But one thing he didn't know about me was that I loved challenges, and nothing would stop me from reaching my goals especially when I was almost going to lose my right hip bone from being injured that day while I was competing against his favorite trainee named Jabbar. But I was glad the trainer was the one who provoked this challenge.

I was determined to do my practices anywhere at any cost. I put a training schedule together for myself for the entire week. As I had mentioned previously, I played basketball on Tuesday's and Thursday's at the AAC club. Going to AAC was quite a distance from my house. I had to exchange two buses to get there and to travel back. I enjoyed playing basketball with the AAC because we had a professional coach who was also training the Iraqi army club named Mr. Mehdi. Professionally, he had a different method of training. He used to invite his primary team, the army club team members (some of the players also played for the Iraqi National Basketball Team), to practice with the AAC team members to strengthen our position in playing basketball. The AAC's number one team was to practice first for an hour, and then the number two team was to follow with their practice. As part of his coaching methods, Mr. Mehdi would mix teams which consisted of players from our club's teams to compete against his professional team as practice to develop skills. Occasionally, I was called from the bench to join in just to do the starting jump at the beginning of the game. I was called to the middle circle at times to do this.

I was nowhere as big and tall as the other team members, but I had one gift and quality. I jumped high for my age, more than the average player could, and I would catch the loose balls in the air from these big players. This amazed our coach and a few of the other players from the army team. The coach was telling them to watch me at times, so he could prove his point. Also, while we were on break at one of the practices, Mr. Mehdi, the coach, asked me if I would consider joining the army club so he could train me with the rest, and this could lead me to play with the Iraqi National Team in the future. Well, I didn't say anything other than that I had to ask my parents first, especially since joining the army was not something I wanted to do at that time. I got to know one of the army club's players named Hassan who was the Iraqi champion in the high jump competition while we were practicing at the AAC, but I was always cautious as my parents had taught me not to be too close to strangers. This was always stuck in my mind at the age of sixteen.

My school's sports trainer didn't want me to practice the high jump in the school field after school hours as I mentioned before, so I had to go through the pain of transferring and carrying equipment with me back and forth from the school to the stadium using public transportation. Now on Monday's and Wednesday's, I was to pick up only half of the equipment, which were two, six-foot wooden poles and were at least thirty pounds each. Due to their shape and size, I had to exclude taking the long bar and the sponge mattresses. My sports bag and my backpack were an added weight to carry from the school to the bus stop, which was about one block walking distance from the high school in order to ride the bus and travel to Al Keshafa Soccer Stadium for the high jump practices. This was a plan from the school sports trainer to cause me some hardship so that in a short time I might give up and let go of this sport so he could bring back his original student trainee to replace me once more. He didn't want me to succeed while I was training myself to get ready for the competition. Despite all this, I'm glad I went through all this conspiracy which had developed will power within me. I forgot to mention here that I was using a short rope as a bar for this sport due to being unable to carry on the bus the original twelve-foot aluminum bar used for this sport. It was impossible to accomplish this. The rope was not an accurate height measurement tool to demonstrate how high my jumps were because it was sagging in the middle, and this was affecting my progress. At times, I had to tie the rope to the pole to stretch it tight in order for me to set a particular height to jump over. But not every jump was successful because I was still learning, and my foot was getting hung up at times on the rope as I was passing over it in the air. The rope was pulling on both six-foot wooden poles and both were crashing down on my back as I was landing on the ground that had only a nine- inch sand fill.

My sports equipment was not complete, and there were no sponge mattresses to be used as cushions for landing. There was only a pile of sand left on that field, and it was the only cushion available for me to land on top of. You can imagine what I had to go through to get there and accomplish my practices, but I believe God was watching all of this as I was training myself without any professional guidance or trainer. Unfortunately, my good P.E. teacher, Mr. Hesham, who was in charge of the school's sports trainer, couldn't change the trainer's decision into training me as he did for the previous school champ. Thanks to Mr. Hesham for getting approval for me to join the competition but, obviously, the challenge was mine, and mine alone, to accomplish.

One Wednesday afternoon and right after school hours while I was training myself inside the main Al Keshafa stadium, I witnessed a big commotion. As I was practicing, I saw the main gate to the stadium open suddenly and several army trucks with about seven to eight soldiers sitting in each truck drove into the stadium. They started yelling at everyone to get out and to leave the stadium. They said practice was over for everyone. There were other athletes doing various other training for track and field sports along with me, and we all had to stop and pack. One of the soldiers approached me holding a thick stick in his hand. I said to myself, "Not again", and for just a short moment, a sudden, unexpected fear took over me once more. It was scary at first, and it reminded me of my elementary school days, but I was not afraid to ask this soldier a question. As I started to pick up the school equipment to overcome my fears, I asked the soldier, "What's going on?" He said, "Hassan, the Iraqi National Team's athlete, is going to start his practice. He is my boss, and he is a one-star officer for the Iraqi armed forces." Then I asked him quickly if this is the same Hassan who plays basketball for the army club. The soldier replied, "Yes." This created some hope and comfort in me to see if I could talk to Hassan to stay in the stadium and watch him do his practice, so I could learn but I wasn't sure if he was going to remember me. I convinced myself to try and ask him personally. I stepped aside and watched the other soldiers unload the professional equipment used for high jumping. The very same equipment was being used internationally, and it was an eye-opener for me to see all of that. Not everyone could afford to have such equipment. I asked myself how I should approach the officer. I knew him as Officer Hassan, a one-star officer who was in the army, which I learned today, and the government was providing him with all these benefits to do his practices. After all, he was going to represent his country, Iraq, in the Olympics.

I saw all the European made thick sponge mattresses, which the soldiers got done placing them over the sand where I was practicing earlier and landing on it. The mattresses covered all the sanded areas as they were big and bulky and sat three feet above the ground, and part of the setup had included two, eight-foot aluminum poles that had the metric measurement written on the side of it as an indicator to show each height a few centimeters at a time. Wow!

All this was new to me. I asked myself if this was a dream or what? Then, as I was observing this new professional set up, I saw the same soldier who answered my questions come back and start pushing me away saying, "Come on, come on, get out of here before he comes." I told the soldier that I wanted to wait to ask the champ a question. Most, but not all, army soldiers in Iraq at that time were not educated. They didn't have a way or style of communicating other than being forceful and yelling loud at the top of their lungs to get their way. As I said before, it was a commotion. But, as I was listening to the soldier's screams, I saw Officer Hassan start to walk toward the high jump equipment area to check the setup. I was still standing there and waiting to see him. He didn't pay attention to me, and later he started to warm up by running. I turned around and yelled, "Officer Hassan, do you have a minute to talk to me?" He waved his hand from a distance motioning me to approach him, and I ran past the idiot who was trying to stop me from running towards his boss.

As I started to run alongside of him, I said, "I hope you remember me, Officer Hassan. My name is Mark, and I'm an athlete from the AAC. I know your coach, Mr. Mehdi, from where we all practiced playing basketball one night at the club."

He wondered for a few seconds, and then he said, "Oh, yes, you're that young man who my coach, Mr. Mehdi, was talking about." I said, "Yes." Then he asked me what I was doing in the stadium. I briefly and quickly told him what I was going through twice a week to train myself for the high jump. He shook his head and said, "They're doing all this to you, and you're not giving up"? I guess this was a trick question. I couldn't say anything against our school trainer because Officer Hassan was also a Muslim himself, so I was not going to stick my foot in my mouth being negative. I changed the way I was supposed to tell him my side of the story. I knew that the hard work was purposely put on my shoulders by the school trainer, so I said, "I believe the school trainer is not being cooperative with me because he wants to see how serious I am about this sport, so he is intentionally creating some obstacles for me."

Officer Hassan was not a fool. He knew and said, "I know you're Christian, and they're not treating you properly, but I want to know what you're going to do about it."

I stopped to think for a moment because I thought maybe he knew what had happened at our school. I wasn't sure. Tears started to rush into my eyes, but I controlled the pain within me so I could present myself in a strong athletic-fashioned mind. I said, "Officer Hassan, I want to be just like you one day, and I'm not going to give up my dreams for any obstacles in life." He liked that and told me, "Listen, kid, go ahead and change back into your sports gear and follow me." I was going to start running around the track to warm up with him first. I couldn't believe my ears; it was like a flash. He ran almost half way down the track. After changing back into my sports gear, I caught up and ran with him. After our warm up we went to the equipment set up site, and he told me he would start to show me how to jump and how it should be done. I told him I knew how! He was a patient person and told me to go ahead and show him how. I guess from my excitement I wanted to show him what I knew first. He looked at what I did and how. Let me tell you, folks, for the very first time in my entire life I felt so good landing on those European-made sponge mattresses. It was heaven for me, and it was so comfortable. Officer Hassan watched me first and then said, "You really need some training. Who is your trainer?" In shy fashion I said, "You're looking at him."

He understood. My heart started pumping fast and anxiety started taking over from the embarrassment, but I managed to hold it in again. He said, "From now on, I will train you myself every Wednesday, and you'll get to use the same equipment that I'm using." Wow! This was a really good deal! He was offering his help to me, and I thanked him for it. In my mind I said, "Hurray, no more equipment to drag along anymore on Wednesdays, and thank you school trainer for making it so hard for me to succeed." After all, a good deed came out of it by practicing at that stadium. That evening I rode the bus back to the school, and I locked the equipment back in its original place and then went home. When I got home, I told my dad what had happened. He was worried at first and surprised at what he just heard. He said next Wednesday he would stop by the stadium to meet the champ. At first, I was nervous about this. Then, in the old days, you wouldn't say no to your dad. Sometimes, you would have no choice and you would have to agree, so I said, "Very well, let's do it together." On the following Wednesday as I was practicing, my dad showed up at the stadium, and I introduced him to Officer Hassan. Officer Hassan was happy that I had a dad who was at one time the champ of Iraq in the track and field sport for the one hundred-meter freestyle run. Then Officer Hassan introduced my father to another Iraqi track and field athlete who was practicing the two hundred-meter dash and the long jump. I can't recall his name, but my dad and this individual had a lot in common to share in regards to sports matters. The next thing I knew, my dad took off his shoes and socks, rolled his pants legs up, and got ready to show other young men how to do the starting position for the runs. After his demonstration had finished that day, this long jump champ liked my dad very much, and then he offered to train me for free. I was thrilled! Ten weeks went by, and I was as ready as I could be for the big competition yet to come. My school trainer, the one who I kept a distance from, asked me if I was ready. One afternoon after school hours, he set up the high jump equipment for me inside the school field in order to see if I was ready to represent the school, and if I was jumping correctly; no thanks to him, of course. His intention was to see me not make it so he could prove his point to the school administration. He was the type of person that held grudges and wouldn't let go. But my objective was to satisfy the P.E. teacher's (Mr. Hesham's) will, and not his trainer's. I informed Mr. Hesham what went on, and he was happy to hear that the Iraqi champs on the field were giving me a hand. After the trainer had set up the equipment for me to demonstrate if I am ready or not, I started to show him a few jumps from what I had learned on the field. He was somewhat puzzled as to where I had learned this kind of high jump style, and, of course, he asked me about it. I replied that I had been watching a lot of sports programs on television. I didn't want to tell him the truth about the learning events that took place in the stadium. I just didn't know why, but I didn't. We both packed the equipment away. He handed me two of the same ID numbers, and the number was #378. I asked him what these numbers were for. He said the school just received them from the Department of Sports Ministry, and they were my ID numbers for the upcoming Saturday competition. I must place them on my jersey with whatever means; one on the front and one on the back. I was happy that I got them. I told myself that this is it. Despite all the time and trouble I went through to get to this point, now I had to finally perform.

During that week, I did nothing but eat, drink, sleep and think only about the competition. That day arrived. I took the bus ride to the same stadium where I had been practicing. There were hundreds of student athletes for every sport, and there were at least ten student athletes from each high school. It was the same for the high jump. We were locked inside a cage like monkeys in a zoo at one of the corners of the stadium. It was funny. Yes, all of us locked in a big cage on one side of the field waiting to be called one at a time by this idiotic guard at the gate and go and do our thing on the field instead of wandering free and doing warm ups. The time had arrived. My name was called by the gate keeper, and, as usual, they pronounced my name wrong. As I came out of the waiting area, and while I ran toward the competition area, I heard a huge number of students cheering, and they were calling my name repeatedly from their seats. For the first time in my life, it was such a great joy and experience for me, and I didn't want to let them down. None of them knew what I had gone through to be present at this stadium that day to compete for all of them and for the school.

I learned that two of my best friends, Mazan and Emmad, had done their share of rallying and campaigning for me by putting out a paper flyer that both had made to encourage everyone to be at the stadium that day. The students that were cheering were all my peers from my high school. The competition started. I had to compete against seven other athletes in high jump and most didn't know what they were doing. They were not prepared well enough for it. There was this one athlete during the competition that I kept my eye on because of his jumping style. He was using the same style that I had learned from Officer Hassan, and his name was "Moonder." As I was waiting for my turn, I asked someone passing by who this guy Moonder was, and I was told that he was the record holder for this competition and was last year's champ. This drew my attention more, so I watched him carefully. He was also the champ for the Baghdad high schools for the four hundred-meter and two hundred-meter free run. As we waited for our turns to jump, someone from the other high schools who knew Moonder previously told me on the field that Moonder didn't study anything in school. He only attended school to sit in the classroom, and all his grades were handed to him without taking any tests. What he did all year round was practice sports. He was privileged because he was the son of one of the top army officers in the regime. This was news to me, but my intention was to win that day. I didn't care about what his life-style was or what he was doing with his life. Defeating and winning over others didn't seem a difficult task for me that day in the beginning, especially since I learned and witnessed the reality that none of them had any training or experience except the top officer's son, Moonder.

I kept in my mind the interesting part of it all, which was to win and take the title from this spoiled champ. I knew it wasn't going to be easy because most of the other athletes started failing one after another. They were competing at the height of three to four feet elevation. At the end, I was left alone to compete against Moonder, the champ. It was not easy to compete against him as he had been training all year round with lots of help and advice, including European style training. I had been training only for three months with some miracle help and advice given to me through Officer Hassan and others. He was well built and muscular at six feet in height and 175 pounds, unlike me at five feet five inches at that time and 115 pounds. But, nevertheless, I put my very best effort in this competition. For the first time in my life, the outcome was not in my favor. I came in second in the Baghdad high school competitions. I was not successful to strip him from his title. I jumped over five feet two inches as my final jump. Moonder made it by jumping a height of five feet three inches; one inch more than my record. It was a very close challenge for me, but my legs were not fit, and they were not as strong as the champ's. This competition had taught me a lifetime experience to not give up and to reach my goals. Each of us were awarded a trophy and the local newspapers published the pictures of the awards ceremony. With a big regret, I had to leave all my awards and trophies behind when we left to run away from the country. I couldn't take any of the memories out of the country to prevent suspicious minds from finding out our intentions for our journey. It was my father's decision to do so to avoid complications in escaping the country. (See the escape story in Chapter 4).

All these athletic preparations took a lot of time away from my studies. I was not Moonder the champ whose grades were handed to him as I had mentioned before. I had to study and be qualified in all subjects and take the tests in the eleventh grade. I had to qualify in thirteen different subjects to pass the eleventh grade. The high schools in Baghdad were not like the high schools in the US because in the US you get to choose some of the subjects you want to study; for instance, you can choose your electives. But in Iraq, it was more like you had to study everything that was set by the ministry of education for each grade level. Naturally, I didn't pass the final examinations completely that year due to the endless involvement in sports. I had to go to a private summer school to retake algebra and chemistry in order to test again in these two subjects before the beginning of the new school year and pass them in order to move on to the next level. Throughout the entire year, our regular chemistry teacher (not the summer school teacher) was so depressing and boring that during his class half of the class was sleeping. He disliked me because I was spending more time in P.E. than in his class. It happened that most of the time while my chemistry teacher was teaching, I would always receive a note delivered during his class by someone from the P.E. Department to attend a meeting and field practice, so I had to leave. One time as I was leaving his class, the chemistry teacher openly warned me that if I should go to practice, he would be sure I would never pass his class to move on to the twelfth grade. He said that I would be taking his class in the next school year all over again. I ignored it because I knew myself well. When it came to studying, and if I put my mind to any challenges for that matter regardless what it was, I knew I would always come ahead winning or succeeding. But I didn't know where he was coming from. I took the finals that year, and like I mentioned before, I failed the chemistry subject and that's why I had to go to summer school. Before the new school year was to start, I had to take the chemistry and algebra tests again and right after the exams, I went home. My mind was still fresh remembering the test questions from the finals, so I wrote them down and answered them as I was taking the finals for the second time all over again. The reason that I did this was because I wanted to present the entire test to my neighbor's son, Mr. Adnan, who was a chemistry and math teacher as well, so he could evaluate my tests. This would tell me an approximation of the test scores before I would get them from the school that next week.

Mr. Adnan looked at the tests that I took and said I should have no problems passing the test with a C+ grade since I had gone to summer school for these subjects. The results from the school were the opposite. I passed the algebra test, but they failed me in chemistry, and, yes, you read it right. They didn't want me to move on to the next grade. Then Mr. Adnan wanted to get involved in this matter. He called the school to talk to the teacher, but no one wanted to answer his call. Nevertheless, I didn't have a choice. I had to continue school in order to avoid serving in the armed forces. After going back to class in the new school year, I learned from others in the first two months that the president of the student body along with the chemistry teacher were both part of the regime, and they forced the principal to accept the decision of making me repeat the whole school year regardless of the fact that I made the school look good in track and field. I put the school's name in the high school history books by earning the second-place trophy. I was not part of their circle because I refused to join their Baath Party ideology.

It was a political game; a hard lesson to learn in life and a hard pill to swallow. I will never forgive or forget them. I learned all this information from a trust-worthy person who was a member of the student body at my high school that year. He told me that the message was that I could win in sports against the Muslim athlete, but they could win in anything they want in life, including making me lose a complete year of school. Naturally, I couldn't fight the system by myself, so I had to sit and get embarrassed in class by seeing all my friends going on to the next grade except me. I had to face new and younger students who were attending my classes with me. Some teachers were sympathizing with me; especially, the algebra teacher. In order to make me feel better, he announced to his class of newcomers that I was the school champ, and I was going to be his aid in the class just in case he would be absent, and that I was to help and answer all questions which they may have regarding algebra. My grades were A+ in algebra that year and had always been since then. I had read and studied the algebra book for the fourth time that year. I studied it twice previously in the regular school year, once in summer school and once during finals before school started. Naturally, I knew the subject as good as the teacher himself, of course, but by practice only. My morale was lifted a bit, and I thanked the algebra teacher for his trust in me. Most of the students in the classroom were happy that they had a student like them who could aid them as well as the teacher. But, in the big picture, I felt I was a failure for some time. I continued that year and never gave up hope. Despite everything, I refused to join their nonsense regime. But, of course, others could think differently about the regime, but this was my opinion about them, and it was mine alone.

Now, as a member of the AAC (Armenian Athletic Club) of Baghdad, I was also a part of their Boy Scout team due to the opportunities available to travel with the group to go on camping and field trips during the summer breaks. Occasionally, the group would plan to travel to the northern part of Iraq where it was mostly populated by the Kurds. Geographically, it's the best part of the country; only if you like nature and mountainous life and where you can see the northern border of Iraq and Turkey. The region is all full of mountainous lands and forests along with long valleys and some waterfalls. It's like California's Yosemite Park with all the waterfalls and rivers. It's a beautiful place, really. In 1969, the club had asked every member on the Boy Scouts team if we wanted to go for a summer's journey to that region. And, if we were willing to participate on this trip, we had to register first with the club administration and pay the fees for the trip. The distance of that trip was about six to ten hours of driving north from the capital city of Baghdad going toward the northern Iraqi border to reach the village called Zakho, which is located at the border of Iraq and Turkey. This village carried in its landscape a historic Christian Armenian church that was still in existence for centuries and a simple, poor looking school that was built on the church's landscape. This school taught the Armenian language and other subjects to the minority Armenian children, which was the only small Christian Armenian population that is still in existence in that village in the Kurdish region. The church's designated priest was in charge of it all. After arriving, we were to use the classrooms as sleeping quarters as this information was passed on to us during the Boy Scouts meeting by the organizers of this trip.

I came home that night and told my parent about the trip, and, naturally, the answer was no because they were concerned about my safety, especially in a place away from home where they had never been there themselves previously. And, to be honest, this was going to be my first time away from home and staying out for a few days. At the end, the big factor in making this happen for me was my Uncle Steve. He was Aunt Sofina's husband and the owner of a big wine factory up north in that region of the country, and he was a third-generation wine maker in his family. This factory was not too far from our destination. He managed to persuade my father to accept my traveling to the north with the group. My Uncle Steve had a big influence in my life, which I can say was more than my own father's influence at the time. I admired my uncle's courage, his intellectual level and for seeing matters always differently than all the rest. He told my dad that he was going to send his own son Jack (my step cousin) along with the group, and he was even going to pay for the whole trip himself. He also told my cautious father that the boys are growing up fast and this was going to be a big experience for them to build their self-confidence as grown men. Then he told my dad, "Let's go ahead and do it; let's send them both." My dad got persuaded and let me loose this time, for a change, to join the Boy Scouts team for this trip. It gave me great joy to hear this, especially since I love challenges. But my dad always underestimated my abilities and judgments. It's natural for parents to do so no matter how old you get in life. Your parents will always look at you like that little boy they raised. In other words, you will never grow up in your parents' eyes.

I started to pack. I was going to travel in two days. I went and slept at my Aunt Sofina's home the night before the trip so that Jack and I could get a ride from their private driver to the bus station. The organization had reserved a private bus and a driver whom they knew and trusted for long years and whose son is also a member of the club. He had an eighteen to twenty-passenger Mercedes minibus. We left town early that morning around 7:00 a.m. It was a long journey, and we got exhausted fast. I fell asleep on the bus the last two hours of our journey. Then a loud voice from our Boy Scouts team leader alerted us by saying, "Hey wake up everyone. We are here at the village of Zakho." We got there around the early evening hours. We were fifteen Boy Scout members in total. All of us, or let's say most of the young scouts, were athletes from the volleyball, basketball, and soccer teams who played for the AAC.

I started to pick up my bags. I had purchased this large green army duffle bag, and I put everything in it that I needed for the next four days; clothing and other necessary items. My cousin Jack (Aunt Sofina's stepson) had done the same with his bag, but he had one item that I didn't have with me and that was his thermal under-wear. As we stepped out of the bus, we were all greeted and welcomed by the local Armenian priest at the gate of the church and were guided to the classrooms where we were going to stay for the next four days. We had a small reception. A table was set up with some food made by the villagers that were all naturally and organically grown in this village as well as fresh baked bread and three different kinds of homemade cheese. We gathered around the table and sat, but before eating we got up and stood around the table because the priest wanted to bless the table with a short prayer. Then we all sat down and started eating and drinking the homemade juices and unpasteurized natural milk.

Right after dinner we were tired, and we all went to the classroom to unpack and go to bed. Every one of us had with him a sleeping bag and a blanket. I didn't have much of a winter protective gear with me other than my clothes and a long raincoat as well as a sweater. But let's remember that I was not from a rich or middle-class family. My cousin Jack had his thermal underwear on him, which kept him warm, but I had my Boy Scout shorts on me and long army socks. I never traveled before on this kind of trip, so I didn't know what to bring. The night had set in, and the weather was very cold with freezing temperatures at that high altitude. There were no wood-burning stoves or electric heaters in these classrooms to keep us warm at nights. These classrooms were built inside a centuries-old structure without any insulation. We had to sleep on the cold concrete floor with one blanket under us. Then I noticed in one corner of the classroom a piece of mattress-like item which was possibly being used by the children as floor mats during the day to sit on them. My body was almost half frozen. I believe the temperature that night was almost 10 to 20 degrees Fahrenheit at the elevation of four to six thousand feet high in the sierras, which was something I wasn't used to. I went and pulled the children's mattress out from the corner of the classroom, and I placed it on the floor. My cousin Jack had a sleeping bag with him, and I placed my blanket on top of it to avoid the cold temperature of the concrete floor from getting to us throughout the night. My cousin Jack agreed with the idea, and we set up our sleeping space accordingly that night, avoiding the cold air breeze which was blowing through the broken classroom window that had caused all this fuss. I took whatever clothing I had brought with me from my bag (things like my long pants, my long shirt, a sweater, etc.), and I had to wear them to keep warm. I was still cold. The low temperature was preventing me from sleeping. I had never experienced this in Baghdad because it was in a low climate region located in the middle of the country. I was not used to it, but, anyhow, I managed to learn this as my first lesson as a young boy on my first night; that is, to know your destination by doing some research and being prepared accordingly before you travel.

The next morning, we were woken up from the sound of the villagers' children who were playing in the schoolyard, and the adults were waiting outside to see all of us at the church field. This was a strange and new experience for me. The word must have gotten around fast in the village a night before because we were newcomers from the capital, we were all Christian Armenians, and we had athletic skills. That morning before going out to meet anyone, I packed my clothes and put them back in the bag. I had to wear the normal Boy Scouts uniform with my beret on my shirt's shoulder patch. Then I took a towel from my bag to go wash up. There was one large bathroom, and the water was so cold you couldn't put your hand in it for too long. I managed to wash up and comb my hair, and then I went to the classroom to put the towel back in my bag. I saw that my cousin Jack was still asleep as well as the others. I tried to wake everyone up, but they didn't like to wake up that early. All of them were cuddled up in their sleeping bags keeping warm, so I went with the others to the breakfast room. Wow, what healthy and delightful food they had. I had never seen a bowel of butter that big, or the huge can of fresh raw golden honey which you could still see some of the bees lying at the bottom, and, of course, all the "tanoor" or fresh cooked bread. (I explained what "tanoor" is in the previous chapters. Please see Chapter 1 or 2.) I tried to stick my breakfast knife into the honey to get some. The honey was so thick that my knife started to bend. I had never seen such thick honey before. While some of us were eating, we met the men whose wives prepared all the food for us. But the hall was full of men, and no woman or girls were present to serve us or put things away. It was a macho and traditional village and a very old-fashioned one. Men come first, and women come second. That's the way it was in Muslim countries in the sixties, and the Kurdish regions are not any different in their beliefs regarding woman. Well, that's what I witnessed, and that's how it was back then on our trip in the late sixties to this Kurdish region of Iraq.

While we were eating, one of the Kurdish men whose family converted to Christianity sat next to me and started to chat with me. What this man told me was that Kurds are a nation like any other with deep roots in that region, and, like every other nation, there was a religious mix among them; although most Kurds are Muslim in faith. But not everyone was followed their faith. What I learned from this man was that a small group of another faith called Yezedee were also living in this village. Their faith believes in the existence of two gods; an evil god and a good god. When we finished our breakfast, our Boy Scouts group leader was approached by this Kurdish man who lived across from the church. He told our group leader that we were all invited that evening to his home. He was hosting something like a bachelor party a night before his son's wedding. Our leader said that we were honored, and we will be there.

Our schedule for the first day was to explore the village and to visit the border bridge which separates Iraq from Turkey, and then we would visit and see the historic sites. We accomplished all these trips throughout the day, and night fell once more. We were getting ready to go to the men's only bachelor party (don't think it's like what we do here), and we got there at 8:00 p.m. that evening. Most of us were not more than fifteen to twenty-six years of age. We all went to the party and were received by the groom's father at his home. We all sat down, and the local ethnic music started. It was somewhat close in rhythm to our Armenian music (for those of you who play music, the rhythms were 4/4 and 6/8) so we all liked it. Since some of us were members of the cultural dance group back in Baghdad, naturally we started one-by-one to show our abilities with dance steps. But, before we could show off our dancing abilities as gratitude, there was a macho man drinking contest, which was dictated by a rule that says whoever can drink the most homemade arak (hard liquor made from white grapes picked from the mountains) will be respected as a mature man.

It was not clear to me what the percentage was of the alcohol level of this drink. Who knows? It could have been well around 200 proof or more. It was a homemade remedy, and no government regulations were in effect to control the liquor making activities of this northern Kurdish town. From what I observed and witnessed that night, the village men were drinking heavily, and the cold climate of the region was helping them to consume it. The region we were in was on very high-altitude ground. I was handed a half a glass full of this stuff, and I believe that was my first time drinking any liquor at the age of sixteen. You have to believe me if I tell you that after the first sip my head started spinning. I couldn't finish it. I handed the glass to the others. But as naive as my cousin Jack was, and mostly because he wanted to feel important and to put on a show, he said since his father was a wine maker, he could handle drinking a full eight-ounce glass of this liquor, bottoms up. I warned him saying, "You're going to drop dead. Don't show off with that stuff." But, as usual, he was a spoiled kid and didn't listen. In the meantime, our group's leader cautioned Jack as well not to do so. He told my cousin Jack that he would personally inform his father about this, if he didn't stop. But, nevertheless, Jack was a spoiled rich kid, and he started to drink the whole glass in one sip. I could see his eyes were already turning red as well as his ears. After finishing the eight-ounce drink, Jack didn't have a chance to put the glass on the table, and he fell down on the floor. He was awake, but he was tongue-tied to talk. Naturally, two other Boy Scout members and I carried him to the church classroom where I had to put his pajamas on him. We all put him in his sleeping bag so he could rest, and then we went back to the party again. By now everyone was half drunk.

The men in the household were used to it. The drink didn't affect them much, or they knew the secret of how to drink this stuff, which they didn't share with us.

The music was on and one of our senior Boy Scout members took a couple of table knives with pointed and sharp edges and decided to dance using the knives. By holding one knife in each hand and while jumping in the air, he moved both knives under each leg one at a time as he was jumping up and down. I don't know where he got all these creative dance moves. It must have been the 200-proof liquor's after effect. I saw it coming. I knew he was going to hurt himself. And, sure enough, he stabbed himself in both arms when he did his first jump. Luckily, it wasn't too deep of a wound, but it was enough to handicap both his left and right arms. The next thing I saw was the homeowner rushing to get some homemade bandages. No alcohol was needed because he used the liquor which was strong and pure enough to sterilize the wounds. At this point, our group leader told all of us to go back to the classrooms and go to sleep while he stayed a while longer in peace to enjoy the rest of the evening with the homeowner and the rest of the men.

The next morning, Sunday, was the second day of our trip. We were woken up by the sound of the villagers' loud drum beats and the zourna, which is a cultural musical instrument made from apricot tree branches by carving it with a machine or by hand which you would play like a flute with your mouth and that would cause a very sharp pitch sound. The people of the village then formed a half circle consisting of men, women and children. They were going around joyfully dancing in the open church field. For me, this was very joyful to witness. What a morning this was that had started with music and fun. I watched the dance and tried to pick up the steps because it was a true cultural dance, and it was performed live by the natives. It was something to see, and it stuck in my memory all these years.

After a half an hour of dance and music, everything ended. Everyone went inside the church to start the wedding ceremony. This time, we were not going to be a part of it because we had to go and do what we came here to do, and that was to explore and learn. As we were boarding the bus, one Kurdish militiaman wearing a belt full of bullets in an X shaped form from shoulder to shoulder, carrying an automatic Russian-made AK-47 machine gun hanging from one of his shoulders and also a holster with a pistol inside it loaded with bullets on his waist approached the bus and asked us who the leader of the group was. I have seen these machine guns in the capital where we lived. Every army soldier had one so it was not something new for me to be surprised about. Right away my intuitive feelings told me that something was wrong. The leader of our group, along with two other older members, stepped down from the bus and started talking to this Kurdish militiaman (freedom fighters). After ten minutes of talking with our group leaders, he left. I saw their faces filled with fear as they were boarding the bus once more. Our group leader said, "Listen up, and listen up carefully. Our exploring schedule is going to be interrupted today because the Muslim-Kurdish Mayor of this village has asked us to compete with their village national or their first ranked sports team. It's the Mayor's wish for us to do it today."

We were going to play three games: volleyball, basketball, and soccer. Then our leader pleaded to us in a fashion that went like this: "Please, I beg you not to take these games very seriously. If we must lose all the games to make them happy, let it be so. Because this village is dominated by Muslim-Kurds in the majority, I'm going to try to avoid complications and hardship for the minority Christians that live in this village, if you know what I mean." He also added saying, "I know most of you are not prepared to do this because we came here for other rea-sons and not for sports competitions. I know we are short of players, and we don't represent all our athletic teams here, but they are looking to us as a step up from their level by playing against us knowing that we're an athletic club. It's a matter that's out of our hands since they control the village with guns and ammos, and not us. So please be careful"

When I heard all this, I knew right away during that ten-minute conversation between the militiaman and our group leaders was that our side was trying their best to reject/negotiate most of their demands and to prevent these games from taking place. We were not on an official sports competition trip from the city of Baghdad, and no official government sports agency had asked us to come here and compete against the Kurds in this village. All we had to do was just comply. I also knew our leader didn't have any choice in the matter. He was trying to stay on course and save the day, especially since we were far away from home, which was about an eight-hour drive by bus, and there were no airports nearby to fly back right away to avoid all this from happening. I can't blame our group leader. They gave him no choice, especially when the messenger was armed with a machine gun. One thing you have to know, and this is by generally speaking in regards to the mountainous Kurdish population, they are a very stubborn people, and they will not take "no" for an answer. This is part of their nature.

We got off the bus and tried to rest and put a team together for the first game, which was volleyball. An hour later, we went to one of the high school fields and played volleyball.

They won the game 2–1 against us. Now we lost the first game on purpose. The villagers were cheering so loud that we were scared they might attack and harm us. They were enjoying their team winning as we had to give the game away. We had to take a lunch break and then go back to play a second game, which was basketball. Three different games in one day! No one had ever heard of arrangements like this before. It was funny. We were the same players for all three games, and we were wearing army boots and no sport shoes or gear.

The lunch break was over, and all of us were mad that we had to give up the game and lose. This would never have been the case in the capital city where our athletic club took everything seriously and passionately to win competitions. No one won that easy competing against us or our teams because we were better structured athletically, and we were well trained to face all sport challenges. But, playing against the villagers created a lot of drama and anxiety among some of our members and players. We (the players) put together a plan right before the basketball game to do the best we could to win the game and to reduce our anxiety without letting our leader know so he didn't panic in fear. The game started. Their players were tall enough for a basketball game, and, as usual, they had their full sports gear on them. Unlike us, we had to play the game with our Boy Scout shorts and T-shirts. We were the same players who played volleyball earlier and lost, and we still had our sweaty cloths on us with no choice. Our team plan was to make fun of their tall players and take advantage of the situation. If it worked, then we could score and win. One thing we noticed during the lunch break was that some of their basketball players were shy individuals and by making them look like clowns where the audience would laugh at them that would give us the edge to lead. We managed to use our shortest player who was four feet six inches in height. We told him we would pass the ball to him, and he would have to go forward and dribble the ball, and, instead of going around the player, he must try and pass the ball under him between his legs.

We used this strategy throughout the game whenever we had a chance, and it created two things. First, it had gotten their forward players off balance while trying to shoot the ball in the basket. Second, this situation encouraged the audience to laugh, which helped us win over their audience, and the audience cheered for us instead. This idea was started by me, and we all did it collectively. It worked, but it angered some of their militiamen who were watching the game. While I was playing on the field, I saw their militiamen shout in their Kurdish language to the audience to stop laughing. Then I, along with another one of our players, started to do some funny movements while passing the ball to each other. This gave the audience no choice but to laugh again and again. Honestly, I didn't care because I don't like to do things or play sports against my will for anyone or for any reason. But that's just my thinking. At last, their players' concentration and their motives for the game was shot down completely. We started getting very tired ourselves as well to continue on, but these were the moments that we were waiting for. We wanted to score, so we pushed to do more. We managed to move forward with the ball more often, and we won the game with a few points more over their best basketball team. We all shouted in Armenian, "Yes, yes!"

Folks, can you imagine how much our bodies were tired by then? We had played two games that day, and all our nerves were shot, but our morale started to pick up. For a moment, we forgot that we were there on a visit and not for competition. I developed a saying, "You can take an athlete out of sports, but you will never take sports out of an athlete." It didn't matter anymore to me whether we were there for a visit or not. The villagers had already ignited the athletic emotions in us. Some of our team members were not putting much effort in the games. They were acting as participants only because after the second game, they went and asked our leader if they could quit because they couldn't go on playing anymore. I felt the same way at one point while playing because the muscles in my feet and legs were tired because of the boots I was wearing. Had it been athletic footwear, it would have made a big difference. But the one thing that kept me going was remembering my high school track and field competition a few months back and how I was treated like a second-class citizen where I was discriminated against because of being Christian, and this was payback for me. I told myself I must go on and never give up. It was a personal matter. I was meeting the challenges head-on to get even by playing the games and not hurting anyone. Some of my group members knew about my past, and they also didn't want to see us get defeated. As a team, they agreed with me about whatever the cost would be. We must all struggle and win the game, regardless what our Boy Scout leader may think of us.

As a group visiting this region, we didn't create this mess to start with, and it was sad seeing that some of our players went back and slept in the bus to rest. They couldn't go on any further. They didn't have any motivation or energy left to go on and help us finish the job. We had yet to play soccer as the third game that day, which is an hour and half long, and it would take a lot of energy to run around the field for so long. This situation created a short-age of players on our team to play this game. Normally, to play soccer you need eleven players at all times. Then you need at least five to six substitute players and one substitute goalkeeper sitting on the sidelines. We didn't have the luxury of having eleven players or a coach. As a matter of fact, we were short five players including a goalkeeper to play. We noticed there were some Armenian speaking Kurds among the village population, and they were Christians like us. They had lived in the village their entire life. Some of them were physically capable, strong and knew how to play soccer. We learned this because they approached us and told us openly but fearfully that they were willing to help and play alongside us, but then we realized that this was a dangerous situation. It was a fearful situation for all of us to accept, especially after we had asked one of them to step into our bus while we were trying to rest in order to find out why and how they wanted to help us by participating. We had to keep him away from the eyes of the militiamen. Our senior Boy Scout leader asked this villager why he was afraid to talk to us in public and to participate playing with us. He replied that the local Kurdish authorities had told them and all the other Christian Armenians who were living in that village a night before not to get involved in helping us, and if they do, they will be facing consequences. This whole conversation was done privately with this young man from the village inside our bus. After hearing this young man's explanation, our group leaders talked to the local authorities to get their permission to use some of the villagers that wanted to play and help us make the game more balanced. We wanted to keep the peace and not disturb it. This was our first reason in meeting with the authorities, and the second reason was we didn't know enough about the villagers as Christians. They could be informers for all we know, and they could possibly be setting us up for something else planned by the village authorities. So our leaders played it safe by asking the local authorities for volunteers to join us to play the game. Our senior group member asked the authorities to give us players of their choice regardless of their religious faith in order to accomplish their objective. We needed at least five to six more players. We all thought about whether the authorities had a special agenda in mind by engaging us into these games, or were they using these games as entertainment only for their village people to enjoy. We didn't know what was going on in their minds. We agreed amongst ourselves to insist and ask for a fair game to take place; otherwise, we would pack and hit the road back to Baghdad that night. The three senior people who were talking with the local authorities were also trying to read their minds, and, somehow, our conclusion of the authorities' mindset was correct that this was a preplanned issue from the previous night while we were all at the party celebrating the wedding. We also had the assumption that they were trying to tear down our reputation as Christians inside their village for some unknown reason(s). Or, was it? Possibly, it was foolish thinking on their behalf by signifying us as weak Christians in the region in the presence of the entire village, so they could still control and govern their local people. All these were assumptions. I was resting in the bus and listening to our senior group leaders as they were exploring these possibilities. As a matter of fact, there was some discrimination that had been going on throughout the years against the minority Christians in that village and our senior members were told about this that very day by one of the villagers who had gotten on the bus and who had privately spoke to our group leaders. Wow!

Our group, formed by three senior members, tried to negotiate with them, and at that point, we were serious, and we were in a very serious situation. We asked them if we could have some of their villagers join us and play soccer in order to make the game more balanced and fun. But since we knew what was going on inside their minds, and it was obvious why they were doing this and for what purpose, we changed our minds and insisted on having only Christian players from the village join us, so we could play. Their plan was a soccer game between Muslims and Christians. Our latest suggestion had stirred the pot. They started looking at each other, and that was a signal to us that we hit the nail on its head through the negotiations. Eventually, they were thinking to elevate tension with it, and right away without any hesitation, somehow, they agreed to go with our plan. We chose four players from their village. Their names were given to us by the very first player who got onto the bus with us an hour earlier that day and gave us all these tips. We understood what was going on behind our backs. We were just peaceful visitors to their region and nothing else. But one more sad fact we learned from this young fellow was that most Armenian Christians who were living in this village were forced by the Iraqi Kurdish authorities not to speak their native Armenian Language, but they kept the church open, so everyone could practice their faith! It didn't make any sense to me after what had happened, but I wasn't going to be involved in this matter. Besides, none of us could do anything about it. We had enough problems to overcome as it was, and this issue was for the government to resolve and not us.

We couldn't get any more than four players from the village. This was still making things difficult because this would have only put us in a situation where if one of our players got injured or kicked out of the game for any reason by the referee, they would still have had an advantage over the outcome of the game because we had no substitute players. But we got lucky. God was watching over all of us, and this luck was playing in our favor. We learned that one of the four players we got was a professional goalkeeper. He played with one of the best soccer teams in the city of Mosul, which was a city close-by in the northern Iraqi region. It was not too far from the village that we were visiting. This had put our hopes high a bit because the most important player in the game is the goalkeeper. We didn't show our excitement much regarding the goalkeeper because you never know what would happen. This goalkeeper was much older than most of us, but he was still fit for this sport as we all witnessed throughout the game.

The soccer field was situated on top of a flat big hill and it was sloped down leaning toward one side of the hill. When you stood at the high end of the field, you could see that your feet were almost in level position with the top of the goal post at the far end of the field. Naturally, whoever was to start playing from the highest point of the slope going downward had an advantage over the other team because the ball would roll down faster. By then we knew these kinds of arrangements were only happening on purpose for the home team's advantage. It was not for us. Why was I not surprised? The game began. The field was not smooth. It was full of natural rocks, the size of a grapefruit, sticking out of the ground, so if you're running without looking down, you could tumble over a rock and get hurt easily. We had no choice. We started playing and pushing the ball toward their goal running upwards just like climbing a hill. This was very exhausting. One thing I laughed and was amazed about was that their soccer team was over dressed wearing full soccer gear, just like this was a World Cup competition.

We put our heads together to win this match at any cost. We got lucky, and we scored the first goal in the game. The crowd from the basketball game watched us play soccer. If you remember, towards the end of the basketball game, they liked us and were cheering for us instead. They did the same thing at the soccer field when they saw we scored the first goal, but this was not going to be a smooth operation. We witnessed some of the men with guns starting to hit their own people in the audience with sticks, and most were getting hit regardless of age or gender. The men with the guns tried to shut the people's excitement down and discourage them from cheering for us. Folks, this started to get ridiculous, especially since their mayor was present. So we stayed with one goal in mind and that was to win and not to be involved with the locals and their agendas and attitudes toward their village people. Throughout the first half of the game, the score was one goal to our advantage. Around half time, we were all sharing our thoughts while resting in our bus saying that the second half would be easier because we would have the advantage of playing from the higher field downwards when we switch to play on the opposite side of the field where the ball could roll downhill easier. And, with some extra effort, we may be able to score another goal and win the game for all the villagers and not just for the Christians, which was our main goal to achieve. But something happened before starting the second half of the game, and it was true prejudice. The referee of the game who was from the village itself informed us as a team that no changes should take place to play on the opposite side of the field and both teams should stay on the same half field and play. Something like this was never heard of in the entire history of soccer around the world. They had changed the rules to gain advantage, and we had no choice but to continue and get it over with.

We also realized that the referee was being partial, or it seemed like someone had threatened him with something. In the second half, his decisions started to be more partial, and when anyone barely touched the home team or passed by them running with a certain speed, a foul was called out. This was unlike the home team who were hitting us with their elbows while we were trying to dribble the ball to pass it forward or tripping us as we were passing them running and advancing toward their goal. They were playing rough with us, and all these faults were not being called out as fouls by the referee. This led to a lot of tension among our team players and was going to lead to violence. This is where I tried to calm our team players down and reminded them to focus on the game and not to lose faith by telling them we only had twenty-five minutes left to play, and we were up with one goal. While playing, I reminded them not to lose faith, but not every player felt like I did. After all, they were men, and they were angry.

God never created two of the same individuals, so, naturally, we were on the verge of a fight. Approximately three minutes later one of our defensive line players hit the home team's offensive player in his chest with his elbow as he was running with the ball toward our goal, and he knocked him down. This hit happened outside the big penalty box area, and not inside it. So, naturally, the call should have been a foul with an indirect kick. In this situation, our team must form a blocking wall to block their kick toward our goal. But the referee called it a penalty kick for the home team. This blew our minds and got us all angry. We walked out of the game and ran towards the bus. We saw our leader come out of the bus and said, "We can't do this. We have to stay in the game, for Christ's sake. Our leader felt our pressure, and he had a lot of it himself, but he calmed us down as well after my attempts had failed. Then he said to take it as a challenge and not as a game. He added that we don't face hard situations like this every day in the city, so this is good practice for all of us to learn.

He said not to forget they were doing this on purpose because we are Christians, and we shouldn't change to be something else. He added for us to be patient as we had one more day before we were to go home, and this would be an experience for all of us to learn from.

That was a good speech. Using the word "home" comforted all of us. We returned to the game. Coming out of the game, listening to our leader and going back to the game all happened in four minutes. This left us with one thing in mind, and that was when we went back to play the game again, we had no choice but to accept the decision of the referee for the unfair penalty kick call. This was uncalled for in the rules. We were all getting in position waiting for the penalty kick, which was about to be executed on the field against our goal. Our goalkeeper was getting ready for the kick. We saw a Kurdish militiaman go behind our goal net and say something to our goalkeeper in Kurdish. Our goalkeeper got mad and started walking away from the goal, and the game came to a halt again. Our captain asked the goalkeeper, "What happened, and what did the militiaman tell you?" The goalkeeper said that the Kurdish militiaman told him that if he saves the ball from entering our goal (which would have been an equalizer goal, if they scored), he would go to his home (meaning our goalkeeper's home), and he would kill him by shooting him tonight. Wow, wow! When we heard this, we couldn't believe it. The idea of killing a man for a friendly sports game didn't make sense at all since these kinds of things didn't happen where we lived; at least I had never heard of any such thing at the time. And, then again, bullying was a favorite game for the new Baath regime which had taken power. But anyhow, that's a totally different story in itself to be told at a later chapter in this book.

We were all standing at the game and moments before witnessing the penalty kick getting ready to be kicked, our leader shouted in Armenian from the far side of the field through his fears, "Don't win this game; otherwise, we could all be dead tonight!" We knew some of the militiamen were fanatics and crazy. Right away, we told our goalkeeper to let go of his anger, to please not catch the ball, and to try to fake jump toward the opposite direction to avoid catching the ball. At first, he said okay, but when the ball got kicked, he jumped toward the direction of the ball trying to catch it instead, ignoring what he was told by our captain. This got all of us worried for a moment. Then, on a split-second decision, somehow he decided to pull his arm back in order for the ball to enter our goal. We realized later that our goalkeeper, despite living in the village, hated the Kurdish militiamen's guts because they caused some difficulties for his immediate family members, especially his Christian sister, but he couldn't tell us why. We didn't want to pursue it, especially since we saw tears in his eyes. The whole team decided to pay a visit and to go to the goalkeeper's home to thank him for his efforts and to visit his family that night.

Now the other team had scored their first goal. The score was an even one to one so far.

We said so be it. Then ten minutes later, we let them score a second goal to win The Senior High School Years, and Our Haunted New Home the game. The game ended, and we witnessed a show of machine guns which began. Most of the militiamen were celebrating by shooting in the air, disregarding the danger of the falling bullets. As we all know, what goes up must come down, and this could have injured or might have killed someone. All of us were in a panic. We thanked the mayor for the opportunity to play the games, and we ran and entered the bus in a hurry to leave the field and head back to the church where we were staying at nights.

I was so happy that my dad agreed that I take this trip. He probably wouldn't believe his ears if I told him what took place those past several days in that village during our trip. This experience taught me a lot of things. I had kept it in my heart to grow up strong toward sudden life challenges, to develop courage and wisdom in me and how to apply them in times of danger. It was a bizarre experience for me to learn from. What I can say is this, "How much we know in life is not important. What's important is how we apply our knowledge in time of danger, and if you are going to lose in order to win, let it be so."

CHAPTER

4

Escaping from Iraq

My father was a great dad. He was involved in the Christian Armenian community as a volunteer secretary for the administrative committee for the cultural club. The primary goal for this group was to protect and preserve the Armenian heritage, religion, and culture in a Muslim-dominated Iraq, along with other brave friends and some of our community members who were caring enough to devote their free time as well. I don't know if you can call this a political group or not, but myself and others certainly don't think so; it's a gray area. My father was a peaceful man. He believed in this cause where no man should be able to destroy or make it extinct (we are referring here to the Christian religion and the Armenian culture of staying alive in Iraq around the sixties). He had to do what it took for all of us in the community as minorities like others before him had done in previous generations in Iraq, starting with Mike's own father back in the day. None of these members were trying to start any revolution, disturbance or violence of any sort to hurt or damage other minorities' religion or faith. They respected all and whatever viewpoints everyone else had. These men were noble in their work ethics and choices. They devoted their life and time to do this for a noble cause as volunteers for all Christian Armenians who were raising families among a Muslim population in all regions of Iraq. As Christians, they all blended in the Iraqi society and had many Muslim friends and co-workers who they respected. But, nevertheless, a dictator like Saddam Hussein and his bullies took power and occupied the country's highest office as the president. When the regime came into power in 1968 under the leadership of Maj. Gen. Ahmed Hassan al Baker as president and Saddam Hussein as Chief for the Homeland Security Department, they didn't care who they had to step on, kill, exterminate or torture in order for them to stay in power. They had caused harm to all Iraqi minority groups and faiths. They even did it to their own Muslim population. They wanted to have control and to plant fear among the society like Saddam's counterpart, the former leader of the Soviet Union General Joseph Stalin, who Saddam considered as his idol. In the past, General Joseph Stalin had done the very same things to his own minority groups and had forcefully changed the fate of mankind. History witnessed that Saddam was following in Stalin's footsteps as well, and for long years when his party took power to govern Iraq. This kind of action killed the morale and demolished the trust among the Iraqi people, regardless of their religion or ethnicity. Brother couldn't trust his own brother, and father couldn't trust his own son, and the regime awarded any person if they could inform them about anyone else's wrongdoings. The accused that were reported to the authorities would get picked up by the regime in the middle of the night for interrogation and sometimes would never be heard from again, or you wouldn't hear about their relatives' whereabouts anymore. It was crazy, and these events were sick in nature, which we all had to face on a daily basis for years. From their fears, some people gave in for some unknown reason, and they decided to join in on all the wrongdoings to help the regime. The regime also had planted recruiters in high schools, colleges and universities to help re- enforce the Baath party membership base. But most people resented joining in the wrongdoings because it was wrong and evil. Most, but not all, who agreed with the regime were nothing more than uneducated low lives and had nothing set in life to follow like goals and destiny, and they were joining in due to their fears in order to gain leverage and feel important. Such individuals were empowered by the regime and were the regime's favorite ones. They existed all over town, just like street lights. They existed all over the city, in streets, inside the taxicabs, restaurants, schools, universities and most public places. You could no longer talk to anyone openly and freely, and you couldn't express your opinions or criticize anything anymore without looking over your shoulder or knowing who you can talk to. Freedom of speech was only for the regime to practice. Iraqi history books rapidly started to change and wrong information started to make it into the history books. People who spoke the truth were hung or suddenly disappeared from the face of this earth through night raids in their homes and so on. Torture was a daily routine for these bullies. A person, even a child, couldn't look into the eyes of the authorities without getting themselves in trouble. We all had to learn how to lie and change our opinion or cover it up with stories by sugar coating our thoughts so we wouldn't get in trouble. You wouldn't know if your daughter would be safe going to school or riding a bus. No one was safe, but yet some, until now, say it was better during the time of the regime. Hmm, that makes me wonder.

It was a sad thing to have witnessed and heard all these evil events living in the city and seeing them on television. God didn't exist in their hearts, nor were they practicing their own religion faithfully. It was all an act, and some of the Muslim mosques were used as government meeting places, and who knows what was going inside the basements of these mosques. I was aware of these things because the father of one of my Muslim friends was a member of the Baath regime in Iraq, and my friend from high school had overheard his father discussing these things with his wife at nights in bed. As you can see, life was not going to be easy, and you wouldn't and couldn't live it in any way you wanted to anymore. It was their way or the highway. You could face death regardless if you were Christian or Muslim or other faith. They would punish you and kill you and your family with any method of their choice. They did these killings without any trace, just like the mobs. In my opinion, they were a govern-ment of mobs and not a government of people.

Our homes and neighborhood were watched constantly, as were everyone else's. You would witness several Russian-made new Volga passenger cars all over town, and when you saw them, you knew for sure they were the death squad, as I had labeled them in my mind. They would follow you for days if they are suspicious of you and waiting for any failure, mistake, angry word or action on your part toward them or toward the regime, especially if they decided that you're not likable or there was something so wrong and obvious to them about you. It was a personality game. It could be your looks, the clothes you wear or the way you walk past them. Once confronted, you had to always follow what they would like you to do and how they would like you to act. Most people were like robots. Yes sir, no sir, you are the best sir, and so on. This was not what I wanted out of life as a young man.

These events affected my life throughout the years. I believe no person should see so much turmoil in his or her country's daily life that was changing towards unpleasant events rather than pleasant ones. As a result of this, the direct impact on your self- confidence was to deprive you from it all. The assurance to grow up as a good, loyal Iraqi citizen was doubtful. Furthermore, I survived for a long time, but the damage to my self-image had carried on the scars within me for years to come.

Spying was a daily routine by these bullies who would never qualify to be a simple boy scout. Spies were individuals who never finished their elementary schools, and you could test them by asking them to write their names on a piece of paper. You would be amazed at how many of them didn't know how to read or write. But, for sure, they could have control over you and your belongings at any given time or day when they get the call from their headquarters to act with such an order. All of them were supplied with guns, communication radios and were given power to act instantly. It's sad when you know how many people were killed and tortured for no reason or for fun by these bullies. Once these bullies were empowered by the regime and due to unspecified rules or instructions communicated to them, some of them took power into their hands and had a score to settle with others through their past experiences. Once captured, many woman and young girls were raped and later killed to get rid of their bodies throughout the city. The country's rape laws were very tough. Anyone committing a rape crime would be subject to a punishable law of hanging to death. But for the regime these laws were only written in the law books and were meant for the poor and the misfortunate and enforced on the average citizen. It was not for the bullies and the gangs of the regime. Although some of the regime members were fair and just, it only existed in a few. What a shameful thing to talk and to write about on the country that I was born and raised in. But, if I or anyone else does not write about it, then the young generation who follows will never know how to fix these kinds of problems. Hopefully, such crimes and evil wouldn't take place anymore in their generation.

One summer evening around 6:30 p.m., I left home and started walking towards the local bus stop to take a bus. I had to attend basketball practice at the AAC (Armenian Athletic Club) that evening. The bus station was a ten-minute walk from my home, and I was accustomed to doing this twice a week. That evening, as I was walking to the bus station, I noticed a Russian-made Volga passenger car that was parked in a dark place a short distance from my house next to a backyard wall a few houses down from my backyard. I looked at the car to see if there was anyone sitting in it, but I couldn't see anything in the dark as I was walking to it from a distance. When I got closer to the car, I noticed two dotted red flames lit behind the windshield. The flames were going from bright to dim. Then I noticed two men sitting in the front seat smoking their cigarettes at the same time. One of them lowered the window, called me in an unpleasant manner and tone of voice and asked me if I knew the time. Out of fear, I couldn't turn back to answer him, and then I realized I had taken my watch off from my wrist earlier that evening for some reason and left it at home. My mind was shot due to the fear and panic of that moment. I ran to the bus station. During the bus ride as I was heading toward the club, I missed getting off the bus at the right station, so I got off two stations further away from the club. I ran fast toward the club building, so I could overcome my anger and fears. That night when I got to the practice site, everything was back to normal within me for some reason, but I still had to return to my house around 11:00 p.m. After the practice was over, I came up with a plan to return home. I would get off the bus two stops earlier and away from my house and use the side streets to walk in the dark in the nearby community. I managed to get home safely trying to avoid any more encounters with these bullies that night.

I told everyone what had happened, and I asked them to avoid taking the bus by walking their normal path. I asked them to wake up early in order to catch the bus by going from the back streets.

I was not scheduled to go to practice the next day. I then called in to practice pretending to be sick. I did the same for the following scheduled practice days. I was trying to avoid the bullies for the next two weeks, hoping that they may lose track of me and go away. After two weeks' time, I was scheduled to go to the basketball practice again. I started walking my normal route hoping I wouldn't encounter them anymore. I turned the corner two blocks from the bus stop, and I saw the same car again and parked in the same place, but this time there were two different men sitting in the front seat. They did the same thing by lowering the car window to ask me for the time. This new team of bullies sounded politer for a change. They asked me to come closer to their car. I decided to take the challenge and meet them face-to-face by approaching their car without any fear. I walked to the car, and they asked me if I knew my next-door neighbor's son's name. I refused to tell them who he was by denying that I had any encounter with my neighbor's son. They informed me that they were aware of where I go and what I do at the club because he said it was their job to know these things. He then complimented me for being a high school hero at my high school. I was speechless. It was better for me to just listen and not say anything. I was confused out of my fear once more. Then the man asked if I could help them get some information about my next-door neighbor, the good teacher, Mr. Adnan, who we knew for a long time. He had previously helped me with my school issues. I told them, "This is not my job, and I can't do such a thing and spy on my neighbor." Then, through my fear, I had to admit that, yes, I did know him. I told them that he was a very honest and good man, and we should be proud that we have a teacher like him in our society. The men shook their heads in disagreement, and they let me go. That evening I didn't take the bus, and I turned back to go home from the side streets, and I went and knocked on my neighbor's door. I asked if I could see Mr. Adnan. When he came to the door, I told him what had happened earlier that evening and what they had asked me to do. He was surprised and scared, of course, at the same time. He thanked me for my courage, and he told me not to worry about him much; he would handle it himself. This scenario was going on every week, and every time I passed by them, they asked me for the time. I had to tell them what time it was and so on by looking at the time at home before I left. One night, I was reading one of the James Bond fiction books, which I had gotten from a friend at school. The book was written and translated into Arabic, the Arabic language was the country's first language, but for me Arabic was considered a second language, since my own language was Armenian.

The year was 1972. I remember one evening in October two months before my seventeenth birthday I was home when my father went to visit his friend in town. The distance was a half hour bus ride. My father left home around 7:00 p.m. and a short time later, a Russian Volga passenger car, which was driven by two bullies, had just parked at our front gate. One of the men got out of the car and rang the bell on our driveway gate at the front yard. The entry door to the main house was thirty feet away from the front driveway gate of the house. I answered the doorbell.

I said, "What do you want?" He said he was looking for Mike, my father, and asked if he was home. I said, "No, he just left and will be back later on."

He paused for a few seconds and then said they will be back later to see him. I replied, "May I ask who is asking about him?"

He said, "Just tell him we are his friends."

Wow, what a lie! I knew my father well. He didn't have any Muslim friends who had a Russian Volga car. I closed the door, and I went in to tell my mom. She was puzzled as well. I then went upstairs to the rooftop where we used to sleep during the summer nights. An hour later into that evening I looked down from my rooftop and saw my dad from a distance running in the streets to get home. He was not walking, as usual. We went to open the backyard gate, and I couldn't believe my eyes. My father's face was as yellow as the skin of a lemon; he could barely breathe. He walked into the house, and my mom and his mom (my grandmother Knar) both tried to calm him down. When he caught his breath, we asked him what was wrong. He said when he went to visit his friend today, his friend told him, "Mike, don't come here. Go away. The Iraqi secret service, El Ammen, is arresting everyone who was involved in working for our community's cause." By putting all this together, anger got into me very fast. Now the picture was clear to me. All this asking me for the time by those bullies every time I passed by them had nothing to do with my neighbor's son, Mr. Adnan. Actually, it had to do with spying on my dad's affairs and us. They were not watching others; they were watching and spying on our home. With a big panic and tears in her eyes, my mom told my father that they had already come earlier asking about him and said they would come later around midnight to see him. I could only imagine how much fear was created in my father's heart and mind. This was something only he could explain. I had never seen my mountain of guidance, hope, love, and the caring person my dad was in this kind of a fearful situation before. I knew he was innocent. He had not done anything wrong and it seemed like another life challenge. Yet, it was getting developed once more for me to face, and it had to do with my own loved ones this time.

My parents went to the master bedroom to talk, and after a short while, they both came out. I saw my father had a small suitcase in his hand with his cloths in it, and he gathered us all in the den and said that he loved us very much. He said he was going away for some time, and he didn't know if he was going to be returning home. He looked at me and after hugging me, he said if he didn't return home, he wanted me to remember him as an individual who never did anything wrong to hurt any human being or mankind. Furthermore, he added saying to the whole family and referring to me as his oldest son that I will be the head of the family to take care of them just in case he doesn't make it back. By now, my heart was pounding hard in my chest, and I couldn't and didn't want to hear these words. I told him, "You are my hero, as always. I don't think they will win, so please stay strong for all of us." My heart never lies to me at all, and I told him, "We'll wait for you, dad. I know you'll be back." Then I broke out in tears and so did everyone else. Then the doorbell rang again. I ran and opened the main door, and I saw the same bullies were at our door steps. They said they wanted to talk to Mike, and, out of anger, I yelled that he was not here. Then my dad pulled me back into the house and said, "Here I am. How can I help you gentlemen?"

They said, "We are here to arrest you and we need to search your home."

As you can see, there were laws, but these bullies were not the ones who were going to respect it. In a just world, anyone who comes to search your home should have a warrant with them or a piece of a paper. But, in Iraq no such paper existed at the time. They did whatever their minds told them to do, or whatever their instructions were from their headquarters.

These idiots were following orders from the revolutionary command council of the Baath party, so my father as honest and as cooperative that he was. He did let them in to search our home. We were all asked to sit on our living room floor while it was requested that only my father should deal with their orders. They took my dad's record book and other documents and without reading them they accused him of treason on the spot. All three men walked out with my dad who was walking in the front to their car, which was a Russian-made Volga. We noticed our front door was closed shut, and we all got up and rushed to the front window of our living room, which was overlooking the street, to observe what was happening. I saw my dad turn around and look back at his home just like someone was looking at it for the last time knowing that he was not coming back there anymore. When I waved to him and yelled, "I love you dad", one of the bullies turned to me and told me they will take care of my father. They only wanted to ask him some questions at the station. I replied, "I hope you do so, or I will make you eat your own words later."

He didn't like that. I was not harmed, but they shook their heads and drove away. They took what they came to take. Sadness took a big place in our home that evening like a waterfall that stopped flowing anymore. I didn't feel that even the ghost that was haunting our home for some time was going to make any moves that night. None of us could go to sleep that night, and, luckily, my aunt (my mom's sister Veronica) and her family was living upstairs in the same household with us at the time. They started comforting my mother that night. I couldn't believe this could happen to us. They took my dad away to prison. How am I going to feed my family? What am I supposed to do? I never worked in my life; I had no skills. I went out to our back yard that night trying to isolate myself. I don't know what happened that night. As I was asking myself all these questions and my heart was full of hate and anger sitting on the grass in the dark behind our house, I heard a voice in the dark which scared the living daylights out of me. It was talking to me. Or was it? I don't know who or what it was. Was it the Holy Ghost, or was it the evil ghost which was haunting our house for some time? I was not ready to face another fear, especially after what we went through about an hour ago with the big trauma. But this voice told me not to worry and that we will be taken care of. I looked around in the dark. There was no one next to me. I got up quickly in a panic, turned around and ran back to my house and hugged my mom strongly. My grandmother's (Mike's mom) head couldn't stop looking at the sky all night. She was praying and praying very hard for her only son. It took her a lifetime to raise him along with her five daughters; a son she was attached to and loved so much. He was everything to her and she was proud of him. What she promised her husband before he died was to take care of all six children with whatever means and at any cost. She finished praying and called me next to her and said to me, "My dear, don't cry or fear anything. God has always been caring and providing for us in our family's most difficult times." She added that she had seen horror and fear when she was nine years old during their escape in 1915 from their village named Van during the Armenian Genocide at the hands of the Ottoman Empire (the Turks). She said, "This pain will pass as well. Don't worry. We shouldn't be angry with God. He must have a new plan for all of us. She said, "I don't want you to forget why your father was arrested. He was arrested because he loved his people. He loved justice and he loved to give and help people in their time of need. Your father was the type of person who took his shirt off and gave it to whoever asked for help."

She added that my father is paying the price for his work, this noble cause, that he was involved with for our community, which he believed in, and whatever the outcome is of his arrest, kid, he always will be our hero. Then she turned to me and said, "All I want is for you to follow what your father believed in and accomplish it for his community (the Christian Armenian community, that is), and don't let your community down. Your father will be very proud to know when he comes back that you are following his footsteps. I realized she was referring to me to carry his torch now, and then she held her tears, so I didn't have to get emotional. She said, "Let's go to sleep with whatever time is left tonight, and tomorrow when the sun comes up, we will think of what to do next." I couldn't agree more with what she had said. It was all true, but I was exhausted, and I fell into a deep sleep.

The next morning at the breakfast table, no one had an appetite to eat, but we forced ourselves to eat in order to gain energy to think and start the day. My mom and my grand-mother decided that I should go and deliver the news to my aunt Sofina personally because they said our phone could be bugged. We knew this, and it was proven to us as well with the very first phone call we received from my dad's boss at work. He told us that he got reports from the field office that the streets were full of people in the front of Mike's office at the Department of Water and Power to pay their utility bills. He asked us where Mike was. He said Mike's office had not been opened yet. My mom had to tell my dad's boss for the first time in her life speaking with him on the phone that last night her husband was arrested with no apparent reason. She said this in a special fashion, so my dad wouldn't lose his job; not just yet. My dad's boss was a very good man, and he loved my dad very much because my dad was very honest in his work ethics and never stolen any funds from the department. Despite all the cash money he was handling, he was on time for work every day. Although my dad's boss was a Muslim, he trusted my dad very much.

After my mom's conversation had ended, she put the phone down. I went and picked it up so I could call my friend when I noticed two people were talking about my mom's conversation and asking each other if they wrote down what she had said. This was even before I could dial my friend's number. They quickly shouted to each other to hang up the phone up now. I put the phone down, and I told everyone not to use it because there were people who were listening, and we had been bugged by the authorities. My mom asked her sister Veronica, who also worked for the Department of Water and Power in the same area, when she gets to work today, to please ask Mike's boss if he can put Mike on leave of absence and to call the Office of the Iraqi Interior Secret Service of Baghdad in order to get the details and let us know what his fate is, if possible.

The next thing I did was I went the same way that I always go to catch the bus, but it was no surprise to me that the watch dogs who I had encountered months ago were no longer watching our home. I could walk freely for a change to the bus station. But it did occur to me that I could be followed. Keeping this in mind, I changed my plan of going directly to my aunt Sofina's home. I went to her husband's work place instead in order to not expose her residence and possibly endanger her and her family. Her husband was a business owner and along with his immediate family they owned a winery, which was located in the northern part of Iraq in the city called Mosul. It was established sixty to seventy years ago around the 1900's. It happened that her husband had a distribution office in the city of Baghdad where he was working.

I pushed the entry doorbell to his office, and his employee opened the door. I asked if my uncle was there. He said I could come in and wait for him as he had not arrived yet but should be there any moment. I sat down for the first time outside his office looking through the glass door into the semi-dark office. All his diplomas were hung on the office wall, and there was a lot of paperwork on his desk. A file cabinet was set in the corner and there was a large heavy safe next to it, black in color, and it was made from steel material.

I was observing everything while I was waiting for him and telling myself I would and should finish my education at any cost one day so that I could end up as successful as my uncle. He spoke four to five languages and had a business degree from a university in England where he had finished his education some years back. Then, as I was advising myself mentally to keep calm, I heard his voice coming into the building as he had just parked his car outside the office. He was very astonished that I was sitting in the lobby of his building early that morning and waiting for him. He told me to come into his office. My uncle asked his employee to bring some tea and some breakfast for both of us, and then he sent him away. He asked me what I was doing there early that day. He asked if everyone was okay at home or was there any need for financial assistance because he helped us before when my dad had to borrow some money from him and paid him back at a later date. I said, "I am not here for money. But is it safe to talk?" He said, "Yes, don't worry, son," with a big surprise and a question mark on his face.

I said, "They took my dad away last night, and I was in fear that I could be followed. I didn't want to lead anyone to your house, and my instructions from my mom and my grand-mother were to go to your house and tell your wife (my aunt) about the bad news. But I came here to tell you instead, so you can tell your wife by informing her about her only brother's fate, that he was arrested last night, and I explained to him what the reasons were. I also told him not to try to call us on the house phone because it was bugged. But he could reach us by calling Mr. Adnan, our neighbor, who lives next door. Folks, as I said in the beginning of an earlier chapter when I was explaining about this new regime which ruled Iraq that in order to survive under their rules, you must learn how to lie and make up stories.

My mom had advised me not to let our next-door neighbors, Mr. Adnan and his house-hold, know what had happened last night at our home, so I informed my neighbors that our phone was disconnected for non-payment, and we would appreciate using their phone for incoming and outgoing calls, if it was okay with them. I also added that we would pay for the calls. I had to remind them that we helped them in the past when their electric services were disconnected for some time due to some financial hardships they had encountered and how my dad had helped them gain power through mechanical connection to our main electrical box for free for two long summer months. I had to do this because, at the time, we didn't have any income, and how was I going to pay the portion of our usage of their phone, if they asked me to do so. My neighbor assured me not to worry about it, and they would call us any time they receive a call directed to us. I thanked them. Then their son, Mr. Adnan, asked me the million- dollar question: "Why was our phone bill not paid?" I panicked that he might have known the reason, and he would find out if I was lying to them. But the situation changed when he asked me a second question. He asked if we needed any financial help. I said, "No. My father left the country suddenly on a business trip, and he forgot to pay the bill. He should be back shortly in a few days or a week, and then he'll take care of it."

Going back to my uncle, he was shocked and speechless in the beginning about the bad news. He shook his head mumbling my dad's name saying, "Mike, what are they going to do to you?"

I asked, "What are you saying?"

"Never mind, don't worry much kid. But I have to tell your aunt about this in a very delicate way because she has migraine headache problems and hearing the bad news will affect her very much."

I asked, "Uncle, please, can you do something? I want to see my dad again."

"It's not in my hands, son, but the only thing I can do is to talk to some of my connections in town and see if they can tell me the condition of my brother-in-law along with the others who were arrested with him at the same time." He said they were our guardian angels for our community, and we can't afford to lose them. He shook his head once again. I left his office in midday carrying a bag of goods like soap and cosmetic samples, which he was selling besides making wine in his factory, and I walked out with these items. I made this visit to portray that I was a customer and had an order to pick up from his office just in case I was being followed and if someone was going to stop me and search me on the way back. I was walking toward the main street going towards the bus station. I created a habit to stop and tie my shoes while, out of the corner of my eye, looking to spot whether someone was following me or not. I learned this by reading the James Bond books in my earlier high school years. Apparently, the James Bond books were paying off because as I left my uncle's office, I noticed a man with a thick mustache looking at me and then burying his head in the local newspaper. I wasn't sure if he was following me or not yet. Using the shoe tying trick that I had learned, I noticed he was the one who had been following me when I visited my uncle's office. Most importantly, I knew then that I had a follower who was most likely a government informer behind every step I was taking. I had to change two buses in order to get home. I took the first bus trying to ignore him. I sat down and didn't care what this man wanted from me. He was a government informer and he was following his prey. But one thing he couldn't do for sure was to find out what was going on inside my mind. I sat still as the bus was moving and was passing by the front gates of the electrical engineering college. I was day dreaming, and, at that time, all my dreams in life were to enroll and graduate from that college as an electrical engineer. I began to review and evaluate myself, and asked myself many, many questions. For instance, are you sure this is what you want to do? Is this true and will this happen in the future? What if you were never to see your father again? What if they killed him in prison? Then I would have no choice but to leave school and start to work to take care of my family; my mom along with my two brothers and my grandmother. What if and what if. There were too many questions, but there were no sure answers for them in my mind. I had to get off the bus and change to another one that went from this college to my home, and I noticed the same man had changed to the second bus and going with me in the same direction I was headed. He sat in the back of the bus where the only exit was located, and he was reading his newspaper. Now this had created another challenge for me. I was fearfully preparing myself to get up and bravely go and ask this man why he was following me. Sometimes, fear makes you do things you don't realize you are capable of doing, and it's possible this could be the automatic survival mechanism, which we all carry with us in times of need. I stood up in the bus to give my seat to another passenger and told her you can have my seat because I'll be off the bus soon making sure the informer could hear this from the back of the bus. I waited until the seat next to the informer was unoccupied. The bus I am describing here was red in color, two stories high, which was imported some decades ago from England by the Iraqi Department of Transportation. I'm sure many of you have seen these types of buses at some time or another on TV, or if anyone has visited London on vacation or on a trip, then you would know what I'm talking about

Suddenly, the seat next to the informer became unoccupied, so I decided to sit down next to him. I asked him the question of why he is following me. The man was shocked, and he said he was not following me at all. I insisted that he was, and I told him since I left the last address in the city that he had been following me. My observation from his facial expression indicated to me that he was not telling me the truth.

Then I asked him, "Where are you going?" He replied, "It's not your business."

I argued, "It is my business because I have been taking this bus every day for the last two years, and I have never seen you on it."

He said he would be getting off on the next stop. Then I had to make this one up, and I said so was I. I guess I was angry, and I was reacting very strange by asking him these questions, and most informers are, in nature, cowardly people, and they know they are doing something wrong. Their conscious bothers them, and when their cover is blown, they try to run away or be invisible. As the bus came to a stop, the informer got up to get off the bus. I did the same, but one mistake the informer made was that he didn't watch his back because I outsmarted him by walking behind him just like I was going to get off the bus myself. But, when he stepped down from the bus and started walking fast without looking back to see if I was behind him or not, I stopped from getting off the bus, and the bus drove away. ("Laughing out loud") He turned around and when he heard the bus rolling away, he saw me on board. He started running to get on the bus again, but the bus took off fast, and he was about twenty-five to thirty yards behind it. He looked at me, and I was smiling and waving back at him. His failed attempt to get on the bus had assured me that I was right about him. It felt good in my gut feeling when I got rid of him. I was heading home to tell my mom what had happened and that I had delivered the message to my uncle that day, and not to my aunt directly. When I explained to my mom all what took place that day, she agreed that it was a wise step, but I should be very careful not to mess around again with these kinds of people. She said, "I can't afford to lose two men from my household at the same time."

Folks, to be honest with you, regardless of how you are judging me on this situation and the way it ended with the informer and whether I was a brave boy or not, I was only acting out of my fears and trying to meet my daily challenges head on. Let me tell you, no one was safe in the city. You could be a winner on certain days acting like I did, but we were all big losers most of the time trying to beat the system. After 48 hours facing this crisis, I felt the entire family's responsibilities were being transferred and to be handled by me. It was a heavy burden on my shoulders at a young age. I felt my life was going down the drain with no hopes and nothing to look forward to. And, no matter how much faith and belief I had in God, the anger was not leaving me, and it was not going away. Day-by-day I had gotten more impatient and uneasy at times. I wouldn't know if they were coming back to arrest other members of my family, or if they were going to free my dad. The regime, unfortunately, succeeded to plant fear and mistrust among all of the Iraqi people, regardless of their faith and nationalities. This was somewhat like communism, as it was done by the Soviets.

The next day, our neighbors called my mom that she had a phone call. The caller was my aunt Sofina who had just learned from her husband about her brother's arrest. I accompanied my mom to my neighbor's house. She talked on the neighbor's phone line with aunt Sofina, and, luckily, they were speaking Armenian, which our neighbors didn't understand. She told my mom not to worry financially because her husband was well off at the moment with his business, and he could help all of us until the situation could be resolved. She assured my mom that she will do her utmost best in order to pay a visit to see her brother in prison. She said her husband had a lot of connections. He knew some of the regime officers. They were all buying and drinking the wine that he had been making and selling. So, it's possible that she will get a special pass to see her brother in prison and all the other members that had been arrested with him that very same night. But my aunt Sofina learned also that this prison was under very heavy security watch where guards were all over. It was a prison that you could hardly and rarely believe that had ever existed because it was a house in the middle of the city of Bagdad, which had belonged to a wealthy family who had previously been evicted by the regime. No one had previously gotten out of this place alive or without any torture marks or scars on their bodies, as we had learned from others.

On the very same day, Sofina's husband managed to contact some officials. They asked him to send his wife to one of his previous partner's home. My uncle had an influential partner in the past who was well respected by the government officials. His partner had opened a branch business office in Baghdad. This subsidiary business was in production for aluminum foil caps that were getting placed on the wine bottles, just like the foil caps on the champagne bottles. After the regime had taken over power, they had given my uncle's partner a certain position in the government. I don't know what his partner's position or business with the regime was because I never encountered him or seen him anywhere near our home or at my uncle's house. My uncle mentioned to my father a few years earlier that his partner was an important advisor for the regime in the commerce field while he was visiting us for tea and snacks one evening. This conversation took place a few years before all these events had unfolded. My uncle had also mentioned to his wife that he had nothing to do with his partner anymore. Since his partner's promotion with the regime, he said the regime didn't allow his partner to run any affairs with him jointly.

This was the plan. My aunt was to meet with her husband's previous partner's wife to take my aunt with her on the same day to a province outside the city of Baghdad to meet with another officer who was controlling the fate of all the captured prisoners in this particular prison. They arrived late that evening to this new officer's home in the city of Baagoba. This officer was waiting for them in his living room. Sofina was given a special pass and the address for this prison and both women were instructed to leave right away and return to Baghdad and to never mention to anyone the name of this officer or the place they had met. This pass was as good as gold, and, rarely, anyone could have such permission unless you knew some high government officials. Sofina was to follow a set of instructions exactly as was given by this officer. The paper pass which was handed to my aunt was a one-time pass to permit her to visit the prisoners, which included her brother Mike. Sofina's instructions also were to take the paper pass to the prison warden, or the general, who controls the prison. The paper pass didn't have any writing on it other than a set of numbers. She was told to go to this prison and upon arrival, she should show the guard this paper pass with the set of numbers without being subject to questioning and to tell the guard to give the pass to the officer in charge only, and then he will know why she is there. But earlier that night and before Sofina had received the pass, this high-ranking officer told my aunt that she cannot mention his name anywhere and told her if they ever asked her at the prison site who gave her these numbers, she shouldn't give them an answer and just wait. I knew all about this from Sofina in 2004 when I visited her outside the U.S. as she had just left Iraq herself to reside elsewhere in this world. I had a chance to interview her to get all the facts from her by asking her the right questions about my father's capture. I asked her if it was okay to publish these facts in my book, and she agreed. Then she continued telling me more facts and said she had no choice but to agree with the officer at that time so that she could see her only brother and the other captured Armenian community group members.

Sofina didn't waste any time. She was away from her own family and outside Baghdad's city limits for over ten hours that day. When she got into town, she told her husband about what had happen and she instructed him before visiting the prison that they should get a large basket full of food, fruits, and some warm clothing for all the prisoners because she wanted to go right away to the prison to see them and deliver the goods that very same night. Then she asked her husband to go and pick up her brother's wife (my mom Elisa) before going back to the prison for a surprise visit. Sofina's thoughts were mostly psychological in doing this because she knew her brother well, and by taking his wife to visit him in the prison on the second night, this would make her brother gain courage and energy to go on with the pain that he's in or possibly is going to endure. She was smart. She knew her brother's weaknesses and his strengths as well. They arrived at my house that afternoon and picked up my mom. I insisted on going with them, and because they didn't want to waste time, they let me get into the car as well. My intentions were to see my dad since I had not seen him in the past forty-eight hours, and this was going to be my only chance. Who knows if there will be a next time to see him? It may be never. I must live my life a day at a time.

After my mom and I got ready, Sofina's husband drove us to the middle of the city where this prison was located. Her husband helped her take the basket and the clothing to the door where the guards helped Sofina and my mom to enter through the gate. I was left behind in the car out of my mom's fear that I was too young (only fifteen years of age), and she didn't want to intensify the situation just in case I was subjected to questioning by the guards at the prison gate. But both my mom and Sofina knew that any prisoner within the first forty-eight hours in an Iraqi prison under this regime would have already gotten been tortured for sure. Another reason was that both Sofina and my mom didn't want me to see my dad in pain when they asked me to stay behind in the car with Sofina's husband. They were right about this one. Sofina was surprised when she entered this prison because it was nothing more than a single-family residence with a basement under the house at four feet in height that didn't have much ventilation, and most of the prisoners were kept there in the basement. Her husband had to stay out because the pass was for two people only, and it was for a short visiting period. My aunt was a very smart lady. She knew her brother's heart very well. When she went in, she told the guard who was just about to go and call my dad out to come and see them, "Please, do me a big favor. Don't tell my brother that someone is here and wants to see him upstairs right now. And, please don't go down to the basement and ask who Mike is either." She told the guard this because her brother was not a very brave person, and this was his first time that he had ever been in prison where, possibly, from his fears he could have a heart attack and die right then and there. She continued telling me that she handed the guard some amount of money for him to follow her wishes. The guard asked, "Sofina, what do you want me to do? How am I supposed to call him?" This guard was naive and shy per Sofina's feedback at a later date to her husband regarding how these events had unfolded that night behind the closed gates.

Sofina was smart and brave. She told the guard to do it in this fashion, "You should open the door and say, 'good evening, how is everybody'? Act very happy to see all of them, and clap or rub your hands together at the same time so the prisoners don't panic in thinking that you're taking them through hardship again. Then you can say, 'Hey, Mike, you have a visitor'." To her surprise, the guard had a heart to listen to her advice. She thought it might have been the numbers that were written on the paper pass, or maybe the bribe money. It was quite possibly the numbers on the pass, which could have been some kind of code telling them to take good care of her requests.

A short period of time later and according to Sofina's input, my dad was brought out from the basement to the main lobby of this converted residence into a prison. The color of his face was yellow, and he was shaking uncontrollably and could hardly walk. Sofina received him along with my mom and they both gave him their blessings and encouraged him to stay strong. Sofina quickly learned from her brother later that night that he was tortured the night before from taking a beating under his feet with electrical copper wires. He was asked right after the beating to walk on a large ice cube for a short period of time, and then repeating the beating and walking on the ice cube as a repetitive process. This was to make him feel the pain and to testify. Saddam's secret service unit had this theory and belief that my dad, presumably, had some hidden secrets to tell them where they thought my dad and the rest of the group were working against the regime and helping the western world from within Iraq.

Nowadays, unfortunately, some of us Americans are still in doubt as to why our troops had gone to Iraq and what was the purpose of the war to liberate Iraq. Some believe that we had no just cause to throw Saddam's regime out of power, and we shouldn't have done that. In my opinion, we had a very good and just cause, and it was enough for me to see history being made doing that. Although there were a lot of arguments in terms of how the war was planned and so on, that is something for the experts to solve and analyze. This is not the reason why I'm writing my story, nor is it my intention to discuss the Iraqi war and throwing Saddam out of power. I personally don't think that, in most cases, war is the answer, but the Iraqi war was enough of a just cause for me to accept its outcomes. We had to put an end to unnecessary evil against humanity, which had haunted innocent Iraqi people throughout the years of this regime which had governed Iraq. The war had put an end to foresee that all others who suffered for no apparent reasons under this regime are now liberated from those animal acts from the injustices caused by evil men and had helped other lives regardless if they were Christian or Muslims to be better and more secure. I say more power to all the men and women in uniform who had sacrificed their lives for this kind of just cause and to save others from an ill-fated regime. Their parents should be proud of them as I am proud of them. And may God bless them all.

In the next few pages I would like to share with you a bit of history about Sofina, her family, and her life after marriage. Sofina married Steve. Steve was a very kind and giving individual, and I grew up noticing this in him. I spent a lot of time with his family and with both of my step cousins (a girl and a boy) by staying at my aunt Sofina's home a week per month at times. My uncle's marriage with aunt Sofina was his second time around. He was unhappily married once before, and after his nasty divorce, he managed to get the children to live with him per the court's orders. This took place in a different time and under a different Iraqi government in power. Sofina was a blessing for him to meet. She took good care of her husband's two step children, a girl and a boy, and she had also given birth throughout the years to five more children of her own. The family had grown from two to seven children in all. As the years passed by, I got along with everyone living in that household; they were all cousins to me. They didn't mind me at all. I respected them, and they always wanted me to be around their children as well; especially the step children. I admired and still admire both until this day. The girl's fate was to meet someone through a blind date, and she ended up getting married to him. She resides today with her husband and two daughters somewhere in the world. And the boy's fate, his name was Jack, was not so fortunate. My step cousin had visited the United States and was educated in the field of art. He was a very good artist with good free hand drawing. He graduated from college in the early eighties. But due to the foreign Arab and Muslim student population influence that backed the Iraqi regime in that college at the time, they brainwashed my cousin through student meetings to go back to Iraq and join the armed forces to serve the country. I tried to talk to him out of it, but he didn't listen. He returned to Iraq back in the 80's, and sometime later after enlisting he ran away from the army and was captured, and due to Saddam's bullies, he was tortured for running away from the armed forces after he found out that there was no just cause to serve in the armed forces of Iraq. Years later I found out from others that he was captured and tortured with electrical equipment. Presently, he resides in a psychiatric hospital in Baghdad as a permanent patient. What a waste of human life and God- given talent!

My uncle, Sofina's husband, was so generous that he made a promise to me years ago while I was attending junior high school. He was telling me if I could score at least three A's as a final grade in any school year in my subjects, excluding sports and art, he would take me out of the country along with his family for a three-month summer vacation, and every summer on one condition, which is that I pass my grade to the next level. I kept my side of the bargain year-after-year, and I scored A's not only in three subjects, but in six to seven subjects as my uncle had suggested. He was an educated man himself from a wealthy family. He was not going to give something for nothing. This motivational method had worked for my own good in the years that followed. The motivation of being successful was always on my mind, and it was driving me to do my very best every time I put a goal in mind to achieve. I have been using this same tactic with my own children. Taking a vacation with my uncle's family lasted for three years, and every summer I went with them out of the country to visit whatever place they went that year. I learned that taking me with them had another purpose and meaning. He wanted his son from his previous marriage to be influenced by my attitude and lifestyle and to be like me. But that was not for my uncle to decide because God never made two of the very same people, but maybe similar. There's always a bit of difference among all of us. I also remember every spring break he used to purchase a round trip train ticket for me as well as for my other cousins in order to go and stay with them in the northern part of the country in the city of Mosul where his wine factory was located. All of us used to go out and have fun as well as work and help during the day in the wine factory to bottle the wine. I was very anxious to know how they made the wine. Actually, they were getting the dry raisins and washing it thoroughly. The raisins were then placed in a large compressor where a big mechanical platform tray looking like a big circular plate was slowly pressing down on the wet raisins. Gradually, the raisins released all its extract and juices in the form of heavy syrup down into a large bowl. Then it got mixed with other liquids and chemicals after being placed in a copper barrel. They had to monitor it day and night for a good fifteen days in order to make the wine before it went to other processes and before it got bottled. During the day we used to work and label the bottles by hand the old-fashioned way. I used to time myself with my step cousin Jack by competing against him on how many bottles we could label in a day and without any mistakes. My step cousin, Jack, was spoiled. He didn't like to work very much. He wanted to manage and order people around only. He had no understanding and had poor judgment for people. I didn't mind this as long as I could do the work and help them achieve the objectives by volunteering my time daily and in small portions. My goal was to observe how everything was getting done, and to have fun with the rest of the gang. My approach to the work had captured the attention of some employees in the factory, and they told my uncle about it. One night he was going to the wine processing room, which was located at one of the corners of the factory. He asked me to go with him in order to monitor the making of wine at some stage. He showed me how and why things were done a certain way. At some point, I felt he was trying to teach me the wine making trade, but I was not ready to observe all these technical issues, so I just listened to what he had to say. Soon enough, he noticed that it wasn't time for me to comprehend yet. He said, "One day, when you are ready, I will explain this again." Unfortunately, that one day never came. He passed away in 1986 due to a tumor in his brain caused by lots of stress on him after the regime took power in Iraq. Some thirty plus years later, Sofina explained to me her husband's fate after the regime had taken power in Iraq. She told me they, meaning the authorities, had come to her husband and told him he can't operate a full day and in full capacity. He had to cut the wine making operation to a half a day of production at first. Then after a year's time they told him he can't make wine anymore, and they forcefully closed his operation completely. The closing decision was not caused by the regime alone. It was also intended by his greedy mother and some of his own greedy sisters who had taken some legal actions one after another against Sofina's husband to hand over the entire operation to them, despite the fact that throughout the years my uncle was the only businessman in his family to run the wine making production and split the profits according to certain agreement among his immediate family based on percentages. But greed had gotten into his family's hearts, and their belief that when he dies, they didn't want Sofina to inherent any of his fortune because Sofina was originally from the poor class of society, unlike them. They succeeded to inflame Sofina's stepson Jack his own father, driving him insane. The family used the new laws of the regime against their businessman and son who was the Chief Operating Officer of the factory. After the factory had been closed by the regime, Sofina's family went from rich wine makers to poor ordinary citizens overnight. She said this had not given her a second chance to help build her husband's dream from the ground up because her side of the family, who she trusted very much, had departed Iraq already. I remember one day I spoke with my uncle Steve over the phone from abroad. I had to choose my words carefully, of course, for what I had to say to him because every word was probably getting recorded by the telephone operators; especially, if the conversation was about business or in regard to an American subject. My uncle was sick at the time, and I didn't know it. He asked me to send him some catalogs on small kitchen appliances and other goods, so he could start ordering them from me, and I was supposed to find the manufactures that make them. He was trying to give me a message, I guess, about starting something or doing something with my life. At first, he wanted me to send the information to him. He said he would send the money to me along with his clients' orders. I was going to be his purchasing agent abroad. I took his offer seriously. I gathered everything he wanted from me together and mailed all the catalogs to him. Again, I didn't know that he was dying in bed at home as I heard about this later, and it was too late. I was told that he had seen the catalogs and that he told my aunt he still trusts her nephew, meaning me, because I was a man of my word. Months later he passed away. As I am remembering and writing all of this, tears started rushing back to my eyes.

It is Halloween 2006 as I continue to write this book. As I am writing these lines, my youngest son, who is nineteen years of age, walks into my office and starts telling me what a hard day he had at work today. He goes to college and works part time. The interruption of giving out candy at my front door every time the doorbell rings is inspiring me more to write this book. I look into the eyes of these young kids with faces full of life, holding their parent's hand on one side and with a bag or bucket in their other hand, waiting for me to give them their sweets. You could see what God had done. He had given them a normal, happy life. I just couldn't resist making them happier by saying, "Trick or treat," even though I'm not a fan of celebrating Halloween. But that's the way it is here. People like it, and everyone is free to choose what they want. It's a great feeling (the freedom of choosing).

My son asked me what I was doing. I said I was writing my memoirs but, I couldn't help not to tear up.

He said, "Why don't you sell it and get rich?"

I laughed and said, "I'm not doing this for the money. It's a personal matter for me. I just want to tell the world about it, and I'm not sure if anyone will be interested to read it."

He said, "Dad, you're always positive. Let me tell you now that everyone will read it." "Thank you, kiddo. I'm so happy you're starting your life here and not have to carry these kinds of memories with you." I told him be positive every day and to thank God that you can move your arms and feet, and you can move around and aim towards the future. I mentioned to him that he can plan for himself for the future focusing on whatever he wants to be. I hugged him as I do that daily to both of my sons, including the oldest who is twenty-six years old so they won't be short of love and courage. I believe, hugging will energize your children more if you make a habit of it every single day. Let's go back to the story about my father being in prison.

It had been eight long days since my dad was imprisoned. I was in my eleventh grade when this happened, and none of my friends knew all this time that my father was in prison. I was counting the days when I could see my father again. I believe it was March 1972 when I came home one day from school and saw my mom very happy, so I ran all over the house looking for my dad, naturally. She called out to me and told me he wasn't there. Fear struck me, and in my heart, I thought my mom had gone crazy or something bad had happened, and she was reacting with strange yet happy moods. I yelled holding her in my arms, "What the hell is going on; what happened." She said, "Your father is free."

I said, "Mom. Don't joke with me." She said, "Sit down, son."

I sat down on the sofa in the den. She told me that she got a phone call from Sofina saying her husband was informed through his city government connections that the government will be freeing all the imprisoned Armenian community group members, and they will be sending them home free because they were all innocent. They couldn't find them at fault for any crimes against the regime or the country's interest. My mom added, "Right now, Sofina's husband is at the gate of the prison waiting to pick up your father. Then, your aunt Sofina is going to send a taxicab to pick us up so we can all go to their house and receive him." I didn't know what to think. I knew all along in my heart that my father and the group were not guilty. But there were also a lot of others who were not guilty in the Iraqi prisons as well, but they were not so lucky to be freed and to go home. They all ended up missing and being killed and their bodies were disposed of either somewhere in the western Iraqi desert, into the river, sewer lines, or basements, who knows. This must be a miracle. I went and knelt in the front of the picture of Jesus Christ, which was hanging on the wall in our den for decades. It was a very old picture of Christ in an old redwood frame, and it was transferred to us from generation-to-generation from my great grandfathers where some of them were priests in various churches in the historic Armenian lands before the 1915 genocide of Armenians had occurred many decades ago. The picture of Christ was hanging on the wall in our den, and as I was praying, I thanked him for saving my father and the others from this evil regime. I got up and ran outside. I couldn't wait for the taxicab to arrive. Finally, after a half hour, the cab pulled up at our door steps. We all got into the cab, and we were on our way to Sofina's house. We arrived at our destination with my mom and my grandmother along with my two siblings. I let everyone go in first. I kept myself back to be the last one to see him at the very end. I don't know why I did this, but it was more comfortable for me at the time as I remember. Everyone was crying from their happiness, but tears were not part of what I had in mind that day. Then when I saw my dad, he had lost a lot of weight in the eight days of imprisonment. I notice he had grown a thick mustache on his face. He looked at me, and I ran and hugged him.

Then with a loud voice I said, "How are you doing, our hero? I knew I would see you again."

This captured my uncle's attention, Sofina's husband, and he said, "Bravo, you received your father like a man. I am very proud of you."

I thanked him for his efforts and for everything he had done for us. We stayed a while longer at my aunt's house that evening; then we went home. My dad couldn't wait any longer. He wanted to be in his own home very much. Who could blame him? He had faced death during the past eight days being in Iraqi's harsh prison. I couldn't believe we were going home with my dad! My mother's sister, my aunt Veronica, and her husband, George, were also waiting at home for my dad's arrival. They all sat down in the living room and chatted for hours. Then, everyone went to bed that evening.

The next morning, which was Friday, everyone was home because in Iraq Fridays were the weekend, just like our Sundays are here in the States. My mom and my grandmother were up early fixing breakfast. We all sat to eat, and a prayer was said. Then, my dad thanked everyone for being strong and waiting for him. He said we could ask him questions, but nothing of what happened behind the prison walls. I understood what he meant, so I didn't ask him any questions that morning and continued eating my breakfast. We were happy that he was alive amongst us and having breakfast together again. It was obvious that my father didn't seem like he was the same man any more, and his appetite for food was not so great. I noticed that he was in some type of pain. You see, unlike in Baghdad or the Middle East, in most of the other countries a prisoner is supposed to go and visit a psychologist or a doctor. It was not a customary thing in Baghdad, but it would have helped to talk to a professional after he or she had been in a prison cell in order to overcome the bad experience of torture. But nothing in this nature was available in Baghdad in those days. It was said that a man should take care of himself and all challenges like a man. But a human being is not made of stone. One would try to handle matters themselves, especially torture in prison, and not know how one should conceal their anger and pain within themselves afterwards. This could transform to worse in some ways and then that person could try to hurt others by exploding their anger on individuals and not know why. Some may even try to commit suicide to cover the shame which they felt. Thank God none of these events had happened with my father, except one thing we noticed was there for sure which were his hidden anger, paranoia and anxiety. The anger was always directed at his immediate family. Then the paranoia symptoms were at the surface of it all. Whenever we were trying to go somewhere at night, for example, to visit relatives who lived close by, my father would call the taxicab, and made us get in the cab, but he ended up walking to our nearby relative's home on foot. Luckily, they were living a short distance from our home; only a few kilometers away. I always walked with him, so we could get there without him getting lost due to his mind being so occupied with his thoughts. Also, the anxiety level with my dad was so much that when we socialized with friends or with relatives, my dad was always getting impatient and restless. These were the things we noticed, or mostly I noticed from the outside. God bless my mom who knew how to take care of her husband and much more. She had to put up with the entire ordeal from inside their bedroom walls, arguing and verbally fighting for long years.

Both of my parents were good in hiding things or trouble from us kids. They always wanted us to be happy and not to worry much. They both were quality parents. My observation of my dad as my role model in life had changed. But my grandmother was always trying to tell me, "He is just fine. Don't change your heart about your father. He will regain himself again as he is disturbed now." She added by saying, "Who knows, son, what went on behind those prison walls. I'm sure he will tell us when the time comes. All these feelings will go away soon. Don't worry, kid, really." Thanks to her, she was a great healer and guidance for me.

One day after a few weeks, we were sitting and eating at the dinner table when one of us asked my dad about his arrest and how he spent his time in the prison. At first, he teared up, but he answered the question by saying that he spent most of the time thinking about us, his three sons, and what we were doing every moment. Did we do our homework? How we were managing going back and forth to school. That's what kept him alive along with the thought of how his wife and his mom were handling the daily life expenses without any money and so on. After breakfast, my father went to his bedroom and came out with a 16 × 20 inch black and white picture which was in his hand. At first, I didn't know who or what was in the picture. He told us that after handing all the prisoners this same picture that it should be hung in everyone's living room. At the time our living room wall had a picture of a nice Armenian symbolic artwork inside a 16 × 20-inch frame for decades. My dad had to use the same picture frame by removing the original artwork from the frame to replace it with this new picture, which they had given him in prison. I still wanted to find out what this new picture was that we were going to look at on a daily basis, which was going to replace the nice artwork that we had. Then, with a big surprise, he unveiled Saddam Hussein's black and white picture with the exact size of the old picture frame. He placed it into the frame and hung it up on the wall of our living room and facing all of us daily. I was the first to get angry.

I asked him, "Why do we have to do this. I hate this man. I'm sick of looking at him every day, everywhere I go and on TV at my school and all over town. Who the hell does he think he is? He's nothing but a president, and not God."

My dad told me to calm down, and from his fears he suddenly covered my mouth with his hand and said, "You know the walls could have ears, son. Don't act like this outside this house. Otherwise, if I get imprisoned next time, you wouldn't be able to see me again; and this time forever. We have no choice because in a week they will come from the prison to visit us individually in our homes and to see if we are following their orders."

I asked, "What orders"?

He said, "The regime's orders."

I went out to the front yard, and I was very upset. Then my father came out and said, "Calm down, son. This is just temporary, and it'll go away. You don't want me to go back to prison again, do you?"

I hugged him and said, "No, of course not."

That afternoon as my dad started to work around the yard, he got tired and he was short of breath. He sat down and started to wash his feet with the water hose at the front yard. Suddenly, I came near him to ask him a question, but he was embarrassed about his feet. I couldn't believe what I saw.

I said, "What have they done to you, dad?"

He said, "What do you think? Please don't shout. We were not in prison for a picnic, son."

I saw his feet were full of scars. The bottom was heavily injured by the copper wires used to beat and torture him, and his feet were swollen about two shoe sizes bigger. He said not to mention it to my younger brothers as he didn't want them to know until his feet get healed. I promised to keep his secret, but every day, as I walked by the living room, I wanted to burn the president's black and white picture which was hanging on our living room wall or tear it up in pieces. But I kept my cool so no one from my family could get hurt for any reason. In an effort to reduce my anger, I managed to chew gum and try to spit it through my mouth on the president's glass-covered picture to see how good my aim was to hit his face. Then I had to stand on the table top to remove my gum from the glass before my mom saw it. This was in a way comforting me somehow. My father was assuring me every day not to worry much about him, not do anything foolish toward the regime, or join any resistance groups, which may cause me harm and disturb my future goals or plans in life. He said he was willing to send me out of the country, maybe to the US, if he had a choice, or if there was a way to do it so I could live a free life with a promising future. My answer was, "If none of you are going with me, I'm not going anywhere. Either we all go together, or we don't go at all."

Well, this was a tough choice my dad had to think about; especially since he started to remember his childhood dreams and wants. He always wanted to come to America because he loved to act and to be an actor. These were his dreams at the age of seventeen back in the year 1946. But my grandmother, his mother, was so protective of her only son that she wouldn't let him accomplish his dreams. She didn't want her only son Mike to go away. It took a big shakeup in my father's life, so he could personally decide to move on toward his dreams. The prison was that big shakeup for him to think about his childhood dreams once more. A year later, my father got encouraged to move on and make a big change in his life in order to reach his goals and possibly make them happen and not wait for tomorrow. I'm glad he started to take matters into his own hands once more. He was also thinking to save his children from serving in the Iraqi armed forces because the armed forces in Iraq at the time were not by choice; it was by draft or force.

A year had gone by, and this new idea of fleeing the country and immigrating to the USA in order to start a new life came to light. A realization of it alone would take lots of money and connections to accomplish it. We were all going to need passports. It had been about one year since my father was released from prison. I saw him daily getting more and more anxious to sell his dream home that he had built and risk everything in order to raise money to save the lives of his three boys. He told us that if he does not do this move toward freedom, then, soon enough, we will be grown, and the armed forces will gladly draft us to fight Saddam's chosen wars. There would be no guarantees that we would survive these wars without being killed. My dad was thinking it right and was doing the right thing.

The decision was made by my parents to immigrate to the US, especially since the word had gotten out in secret among all the Christian minorities including Armenians and Assyrians. The word was if you were Christian and had faced prosecution in your country, and if you could manage to get a passport to go to Beirut, Lebanon, you would be able to sign up as a refugee with a United Nations and the World Council of Churches' (WCC) offices. This organization was registering or signing up only minority Christian groups from Iraq as refugees in the mid-seventies who faced horrible abuse or treatment by the regime which was ruling Iraq. So there was great hope for all of us. The name of the game was how to leave and get away from Iraq. We all started to explore the possibilities with total secretive-ness. We didn't want to discuss this matter among us or with our relatives at any time. This was not because we didn't trust them, but if they got caught with this information about us, they could be facing harm too, for sure. People didn't want the authorities to know because the chances were that once the secret was revealed, the authorities would work to block the path for everyone to travel, and in order to protect themselves as a government from facing an international human rights crisis.

It was January 1973 and right after the holidays. My family sat down together at the dinner table, and we decided to take this step at any cost because life was getting to be unbearable anymore. For example, the average Iraqi citizen had to stand in long lines in order to purchase fifteen eggs once a month for the whole family to eat or to stand in line for one or two chickens for the entire family to consume for one month, where before this regime everything like basic necessities were available for all Iraqis to purchase and use. But the regime was sending everything from basic needs to major needs away from the average Iraqi citizen to the Soviet government in exchange for arms and weapons. Those who were part of the regime and had enjoyed living above the scale of necessities were never short of money and goods, and yet nothing had affected their living status. They were serving the regime on the wrong side of history at any cost, as long as their own families were kept unharmed and they were not short of any daily life needs by selling their brother's and sister's blood to achieve all these privileges, which they had enjoyed for some time.

This regime had converted the country's economy day-by-day for the average Iraqi citizen into a third-world country and reached poverty level conditions. Some Iraqi's who would read my life story here wouldn't want to explore these facts about the regime due to their national or self-pride. But one shouldn't hide the truth and lie to themselves for the sake of loving their country. Living abroad in a different country does not diffuse the fact that you wouldn't miss your homeland. The land which we were born in and childhood pleasant memories are always there to remember. But, nevertheless, the story must be told so humanity can learn from it and not to repeat past mistakes damaging future generations to come in Iraq.

Now, the decision had been made by my family and we were going to leave Iraq soon. The next step was to get passports. There were several questions in mind which needed some answers. One of the most important questions on everyone's mind was can my father travel out of the country? It has been only one year since he had been released from prison. Well, he must go and ask the Iraqi Security Service Unit (ISS Unit), the same unit who was in charge of his arrest, if this obstacle was going to be overcome and then the rest of us would be at ease to move on and get our passport process started.

In a year's time, my father had more courage since he left the prison. He took the initiative to go and inquire from the appropriate department and not expose the entire truth about his plans but tell them only about going outside of the country for vacation purposes. The answer from the ISS Unit was a positive one, and they issued a document saying they would allow him to travel outside Iraq for a short time only with a guarantee from him that he would return on a certain date in order to report back to the ISS Unit regularly, which they made him sign a document to that effect. In order for my father to get a passport issued in his name with the return date printed in it, he must present a co-signer and must notarize his return on the designated date; otherwise, the co-signer must pay fines, which was equal to 1,500 Iraqi dinars currency, and, in addition, the co-signer will face interrogation and hardship.

The name of the game, folks, was to leave first at any cost, and the rest should be easy. We could ask other Iraqi's once we were out of the country as to how they had done it staying abroad and not having to go back. The first step was to get out of the country. Then, once at the Iraqi-Syrian border and crossing it, we didn't have to look back anymore. Okay, this was a big obstacle, but we knew how to overcome it.

My mom's passport issue was another obstacle. She was born in Iraq. Her mother (my grandmother) was born in a city in the neighboring country of Iran. This had created a big problem for my mom because her birth certificate stated that her mother was born in Iran, and, as a matter of fact, the Iraqi-Iran foreign relationship had been declining for some time and a general opposition toward Iranians was escalating towards getting worse. The passport agency didn't want to issue my mother an Iraqi passport even though she was an Iraqi-born citizen, and that was her entitlement. The Iraqi passport agency told her she should get her passport from Iran, which was unheard of, but, again, with God's help, we managed to find a big connection inside the passport agency who was accepting favors and money as a bribe in return for getting my mom's application approved. Then, in the end and after several months of going back and forth to the passport agency office, we did get her a passport. Now another mission was accomplished, but it had delayed the process of us traveling and fleeing Iraq with a big anxiety.

The other members of my family were my two younger siblings and my Grandmother Knar (Mike's mom). They didn't have any problems getting their passports. But the biggest problem of all was my passport I was almost eighteen years of age, seventeen and a half to be exact, and I was due to report and register with the Iraqi armed forces as all young male citizens must do, which I had not done yet. I spoke to my dad to remind him about this issue. He refused to go with me to any passport office at first. He told me that I should try to get the passport myself by filing the application first and paying the fees, which he was going to provide me with the funds. He told me if they asked me about my military registration book or ID status, I should act dumb and act like I don't know what it's for and see if that will work. I would like to state that before and after this regime had taken over, the organizational aspect of the government agency offices had not been at its best including locating, filing and searching for any informational files for the average Iraqi citizen, which was advantageous, at times, for some of the people. My father's idea was not so great, but I had to listen and follow my old man's request. I believe I had mentioned before that in Iraq, as I was growing up, a male individual at the age of seventeen must register with the Ministry of Defense, and then the ministry will issue a type of military ID book in order for all males at that age to report back to them every year and get the ID book stamped and marked as current. The bearer of this ID book must be a student in any educational institution to avoid instant draft unless the student graduates and decides not to continue their education. In that case, they will be eligible to get drafted. A violation of not registering with the Ministry of Defense was punishable. Serving in the Iraqi armed forces was not by choice or through volunteering, but it was by force and the draft system. There was no escape from the military service, and the duration of time for an individual to serve was based on their educational level. If, for example, an individual had a college degree, they would serve a shorter duration of time, and they would be allowed to have better living conditions and daily duties inside the army camps. This was a system set in place before this regime had taken over.

My father knew all these rules, and since he was just released a year ago from prison, he didn't want to accompany me to the passport agency office yet as he had a different plan. Well, I didn't know any better. I had to trust my dad with what he knew about these matters. My instincts were telling me that my father could be wrong, but I took my chances as he advised me to do so, so I went to the passport agency office and started my passport application.

I paid the fees. I encountered difficulties around some of the Iraqi passport agency office departments. What I mean by this is that in 1972 the passport agency of Iraq was a building with many offices. Each office had a window overlooking the outside yard and the officers were dealing with the public through these open windows, preventing anyone from going inside the office buildings. We were standing in a big crowded line to deal with the agency's employees through iron bar framed windows isolating the public from the employ-ees. Again, we were not allowed to go inside any office unless we were asked to do so by the officers. That's only if they wanted to see you or talk to you in private for any reason, or if you were already informed by others ahead of time about which officer would take a bribe and how to participate in the act. But, at times you would have to be very careful because there were some individuals who were designated by the authorities to find out about these kinds of unlawful acts in order to capture and punish these criminals who were encouraging bribes which could infect their system. I knew about these types of arrangements from my friends at school who had gotten their passports before me, and they had warned me about it. I never told my dad about this. I wanted to experience it myself first as an ambitious youngster and a young teenage fool at times. As you can see, no just and fair system was in place to conduct any business as usual for the ordinary citizen, and we wonder why, in some of the Middle Eastern countries, some people are not fully reliable. Some of the Middle Eastern governments were supposed to practice what they preached, and when a government does put a rule in place, it must be respected and honored, but most of the time these rules were bent by the same people who wrote them due to empowerment, and those people were the authorities themselves. People never trusted their own government because government had never been bound by these rules for themselves or for their families. Most authorized personnel in these offices could hear but wouldn't want to listen very well because they were trying to catch a hidden meaning in your words. They listen to the individual with mistrust, and this was the case with my passport application.

The Iraqi passport books need several signatures before it gets issued. Each office window was placed for a different and a special signature needed. In my case, one of the tasks to be performed through an office window was to check first to see if my parents were Iraqi-born citizens or not. My life was never short of obstacles. My mom's parent's birthplace issue had surfaced again regarding my grandmother's (her mother) birth place which was Iran. After submitting my application, I was standing and waiting outside these windows for answers and results to check and see if the information in their files were right, and if a pass-port was issued to my mom at its full validity. It took them two and a half hours while I was waiting under direct sunlight in the Iraqi hot summer days. All this was done manually in those days and no computers were involved at that time. Finally, they found my mom's pass-port number and her record in their books, and it did match with the needed information, which was required. I got the signature from this life-shortening passport agency's window. Now, off I went to the next window, but my heart was full of fears knowing that my mom did pay a big bribe in order to get her passport going; otherwise, it was impossible to obtain one for her. My mind was busy with the fear of "what if they find out about the bribe?" My family could go to prison and get tortured, and my passport chances would be revoked. Well, all these thoughts were passing through my mind as I waited with a big anxiety for another hour and half in another line under the sun for one other signature.

I was really scared and tired. I calmed myself down by accepting the fact that finally I'm going to the next step of the process. It was one step before the very final signature in order to get the final passport completed for myself, which was going to entitle me with a passport without any help from my dad. But, as usual, nothing was going to be easy for me to accomplish without any new challenges. Nevertheless, I went to the next window. They looked at my papers, and they asked me to give them my military registration ID book. My heart started to beat very fast, my face turned red and I was speechless. I asked the officer what he meant by a military registration ID book. He grabbed all my papers from his desk and with as much throwing power as he had, he threw all my papers back into my face. All the papers had hit my face and fell to the ground at my feet. I bent down and started to collect them, so the wind doesn't blow them directly into the street. Then the same officer approached the window from behind his desk and started to yell in my face, asking me how the hell I got this far with signatures and no one had asked me for my military ID book yet.

I said, "Sir, I apologize for this. I'm new in these matters, and I just don't know what I'm doing." I told him that I would go and register, and I would get him the book later, if he would let me go today. I was almost at the stage of crying from panic and fear. He asked me to wait for him. He was going to be back in fifteen minutes.

I listened, but one of the clients in the line behind me felt sorry for me and said, "It looks like you're new in this business." Then he advised me by suggesting I leave and run because this very same thing had happened last week to others where the same officer asked another young man to wait for him for fifteen minutes the same way he had just told me. But after fifteen minutes the officer came back with two soldiers and arrested that young man, and they kicked his butt all the way to their army truck and arrested him for questioning. He said they loaded this young man on the army truck and took him to where, he didn't know. After what I had just heard from this man I didn't know if he was joking or not. Right away, and in a hurry, I started to walk fast towards the entrance of the building trying to avoid confrontation. But before I left, I looked back at the officer's desk to see if any of my paperwork was still on his desk. Fortunately, I noticed that all my papers were with me and nothing was missing or was left on his desk. After I got out to the front yard of building, I ran and ran fast. I took the very first bus at the bus station ahead of me. Even though it was not the right bus, I just wanted to get on it and get away, if you can imagine the fear that took over me at that moment. But I wanted to vanish quickly, so I couldn't be captured. I don't know! God must really love me because the nice man who warned me and advised me with all of these happenings just happened to be in the same waiting line that day. After I got off the bus in an unfamiliar neighborhood, I then got into a taxicab to take me home right away. When I got home, I told my dad that I had to get my military registration ID book before I could go back and get my passport. I had to explain about all the events that took place that day at the Iraqi Passport Agency. He said not to go again near any defense or military government office. He will ask his friends if they ever knew of anyone inside the Ministry of Defense who was involved with issuing a military registration ID book for young men my age. Wow! Thanks for the warning, Dad.

In 1972, the country's military system dictated that if you were seventeen and a half years of age and a male, you had to register in the armed forces. As I have mentioned before, the Iraqi military system was by draft and force and not by choice of volunteering, and regardless of your educational level, you had to serve the armed forces for some time. There was always an exception to this rule. As I had mentioned a few pages back, this same government who put the rules for the ordinary Iraqi citizens was just about to break them to benefit the males in their families by excluding them from enlisting. Who knows who was very much in effect, and those who were sons of big ranking military officers got their way out of serving in the armed forces by only having their names written in the books, but without physically attending; meaning there were double standards. Normally, for a male citizen to be exempt from serving the armed forces, the rule was if he was the only born son of his family, then he was exempt from serving, and that was a rule which carried lots of weight and no one could alter it for ages. You see, you go through life and there is no honest system to follow, and you always feel betrayed and cheated. Therefore, the majority of people didn't have faith in the Iraqi government and in the system, which was put in place by the regime. Furthermore, the Baath regime didn't help to make things better, but drove everyone crazy and raised a lot of hate and anger among the innocent Iraqi population by creating a division among their own people for the sake of controlling and power gain over minorities and tribes.

It was a weekday on July 2, 1972 and my father told me that I had to go that morning to the Ministry of Defense building, which was a half an hour bus ride from our residence. He said to go ahead and start my application for the military ID book and go around the offices to get the book initialed by the designated military officers. He added by saying to me, "They will tell you to have your picture taken, and please don't hesitate to comply." It was puzzling me at first, but I followed his instructions once more. He handed me a half a dinar (in Iraqi currency) to pay for the transactions. He said, "Upon obtaining the initials in the book, excluding the finalized signatures, bring it home with you." He was planning to go with me to the Ministry of Defense and to the military officer's building, and then he would help me get the final signatures, so my military ID book can be finalized in order to accomplish my passport transaction. You see, so far, my father had been advising me to do everything myself. His fear after he had left the prison had not settled within him yet. Anyway, he would try to avoid any visits or going to any government agency offices if he could help it, but he promised me that he will go with me for the final process of my military ID book. He must know something that I don't. I will find out when the time comes. I decided on that day to go after school hours to the Ministry of Defense military registration office building, as my dad had told me to do. It was not too far from my high school, so I went to said building alone. This was enough to give me chills in my bones and plant a big fear in my heart. There were so many soldiers with machine guns and a few tanks on the front yard of this place. The look on every soldier's face was very sad and sour. It felt as if you killed someone and you're going there to turn yourself in. For me this was image demoting rather than promoting to join the armed forces. I entered the building from the front gate, passing by the unwelcoming soldiers with machine guns on their shoulders. At first, they stopped me by asking what my name was and where I was headed and why. I replied that I needed to register, and then I asked them, "Can you tell me where the registration office is?"

They didn't show any sign of helping because when he learned my name, he knew I was a non-Muslim and he cared less to show me the way. It was not an unusual discriminatory response for me to comprehend, and I had to accept it. I walked into the front yard. As I mentioned, I noticed a long line of young men like myself, and I also noticed some of them were non-Muslim in appearance. I approached one of the young men standing in the back of the line on that hot summer day with 103F degrees temperature and asked him if this was the line for the registration. He replied with a firm "yes" answer, which helped me a bit to be at ease. Then, while I was standing in the line and, to my surprise, he spoke to me with my own language in Armenian. Wow! This made me more relaxed and confident. I found a friend from my own people. What a coincidence. We talked to each other in Armenian. I asked him why he wants to get the military ID book. He said he was going to travel out of the country with his family on a summer vacation and needs to obtain a passport; that's why. Since, as a society, we were broken due to implanted fears and couldn't trust each other's words, I tried not to say too much about my plans to him. At first, I didn't trust what I had just heard because no one would dare to say the truth about anything anymore, especially if you are going out of the country. I didn't know if he was testing me or not, so I kept my answers short when it was my turn to answer him as to why I'm getting the military book for myself. I just told him that I had to register myself because it was the law to avoid giving him any hints about my situation. After spending more than an hour standing in line under that hot sun, we found out that we were not only going to be registered, but we must have TB shots in our arms that day as well. More anxiety was created within me because it was unexpected. I was just registering that day and not joining yet. Why would they do that to us? Some of the men were not ready to take the shots, so they fainted and dropped down on the grass and were left there until they woke up without any help. I had no choice after seeing all this. I asked myself what other challenges were there that I may encounter that day. I was fearful myself when I noticed they were using long needles to inject everyone.

I got over this unexpected challenge as well. We were directed to take ID pictures and, again, there was a long line. Every now and then, we were all getting pushed from one side to the other due to a big crowd and an uncivilized one. After paying the fee, I got to the chair where I had to sit down so that my picture could be taken. We all had to wait for a half an hour for our pictures to be ready for pick up. Everyone sat down in small groups on the lawn in the front yard of the building to wait. The Armenian fellow who I encountered in the long line earlier that day had found me and came to join me. We both sat down and talked the whole time about the outside world and not about our country, which we were born in. Both of us, as Christians, didn't feel this was our own country anymore. We always felt we were strangers by the way we were being treated by others. This young man asked me again, "Are you going to travel or are you going to get your passport only." Again, I didn't trust him, and I asked him, "Why do you want to know what am I going to do? What is it to you? And who sent you to ask me these questions?" The fellow got uncomfortable with my questions and with my mistrustful manners towards him. Then he said, "Look, no one has sent me to question you. You can trust me. I'm on your side, but I want you to know if you are traveling out of the country for the summer, try not to come back." Then he added by saying that he and his family were planning to travel to Beirut, but they had been telling everyone a different story, so they wouldn't get exposed with their intended plans to not return. He told me his family had been telling our relatives and friends about their travel plans differently. Rather than telling the passport agency that they were going to travel to Beirut Lebanon, they told them they were going to visit

Turkey. I asked him why. He replied that Beirut Lebanon is a semi-Christian country and there was a way to reach their final destination like…! Suddenly, I felt the word that was to come out of his mouth was "America." Because his back was turned and couldn't see the soldier approaching us while he was talking to me, I stopped him by asking, "What is your name"? After the soldier had passed us, I said to him, "Let's finish the process of getting a military ID book here, then on our way to the bus station, if we're not followed, we can continue our conversation. I told him, "Take this phone number that I wrote on a piece of paper with you, but don't call me and talk to me about the outside world over the phone because who knows who's listening on the lines these days." I was trying to alert him.

We both agreed on this plan since there was great danger talking on the land lines, especially since my father had left prison. We exchanged our home phone numbers, and as we were waiting inside the Ministry of Defense complex walls. Our head shot pictures were finally ready for pick up. Everyone's name was a native Arabic name, and when it came to mine and my friend's name, some of the people in the crowd made fun of our names because the army photographer didn't know how to pronounce them, and he laughed and so did the people in the crowd. We couldn't do anything about those idiots but listen to their insults and move on. It was strange to live in a country which you were born and lived in, yet you were discriminated against because you were a Christian minority. This was not motivational for young men like us to join the armed forces and defend the country. I cared less and less every day to take a task like joining the armed forces. I took my black and white ugly looking picture to the next room where the books were issued, and there was another name calling drama that happened without any dispute from us. My intentions were to get it done and get the hell out of there. Finally, after several hours of this kind of ordeal, I managed to get the first part of the military ID book signed, and it was ready to go to the next stage on that same day. But my dad had told me he would be going with me for the next stage of the process, and, until now, I didn't know why he wanted to do that. I waited until my new friend got done with his process; then we walked out of there. We both felt like we just left a prison cell. As we were walking away from the Defense Ministry complex, we went back to the conversation we had left halfway, and I asked my new friend what it was that he was going to tell me about Beirut, Lebanon. He turned around several times to make sure no one could hear him or follow us, and he told me there was this office called the World Council of Churches, and it was a world-wide organization located in Beirut. They were registering Christians and Armenians who were fleeing the Iraqi regime or the country; specifically, those families who had been harmed or discriminated against by the regime and who feared living in Iraq under the government's Baath regime. He added by saying this organization would take you to America as a refugee. I couldn't believe my ears. Then I asked him, "Are you sure, or are you messing with me? How would you know this is not a trap like any other which the regime is fabricating in order to see who has ties and love for the west?" He said he had an aunt who lived in Beirut, and she called them two days ago telling them this story, and she was no liar. He said he didn't want me to tell anyone yet, other than my father, because this had to be done in the secret as we all knew how to survive doing things secretly being a minority.

I thanked him and gave him my word that I wouldn't talk about it, but I would inform my father only with this new information since my friend had asked me to do so. As a matter of fact I still hadn't trusted my new friend yet. What if he was putting us on, and why should I tell my dad only and not anyone else? All these thoughts were causing me to have more headaches that afternoon. The regime didn't teach us to love and care for one another, and they loved to create divisions among all the people whether you were a minority or not. I believe it was another control tactic, so we could be in fear and not trust each other or others. A tactic like this could possibly create more informers to help their cause. In other words, by doing so they loved to see bloodshed to scare and control the Iraqi population and having people wrongfully accuse each other on matters that your brain wouldn't imagine normally. I believe the entire world was on a mission to advance and serve humanity with all the accomplishments that they could achieve. But the Iraqi people were cursed to go backwards, possibly to stone ages with bullies controlling their fate.

Folks, you had to live there to know what I'm talking about and to experience the pain and agony of a nation that had no future. Here, in the states, just watching television and listening to others talk about Iraq is not enough to fully understand about the life of the people there and their daily routines 44 years ago. What I'm trying to do is write and portray for you as best as I can the real situation in detail because I lived there, and I experienced most of those pains for years. You don't have to travel and endanger yourself just to know what's going on. Believe me when I tell you all these things described my life and other people's lives word-by-word.

I took the bus ride home after both of us finished talking about the travel issues, and I'm thinking what and how I should tell my father about the refugee subject and traveling to Lebanon. I knew he would be in fear that I had opened my mouth to strangers, telling them what our family plans were. But the truth is, I didn't give out any information other than my phone number, but I warned the person that he can't talk to us freely over the phone lines regarding this subject. As I was swamped in these thoughts, the bus arrived at the bus stop where I had to get off. I got off the bus and walked to my house, which was a short five-minute walk. I entered my house from the side door to the kitchen, and, as usual, my mom was cooking, and the first thing I did was to kiss her, and then I told her, "Mom, I have to talk to you."

She said, "Go and put all your stuff down, wash up and then I can be ready to talk to you."

"Mom, I don't want to do all that yet. There's something very exciting, and I want to talk to you about it first, so you could tell dad yourself."

She stopped her work, turned the stove off and washed her hands, and then we sat down in the kitchen where there was a small breakfast area with a table and chairs. Some of the chairs were made by my dad, and they were not so great or safe to sit on, but, nevertheless, that's all we had. She sat down next to me. I love my mom dearly because when it comes to her immediate family, she will stop the world just to listen and help. I went on and told her exactly what had happened, and I gave her the phone number of the friend that I met so they can have it in order to talk to his family regarding traveling to Beirut, Lebanon.

She paused for a moment and said, "Maybe it's better that you and I go to Dad and tell him about this news."

I said, "I'm worried that he'll be upset about the whole thing, especially since you know how he has been acting lately after coming home from the prison. My mom comforted me, so I wouldn't worry and said, "Let's go to the den and tell him anyway." We both went and sat down next to my dad. He noticed there was something we needed to tell him, so he lowered the television's volume. Then he asked what was wrong. My mom opened the subject and for the first time and to my surprise, I saw my dad start to smile. He said, "Son, I'm also going to tell you something, and I want you to keep it a secret as well."

I felt that the whole world started to trust me with their secrets. But never mind, this was my own father, and I could trust him. He said what I had heard from my friend was true because he and mom had been informed about it by other trustworthy families. He knew about this subject two weeks ago. He told me not to worry, and then he said, "I know how hard all three of you are trying to make it in school so that none of you will serve in the Iraqi armed forces; especially you. You're working for the next level of your education where you want to finish your high school and attend the electrical engineering college to be an engineer. But, son, there is no future in Iraq for us anymore." He added by trying to make me remember by asking, "Do you remember some years ago back in 1967 we had a guest living a short time in the storage room in our backyard"? I said, "Yes." Then my dad told me, "This man who worked at the Department of Water and Power as an assistant clerk with me was one of the Baath regime's people, and he had been trying to help us understand that in the coming years once the regime could take over the government again, Iraq was going to be nothing but a war zone and things were going to get worse. Then you and your brothers, being boys and all, would be easily drafted into the armed forces to fight wars that no one could predict why they even started to begin with. These are the things I have been told, so we have no choice but to sell everything, including our home, so we can all leave this country to a better world for all of you and the family. I don't want you three brothers to go through what I had to go through in my lifetime."

I said, "But, dad, I worked so hard on my grades, so I could join the engineering college. I need to get my degree."

He said, "I understand, son, but that will jeopardize the entire family's survival. Do you know why I want to go with you to the next stage of getting your military ID book?" I answered, "No." He said, "The man I was talking about who helped me with all this information is a one-star officer in that office now, and he's going to help us to get the final signatures for your military ID book so you can go back and get your passport done and without any trouble."

Now the whole picture was clear in my mind, and I was very happy to see we had a choice after all. This started to brighten my days. I knew it was not going to be as easy as it sounds because one wrong move from us and someone could inform the authorities about my family's plans regarding what we were thinking to accomplish. Then our whole family could get wiped out by this regime. Come to think about it, since this regime got into power again a few years ago back in 1968, they were like a mob for sure. In order to accomplish this, I had to keep everything a secret and never talk about it to anyone. Then I asked my dad how this was going to be possible. If we sell the house, everyone will wonder why. He said we will tell them we are moving to another area. Then I asked about our relatives.

He said, "Son, don't worry. They are all worried about the three of you, and they are encouraging me to take this step. But their worries were how we were going to survive out of the country with no jobs and limited amount of money." My dad assured them that whatever was going to happen then let it take its course. We would find work regardless of its type. I guess my dad had all the answers. He was motivated enough to accomplish this goal.

"Well, let's do it," I said. Then I left the den and went to the backyard.

The very next day I went with my dad to the other military office where his friend was working. We both noticed there was no one entering his office, and the door was closed. When my dad approached the door to his office, he was stopped right away by a soldier who asked him, "Where do you think you're going, sir?" Then he called my dad names. He told him you are an idiot. He was trying to push his weight around as a guard. Since by now all of us as a minority were conditioned to accept verbal abuse, this didn't bother us very much. My dad replied that he had an appointment with the officer in charge, and we were told that this is where his office is. The soldier asked my dad again if he knew where his office was located. At first, we didn't know whether he was testing us or not. Then my dad said, "It's the one that's behind you, soldier." The soldier turned around and knocked on the office door himself, on the very same door my father was going to knock on to start with. We were in the right place at the right office. Then sometimes you wonder who the idiot is in this matter. After the knock on the door by the soldier, a voice from the inner office asked, "Who is it?"

The soldier replied, "Someone here to see you, sir, and he said he's a friend of yours. The officer walked out of his room to receive us, then asked this idiot who was working for him to get some refreshments for us. I followed my dad to the office. It was nothing but approximately ten feet by nine feet in size, so, like old times, they exchanged notes about the past and future, but the officer didn't want to talk much regarding what lies ahead. He asked me to show him my unfinished military ID book, and I did.

He said, "Please, sit down."

Suddenly, my dad reacted to me to not sit down as I was told by the officer. My father diplomatically said that I should be standing up like a soldier. I was puzzled, but I had to follow his wishes. I didn't want to embarrass him and then, again, I didn't know what was going on in my dad's head once more. Was he preparing another drama to make a point to his friend by using me? I was mostly right about my doubts. The officer paid a compliment to my father that he had been raising fine men to serve this country. This had planted more fear and confusion in me as to what I've been hearing. We were there to get my ID book completed and nothing else. This officer was the one who advised my dad about leaving and fleeing the country. Why in the world were they talking about me being a future good soldier; beats me. A few moments later, this officer had signed a note on a piece of paper and put it inside my military book. Then he instructed me to take my ID book along with his note to the other office building which was located right across from his. I went out and entered the other office building. There were three men standing in line ahead of me. The receiving guard at this other office door asked me for my papers. I showed him the note. He took the note, left his post and then went directly to the clerk. When the clerk saw the note, he asked me to approach his desk. Both the soldier and the clerk ignored all the other applicants who were ahead of me including the one whose papers were being worked on. Wow! My dad's friend must have been in a very powerful ranking position. This demonstrates that if you have any connections anywhere in that country, you were going to be taking care of. I didn't think this was fair or justifiable. But what am I saying here? There was no fair system or guidelines to follow when it came to have a middle man connection within the regime itself, then this would allow you to get your way, regardless. The clerk had put aside the application that he was working on and started a new application for me. A few minutes later more people had rushed into the line, and the line grew to almost twelve people in total. After registering my information down in his book, the clerk said he had to write my name down. He turned to a page inside the ID book, and then he started to smile and laugh. He said with a loud voice I should repeat to him my full name by first name, middle and the last name. I said my full name, and I noticed that everyone standing behind me started to laugh gradually. Then he managed to write it down somehow. Half of the spelling was wrong, and I thought I was done. Before he handed the book to me, he made one cynical remark by saying, "If I was a criminal and if the authorities ask me to testify for my crimes, I will gladly testify, but I wouldn't want to write down ten names like yours in the government's registry book." This provoked more laughs from everyone standing in the line. I was very upset because this was the second time that I heard this in one week from two different soldiers working in this ministry building. They were making fun of my name, and they were supposed to be working as government employees. He didn't know what was going to be coming his way because he had forgotten about the note which was written by my dad's friend, the high-ranking officer, and given to him by me earlier. I went back to the office where my father was still chatting with his officer friend, and my face showed some signs of anger. Right away the officer noticed something was not right, he asked me if I had been taken care of.

I said, "Yes, sir and thank you, sir. But I have to tell you something that just happened."

He looked at me puzzled, and then I continued explaining about what the clerk had said about my name. The officer was very embarrassed by what I had just told him. I noticed my dad was trying to shut me off by telling me not to say things like this to the officer. But the man was smart and asked me to go back and call the clerk to come to his office. No matter how much of a nice and God-loving person I was, I felt this was my day; I had to get this clerk in trouble. Maybe I was not thinking right at that moment; I was perhaps being selfish. I went and told the clerk that the officer sent me to call him to his office. Right away he knew what kind of mistake he committed since he was so brave with his insulting words without thinking that I was an Iraqi citizen just like him; no more and no less. He shouldn't have to make fun of anyone that needs his help. Right away he said, "I hope you didn't tell my officer what I just said to you back in my office." For the first time in my life I felt justice will be served somehow, and I replied to him, "Yes, I did tell the officer about what you just did, and he wants to see you."

I wanted to plant some fear in his heart, just like what we had been experiencing every day. We walked together to the next office, and I already saw this clerk was stumbling in his steps, but I didn't care. This time around I opened the officer's office door, and we both went in. The officer in charge asked me to close the door, and I did. He got up from his chair and without asking the clerk anything or his side of the story, he slapped him very hard on his face. Then he asked the clerk to apologize to me in front of him for what he had said and done. My dad started to get uncomfortable. The clerk told me in his native Arabic language how sorry he was for offending me. I accepted his apology, and I thought justice was served, but it didn't stop there. The officer then pulled a big stick, which was hidden behind his desk, and turned to the clerk and asked him, "Do you know who these people are?"

When the clerk saw the stick, he started to tear up and answered, "No, sir."

The officer said, "That's good, because I'll tell you who they are. This man (referring to my father) saved my life, and he's like a brother to me, and his son that you made a joke about his name, he's like a son to me." As the officer was explaining all this to the clerk in our presence, I heard the clerk constantly being apologetic as to what he had done. The officer struck the stick on the back of the clerk and started to beat him up vigorously. My dad stood up and tried to hold the officer's arm from hitting the clerk, but the officer continued to hit him and reminded him who we were and what we meant to him as people. Wow, I felt very bad for what I did. But how should I know this was going to happen? At the end, the loud crying of this clerk made the officer stop what he was doing. Then he opened the door and told the clerk, "Get up and get the hell out of my office and go back to yours. I'm not going to sign your time sheet today because this is going to cost you a day's worth of pay." Regardless of how bad I felt, the message in all of this was that we, as minorities, should be treated as equals by others, but this was mean and not a way to solve it by beating another human being. Everyone in this country was impulsive and acted through their emotions, which was not a good ingredient for a leader like this officer who was my father's friend, but this was their method of treating their own people, unfortunately, at that time.

After a short break the, officer told my dad and I that he was sorry this happened, and he didn't know why he was so hard on the clerk. We didn't say anything to him hoping he would calm down. Then he took my military ID book as he walked out of his office and told us he would be back shortly because it was time for him to return the favor by taking the book to the next and final signature stage where I, personally, couldn't accompany him. He told us it would take two months if we had to go through this process without his help. Naturally, we thanked him. He left to go to the next building, and he asked me to follow him and stay behind him. We walked up the tall staircase of this building. He opened the door and asked me to stand outside and wait just in case I'm needed to be seen by his superior officers. When he opened the door, I noticed five different short desks in a circle-like setup and sitting behind each of the five desks there were high-ranking officers two to three hundred pounds in weight with their fully decorated uniforms. Our friend closed the door, and he went in. I couldn't move anywhere due to a different set of fear factors. But after twenty minutes he came out and handed me my military ID book and said, "Congratulations. I got this done for you. You can go now to meet your dad at my office. I will be there shortly."

I went back to the officer's office where my dad was. I noticed my dad put his index finger on his lips signaling to me not to say a word. I quietly entered the room and sat down next to him. We didn't say a word to each other for a good ten minutes. Then our friend showed up, and my dad hugged and thanked him for his efforts. The officer told us we shall meet later and wished us good luck. We both left his office walking toward the bus station in the Iraqi summer heat of 115 degrees. I asked my dad about several issues. First, why was I called a good soldier in the beginning? Was I going to join the armed forces or what? Why we didn't exchange a word for ten minutes. He said, "I called you a soldier because I was playing politics with the situation." The reason we couldn't speak a word for ten minutes was because his friend had told him previously about his office being bugged by the people in their own regime because the regime didn't trust anyone including their own officers." Then he added, "Son, don't worry much. We got what we came here to get, but you should have told me about what had happened next door before telling the officer. That was a very ugly situation which you had witnessed." After taking a deep breath, he said it reminded him of his prison days, and then he put his arm on my shoulders and said, "Let's go home, son, and tell your mom about our success for today."

We both took the bus to go home and thirty minutes later, we got off the bus at the station near to our home. The heat was unbearable at 115 F on a hot summer day. The buses or the public transportation were not equipped with air conditioning and human sweat and other unpleasant odors were unbearable at times. In Iraq it was not customary to use under-arm deodorants especially by men in general, but not by all men. Shorts were not a part of the dress code for men in public on hot summer days. We were all excluded from these comfortable measures, possibly due to the country's religious culture or customs.

After we got off the bus we started walking toward our home where my mom was waiting for the news. The moment I got in, I changed into my soccer shorts. I went to the kitchen to pour a cold drink for me and my father, and then the three of us went to the den where my dad explained to my mom what had happened today and why we were late. My mom was proud of me for what I had done regarding the soldier who was a clerk and getting him into trouble, but my dad was saying the opposite. I believe my mom was trying to express her anger toward the regime as well for the incident where she suffered too much emotionally while my dad was in prison. I guess this was her way of saying they deserved what they got in punishment.

The dusk was settling in, and the sun just started to fade out with the normal, beautiful Arabian summer sunsets. We received a phone call from one of our relatives who wanted to come over for tea or coffee. My mom rushed to the kitchen, as usual, and started to bake a cake from scratch; it was her specialty. She made it so good and tasty that most of our relatives used to ask her for the recipe. It would take our relative a minimum of an hour and a half to get to our house because they had called a cab to get to our home, and it would take at least an hour or so to bake the cake. That was enough time for my mom to get things going and get ready for our guests. After an hour and a half our relatives were at our doorstep, and they settled in. The adults chatted with each other in the living room, and the kids went to the den and played board games. Then after a while, my mom called me to help her carry some stuff from the kitchen to the living room, and as I was entering the living room, I heard that the subject of the chat was the refugee issue, which I had told my parents about a while back. My dad asked me to stay and listen to the whole subject as they were discussing it. I was shocked at how much these people knew about this issue. Everyone had finalized their conversations regarding going to Lebanon. They said they all had to sell their homes and belongings and carry only their clothes in suitcases with them. Also, everyone decided not to put some items in their suit cases like photo albums, daily diaries, home movies, valuable books from their home library, etc., since doing so would make the guards at the checkpoints inside the country suspicious of you as you head out towards the Iraqi western borders. This would signal and would give them a hint that you would be going away for good. This was a big no-no, and you could be forbidden from proceeding forward, especially when trying to cross the last checkpoint, which is the border between Iraq and Syria. When I heard this, sadness took over my heart, and I felt very bad. All my books, all my sport memories and victory trophies, and all our valuable books from the bookshelves, where they got kept for generations from my grandfather's days were to be left back in the country. This was not good news for me to accept. There were other ways to not keep anything behind for instance we could send them out of the country before our journey. But how were we going to choose which items; such as, books or trophies were going to take priority over others. It was puzzling for me because there were so many items. Soon after our guests went home that evening, I needed to ask my parents how we were going to choose which items to take. Both of my parents assured me not to worry too much and that tomorrow is just another day. When the sun comes up, we should be thinking how to get out of the country first, and the rest shouldn't matter. That was not a good enough answer for my question, but I had to sleep on it that night.

The phrase "The rest should not matter" stuck in my mind the whole night. I didn't sleep well. My brain was in a big traffic jam, and my mind was going around every corner of our house trying to envision everything we had as items and belongings. After thirty minutes, I fell asleep. I had a dream that we were already out of the country and that material items didn't matter. I saw in my dream that everything was replaceable, except for my grandfather's books, which he left behind for my dad to use. I saw the places that I was going to be in, and it was like a big déjà vu for me. The next morning, I woke up to the sound of our neighbor's rooster which was a daily natural alarm system. The roosters used to crow first in the early morning hours around sunrise, and then a short time later the Islamic mosques would start their morning prayers as it was their daily routine every day and every evening. Since Christians were a minority, and geographically speaking, they only had a few churches in the entire city of Baghdad unlike the mosques in every neighborhood, there were no church bells that you would hear every day. You would normally hear them on Sundays when you visit the church some kilometers or miles away. These mosques were a walking distance from each other. Why so many? We just couldn't comprehend.

The next morning was a Friday and a weekend. The usual weekends in Iraq in the 1970's were a half a day on Thursdays and a full day on Fridays. The morning sun had risen, and you could hear the rooster's crow from several different directions as well as all the Islamic mosques' mullahs (religious priests) who were praying the same prayers. All these sounds and voices made me get up from my bed and wander around before anyone else was up. I looked at the sunny horizon and at my nearby elementary school which was located next to my house from my rooftop, which we all used to sleep on during the summer season. Those of you who have traveled to the Middle East or Egypt know what I'm talking about when I say sleeping on the flat roof of a home, and those who haven't had the experience, try to imagine your home has a flat roof where you can walk on it. There was always a staircase leading to the rooftop from the inside of the house. On hot summer nights you have your bed set placed on the rooftop and you could sleep in your bed on the rooftop under open skies with a cool summer breeze cooling you off. It sounds exciting, doesn't it?

Now, some negative questions had rushed into my head as I looked down at my elementary school yard from the rooftop of our home. I asked myself how am I going to leave all this behind? What if the new world we are going to is not so kind? What if we can't find jobs, and are we going to fail our life's mission? What will happen to us and to my family? As I was thinking and looking into the direction of the sunrise with complete deep concentration, I felt an arm had landed on my shoulder from behind, which disturbed my thoughts with a shock.

It was my grandmother's hand. She said, "What are you thinking about? I have been watching you for the past fifteen minutes, and your eyes have not blinked yet."

"Grandma, how was it when you were young, and you had to leave your village called Van at the age of nine and fled to another country?"

She took a very deep breath, hummed and said, "Son, I hope you don't have to face what I had to go through with my family in those horrible days. I hope God will always have mercy on all of you. Then she began to tell me her story. She said in 1915 (historically, April 24, 1915 was when the Armenian Genocide took place at the hands of the Turks during the Ottoman Empire, which is still being denied by the Turkish government as of today), she was only nine years old, and the Turkish militia didn't give a choice for the villagers to stay. They mass murdered everyone; men, women and children. For them it was all the same. She added that there was no war taking place in their village. She said she was lucky her mom found a way to flee all the killings and injustices using the only transportation they had, which was their donkey or mules with carts. Those who didn't and couldn't flee fell behind dead from hunger and thirst and some were abducted by the soldiers for their own pleasures and then were killed later. She said, "I don't want to spoil your morning with my life story, son. Unlike nowadays, everyone has a choice to change their life for the better or decline to do so, but that choice is not by staying in Iraq anymore. We must migrate elsewhere to find freedom and opportunities for all you young people." When I heard all this, I knew God had mysterious ways to work through people's lives and relay a message. This morning the message was clear to me: let's leave everything behind and go. This was coming from my grandmother Knar.

Our conversation came to a halt when everyone started to get up and rush downstairs to the one bathroom we had. We all had to take turns. Breakfast was being prepared, and the teapot was always on in our house. You could have hot tea any time during the day or night. We had stored most of the rice, tea, flour and sugar in fifty to sixty-pound bags under the main staircase across from the kitchen for emergencies. Sometimes when we would wake up in the mornings in Baghdad, we would witness a revolution that had taken place during the previous night without anyone's knowledge and the ruling government had been thrown out and replaced by another while we were asleep, or hints of a revolution were being sparked in the air. These events had made the local grocery shops and markets close for days, and sometimes for weeks, which, in turn, had created a shortage of food and necessities. No one could go out to purchase any goods for some time because of tanks and army personnel guarding every neighborhood. We had all experienced and learned from this in the past. This was a big reason for us to keep extra food at our house for emergencies. But this time around, since the Baath regime came back into power in 1968, the Iraqi people were not so lucky to see a revolution take place in order that this regime and its bullies could be gone soon. However, everything has a cause and effect in life. The cause would be that this regime got into power and was going to stay for a long time and had made life so difficult for everyone to accept and survive. The effect would be that we all had to sell everything in order to survive and prosper. A good example would portray that my parents had worked all their lives and maintained certain standards in life by providing for all of us in the family. Now we all must flee in order to exist and enjoy a better life following the effect symptom, which was going to put me in a situation where I was going to miss out on everything by leaving it behind, including my friends and relatives. It was not so easy for me to let go of everyone and everything in 1973 when we decided to leave.

The morning conversation or chat among us had begun around the breakfast table. It was about our journey and the issuing of passports. After the ordeal which I had encountered to obtain my military ID registration book, now I was told by my parents that I should be able to go back to the passport agency office and get a valid passport issued to me without any fear. They were right. All that was needed next for me in order to get a valid passport was to file a new application to accomplish a renewal of an old and expired passport. You see, I had in my possession an old passport that I needed to renew. My old passport was obtained many years ago by aunt Sofina's husband from the very same government passport agency. Sofina's husband didn't have any trouble back then to get it for me because of my age. I was not old enough to be drafted into the army forces. I was a minor. He had obtained it for me originally when I was at the age of thirteen because I had traveled with them out of the country in the past during the summer breaks. Since the original passport was issued and since I had turned seventeen and a half years old, the rule was no passport would be renewed until I had my military ID book with me, and I must be registered with the office of the Ministry of Defense as a draftee since my status had changed.

The very next morning I went to the passport agency early so that I didn't have to encounter the summer mid-day heat, people and traffic jam. I arrived at the gates around 7 a.m. in the morning, but the gates didn't open until 8 a.m. I ran inside the gates and rushed towards the building along with others to stand in line at the appropriate window and like in the past, a lot of anxiety had taken place within me once more. I was thinking what if they were still looking for me in order to arrest me because I didn't have my military ID book with me like in the last visit three weeks ago. Well, I told myself I must be brave, and I should take this challenge again. After a short twenty-minute wait outside his office, it was my turn to approach the window. The officer inside the room called out to me saying, "Next customer, please!" I approached the window and presented my paperwork including my old passport. The officer was not the same one I had dealt with three weeks ago. So far, so good.

He said, "Let me see your military ID registration book."

This time, and with great pleasure, I pulled it out from my back pocket and I handed it to him. He looked at it and after several minutes of examining my papers, he said, "Excuse me for a few minutes." Again, I felt like a cold bucket of water got dumped on my shoulders once more, and my body started to shake. I didn't know if I had done anything wrong, or if anything else was missing from my paperwork. They never took the time to explain to you about mistakes. As a matter of fact, they looked for mistakes, and they wanted you to fear them because they are the authority. The human touch or the care which was expected from them was not part of their mentality or routines. I had no choice but to wait and wait for my new fate. Fifteen minutes later, the officer came back to the window and said, "Here are your papers. I will have to send you to the final signature room." I was so surprised that this officer started to explain to me what my next move should be, and he didn't even pay attention to any mistakes. He told me in order to obtain a finalized signature and renewal I should have sponsorship paperwork (called "Kafala" papers in Arabic) in the amount of 1,500 Iraqi dinars that must be paid to this agency. This equaled approximately $750 US, at that time. When I asked him what were the sponsorship paperwork for, he replied with an unpleasant voice that it means someone must sign for you and take responsibility for the 1,500 Iraqi dinars. He added that this person should stay behind in the country, and he wouldn't be able to travel anywhere until you come back. And, if you didn't return back to Iraq after your trip, this person would first face paying the penalty for you; second, he should be able to explain why you couldn't be back in time; and third, he could be jailed as well for taking the liability for you in agreeing to your traveling purposes abroad. And this is if we could prove that he knew in advance that you're not coming back. You see, the regime made it difficult for the young to leave the country, and they wanted to punish the ones who could help you too. So much for freedom.

I had no choice but to say thank you, sir. It was all new news for me and almost impossible to accomplish. This meant I was to be an obstacle for my whole family in order to travel and change countries for good. A big dark cloud-like sadness had taken over my heart once more. I had to take my paperwork back and leave the building with no hope. I didn't know where I was going. I started to get lightheaded and a big anxiety started to cave in. I couldn't feel my hands; they started to get numb. But what could I do to change this? They made everything so difficult to achieve anymore. They wanted to keep all the youth in the country, and who knows what military decisions they had been calculated and planned for us for the future. But my family had to know this. I couldn't go on with this all by myself. I walked all the way home that day trying to exhale, and I didn't pay any attention to the weather or the time. It was exactly a two-hour-and-ten-minute walk from the passport agency building to my house. I felt guilty, and I was blaming myself all the way home. After a long walk, I finally got home. When my mom saw that I was all upset, and my face had turned red sweating from the hot sun, she got worried a lot about me. Then she gave me new dry clothes and told me I should jump into the shower and get all that sweat off me. I did as she said. I had no control over my decisions anymore. I felt like a big rig truck had hit me and made me lose control. I said, "Whatever." After I finished with my shower, I sat in the TV room where my mom and grandmother were. They sat down next to me, worried sick, and handed me a cold drink. My mom asked me what happened and why I wasn't saying anything to them. It took a good twenty minutes for me to come back to reality, and I just said I was a failure to them. I told them both to please leave the country without me. I didn't want to hold all of them back, especially my father who had suffered so much. Both my mother and grandmother still didn't understand what the hell I was talking about. Then I went back into a long silent period without talking to them once again. I fell asleep as I was very exhausted. I woke up that evening from the sound of my parents talking next to me, and they were both happy to see me wake up. I smiled back as I was getting up.

First thing my dad said to me was, "Son, don't worry, and whatever it is, we will overcome it."

I ran to the bathroom first, and I vomited. I then washed my face and went back to see my parents. I felt better, and I started to tell them what had happened that same day. At first, my father was surprised, but it was nothing new to him as to how this regime made new rules never heard of before, new laws day-by-day and to confine everyone within their borders so no one could have contact with the outside world other than them. They already had a ban on the FM radios. No one was allowed to have them and use them, or else you would be serving time in jail for it, if they catch you with one.

My father said, "It's okay, son, I'll find someone who will be willing to help us, but it's better to have a plan as to how well this can be orchestrated so the person who will sign for you will not get harmed when we don't come back. All this can be arranged."

Wow! When I heard this, a sigh of relief finally came over me. I told my mom that I was very hungry. She laughed and went to the kitchen to prepare some food for me. That evening my uncle George had come home early from work. He was working two or three jobs. In the mornings, he and his wife worked at the corporate office of the Department of Water and Power, and in the evenings, George was going to homes and tutoring math and other subjects, but, soon enough, he found a better evening job working with a big metal supply merchant. Later, this latter job took over the first one, and he was getting paid better, but it required traveling out of the country. This positioned him to know more people all around, but how deep he was with relations of knowing people, only he can tell. Also, on some evenings I stayed up late and waited for him in order to get help with my math and algebra lessons. We were two families under one roof but a big, happy family. He was a good and responsible man. His wife, my aunt Veronica, had set the dinner table for him one night, and after he ate his dinner, she opened the subject of my being sponsored by him, or if he knew anyone at the passport office, and if they could be of help. He was surprised as well that such a thing could take place, and then he said in the morning he would see if he could find anyone from his contacts that might be able to help us for my situation.

A week later my father and my uncle George were discussing my fate, and I noticed my dad didn't want to impose. I overheard him saying he would try it himself first, then if all options were out, he would consider my uncle's offer. Then I learned that my uncle George told my dad that he personally would take the risk of signing my sponsorship paperwork, so we didn't have to stay behind. Hey, I was happy to see things were moving along, but one thing my father had as a negative was that he was a hard-headed person, and he never wanted to listen to others and was always doing things the hard way. When I approached him, I asked him about my situation. He said he had a friend and his friend had told him that he had some connections with the outside world, but it would cost him some money for me to be smuggled out of the country. When I heard this, I told myself, yes, it's an option, but I never trusted his friend. He had a criminal look on his face, and he was living out of the country for some time because he stole some funds and goods in the past and there was a judgment against him in Iraq. He was on the watch list or on the wanted list; I'm not sure. But when Saddam's regime took power somehow, he claimed that he was part of the Baath party and whatever crimes he had committed in the past, he had gotten himself excused for it. I never liked him, but he was involved somehow doing good deeds for all Armenians in our community. I asked my father where his so-called friend was living out of the country. He told me his friend was living on a ship near the port in Beirut. Then I asked if he knew if his friend had killed anyone in the past. There was a big pause from my dad, and then he said he didn't know, but he had heard that it was possible that this man committed a bad crime, and not just stealing and that's why he had lived five years close to a shipyard out of the country. This, again, was not adding up for me, so I had to ask my father how many people he knew of that his so-called friend succeeded to smuggle out and who were the actual people who were doing the operation.

He said he didn't know, but he would ask him. A week later he told me that the actual operation was being done by Bedouin Arabs across the Iraqi desert into Damascus, Syria. I hummed and then said, "I will not do it, and I will not go! If you really love me and you want to see me again, please take Uncle George's option. It's much safer for me because I've been hearing about these smuggling operations from my school friend whose parents were also hiring such services to send their male children outside Iraq so their kids can avoid serving in the Iraqi armed forces, but some of these operations are getting these young men killed and dumped in the desert with no trace." My father was not in touch with the world sometimes. Generally speaking, it would be helpful to listen to your children, especially if they are grown boys or men; it won't hurt. The only thing which was holding my dad from taking his broth-er-in-law George's option was money. What this meant was that the Iraqi Baath regime just made it difficult by creating a rule like this where not only the sponsor would be jailed, but they also wanted the whole 1,500 dinar sponsorship money paid up front. The difficult part was to come up with the entire amount. The word went out about the need for this money within our relatives, and my other uncle, Sofina's husband, heard about it. He called my dad and blamed him for not letting him know about his being short of funds, especially since this concerned my fate. I was his favorite brother-in-law's son and the one he was hoping one day he could teach his wine business to. My dad talked to him, and they all got a plan in place, meaning that Sofina's husband would supply the funds and George would sign the sponsorship papers. So far so good, but this was to happen at the last minute or at the eleventh hour before we all traveled. In the beginning I didn't know why, but I learned later when the travel date had been firmly set. The plan was that my Uncle George was going to take me with him to the passport agency office. He was to sign the sponsorship paperwork and was to give them a check for the required amount under a different name and not his. In other words, the check would bounce by the time it would get to the government's bank because no banking system in Iraq in the '70s had any computers which were being utilized to do banking transactions; they were all done manually. There was another option, which was for George to leave the country himself before we could. All of these events would take place approximately twenty-four hours apart. In this way, no one could trace his whereabouts and look for him. The latter plan was being considered as a backup plan because the mentality behind it was that by the time the Iraqi authorities learned that I was not coming back for good, my Uncle George would already be out of the country and would be untouchable. In the event the authorities were to investigate his wife and his children, they were going to say that George had abandoned his children, divorced his wife and ran away suddenly, and the family didn't know his whereabouts.

Keep in mind that such a plan was the first of its kind to deal with. No one had thought about anything like this before. But, folks, it worked. The reason it worked was because of the main key element of this plan, which was the head military officer of the passport agency office who happened to be a friend of my Uncle George, or contact in this matter, and he was the one who told George to do this type of move accordingly in order to help him and us in return. Every time George had traveled out of the country on business trips in the past, he brought him gifts and whatever this officer desired to have, and George was the one who made it happen for him. This had created some type of trust and relationship among both men.

Well, the day had come for this head honcho officer to return the favor when my uncle and I went to the passport agency office. I saw my uncle give him the bad check, and he also signed the paperwork. Then I learned later that both the check and the sponsorship paperwork were pulled out of the passport agency's files and were destroyed. There were only photocopies that were kept as record just in case someone should verify or ask for them from this head honcho officer. I never met him, and I don't know what he looked like because I was waiting for my uncle to go into his office and come out as he had instructed me to do so. This was possibly the cleverest thing that ever happened. No money was paid, and the original signed papers didn't exist, only a photocopy for the record books. Wow, it worked. This had created a very helpful situation for my uncle George and his family to decide like us and flee the country later. As for now and in the short term, he had no liability for me. The next step was that my uncle George must travel out of the country first to avoid all hardships as the plans had called for; otherwise, time would be his biggest enemy and would catch up with him, and, ultimately, he would be penalized and/or imprisoned. Now, I got my passport signed, but, again, one last obstacle I had to overcome, and, as I mentioned before, my life was never short of obstacles. The passport agency stamped a big stamp in my passport showing that it was okay to visit all the Arab countries, except the most import-ant country that we were supposed to go to, which was Lebanon. The law said all females regardless of age and only males sixteen years of age and below were allowed to visit Lebanon, and their passports were stamped accordingly. But it was forbidden to have the same type of visa permission stamped for males seventeen years of age and over in their passports, which automatically separated our family into two groups. My dad and I in one group where we couldn't enter Lebanon, but the rest of my family could, including my grandmother. This didn't stop us from moving forward; we did just the opposite. Our minds were very set to leave the country a day ahead of schedule.

Weeks passed, and things started to get clearer to me. Our furniture was getting sold, but not delivered to the buyer because we told the buyer we needed them until we travel. They were a good Muslim family, and they said they could wait for it. The house was not listed, but we found out our neighbor across the street wished to buy our house for his brother to live across from him. But, somehow, he and his real estate-like agent had heard that we were going out of the country and not coming back. We were blackmailed by them saying they would report us to the authorities if we didn't sell the house specifically to them. And, they put a cap on how much they would like to buy it for. We didn't know how the word got around, but my father defused their mentality regarding us not coming back by telling them we were selling the house to move and live closer to his sister's house. He also told them that we were travelling to Istanbul, Turkey for a visit this summer with the whole family, and that we would be returning in two weeks. Nevertheless, they insisted they would report us all if their wish couldn't be granted. My dad didn't have any choice. We had already sold everything we owned, and we were not going to look back. Instead of jeopardizing every plan that we put in place to escape the country, my dad decided to sign the deed over to them to convince them that we would be back, and we were going to move to another area. He also put one condition in the agreement that my aunt Veronica and her husband George along with their kids get to stay in the house after we leave for two weeks until they can get themselves a new place to live in as it was stated in the final agreement. We knew this was not the actual plan for George and his family. It was just a camouflage for this uninformed buyer. The buyer agreed to do so, and the deal was done.

The next step was to decide on material belongings. Our septic tank in the backyard received all the books which we couldn't possibly take out of the country with us. We filled the tank half way then covered it with dirt and concrete because there was no more use for the septic tank as a few years earlier the city had installed and connected a sewer system in our neighborhood, which was functioning instead. It was an unfortunate and tragic thing for me to see throwing valuable books into the septic tank, but it was a small token to pay in order to flee to freedom.

On the morning of July 1, 1973, we were at the bus station. Some of our relatives visited us the night before to say goodbye and some were at the bus station waving goodbye. Tears were a normal thing for all of us that morning, but we had to be careful not to be very emotional because it could raise a flag with the soldiers guarding the station. I saw some of my cousins for the last time. You know, it was very hard not to cry because I was leaving my childhood place, childhood friends, and my cousins behind. I saw them from the bus windows for the last time, and who knows when we would meet again. We all sat down and after the guard had done his routine check for the tickets, the passports and the valid visas, he got off the bus. The bus started moving and rolling out of the station. Some of my cousins were running behind the bus and still waving their goodbyes. I said to myself, the hell with it. I didn't care what anyone wanted to think. I started to cry and wave back the same way to them. I felt I was getting torn from a land that I was born in because that land had no more life in it to give, and I felt in the years to come bloodshed was the only thing which was going to irrigate to keep the trees green in that land anymore. I was right about that. The Iraqi people had been impacted by a great deal of human loss and suffering under this regime. Throughout the years this had changed people including my relatives and the Iraqi population's attitude towards each other and toward the outside world. It was a black chapter in their lives which they didn't see coming their way.

The bus driver, for a change, was a good and funny man. He turned his radio on and asked us to be silent for a moment because the government-controlled radio station had just broadcasted that the previous night there was a revolution attempt against the Baath regime and most of the revolutionaries were captured and executed during the night with no trial, of course. Some of them escaped death. The radio announced the name of their leader was a man called Nadem Geezar. The whole bus was silent for a moment. Fear couldn't be a factor anymore, but anxiety was, and on its highest level. Everyone was getting impatient to get to the border, but the bus had just started its journey, and we still had to travel twelve hours until we reach the Syrian border. The bus drove away leaving the city of Baghdad going towards the western desert heading to the border of Syria and Jordan. We had two teachers with us on the bus, and both were going to Syria on vacation as well as a Christian Assyrian family with a young three- year-old daughter. She had run in the bus and had fallen. Her nose started to bleed. As we all witnessed, her parents managed to stop the bleeding, but her father's white shirt had some blood stains on it around his neck and on the left chest area. I remember our bus had stopped at least fourteen different times for checkpoints and every time we were stopped this poor man was pulled out of the bus and questioned about the blood on his shirt as to where he got it from. No passenger from the bus dared to help this poor man or get involved after several stops with the same type of questioning to him. After a six to seven-hour drive, the bus reached a bus stop rest area. We got out of the bus, so we could stretch out and walk around a bit. The scenery of the desert was a real beauty. The air was crisp and fresh, and everyone got a chance to open their suitcases in order to get some stuff, and if they wanted to change into clothing, they were allowed to do so. The one good thing that this Assyrian man did at the rest station was that he went and changed his bloody shirt and tie that he had on from the start of our journey. He put the bloody clothing into his suitcase, picked up a small plastic bag and approached us knowing we were Christian like him. My mom knew how to speak their language, and they both chatted in Assyrian. Then this man handed my mom this small plastic bag which was put into a paper bag. My mom took the bag and gave it to my grandmother and asked her to place it between her legs and never move around, if my grandmother could help it. The bus continued its journey for another two hours. I asked my mom what the bag was about, and she said in a low voice in our language that it was their gold possessions. They were trying to take it out of the country, and since he was being questioned every time and thinking if the soldiers make him open his suitcase, they would see the gold and they would take it away from him as well as it could be an obstacle for him and his family to continue the trip. The chance for them to search an old lady like your grandmother is slim. But it never fails. He was right. After a half hour drive, the bus stopped again. The new checkpoint soldiers entered the bus, and they did their routine check with everyone's passports, etc. We knew they would get off the bus fast because there was no bloody shirt on this Assyrian man whose name was Aamo Yousif. But, to our surprise, when one of the soldiers turned back before getting off the bus and asked who is Aamo, Aamo panicked, even though he had done no harm to anyone. He had to raise his hand. They asked him and his family to get off the bus. They wanted to search their suitcases. His instincts were correct with what he had done earlier with his gold. The whole family went down and started to open their suitcases. It was not an attractive picture seeing people in fear trying to prove that they are innocent. When Aamo opened his suitcase, the soldier got even more suspicious when he found the bloody shirt stuffed in a bag in Aamo's suitcase, so when he started to explain, the soldier started to give him a hard time. Then we saw Aamo entering the bus and asking the bus driver to help his situation. The bus driver told the soldiers that they were stopped several times that day and Aamo was questioned about the blood on his shirt. The driver told them the blood they saw on Aamo's shirt was his young daughter's blood. He had personally seen Aamo entering the bus with his family with the same white shirt earlier that morning when there was no blood stain on it. This got Aamo off the hook for the moment. It took exactly one hour for this whole thing to unfold. The bus started moving again. Aamo and his family were sitting next to our seats. My mom asked him what that was all about in his own language, Assyrian. Aamo told my mom they were looking for a man whose name was Aamo as well. The Aamo they were searching for was a fugitive who had committed a crime and fled a night before. Then my mom asked, "How did they know your name is Aamo?" He told my mom that at the last checkpoint when we were stopped, the Baghdad security headquarters had contacted all the checkpoints to look for a man named Aamo, but they didn't have a clue as to what he looked like., the soldier in charge at the last checkpoint had confirmed that he had seen a passenger riding on our bus whose name was Aamo. Aamo told my mom that he was very thankful to the bus driver for his help and his testimony regarding his shirt because at one point one of the soldiers had ordered a truck to come by and pick him up and all of his family members in order to return them back to the original bus station in the capital city of Baghdad where we all had started our journey. The driver's testimony got him and his family off the hook for sure. Aamo was a brave man. He had handled the matter very wisely, but I believe God had something to do with his bravery as well. How would Aamo know his suitcases were going to be subject for search when he handed us his gold to be looked after? Think about it.

Fear and panic were evident equally among all of us, Muslims and Christians, inside the bus. Everyone felt close to each other like one big family. Everyone decided to help each other to avoid harm because every one of us, as we found out by interacting, were going on a one-way trip and not look back. All of us, Christians, Muslims and others, were escaping Iraq, our beloved homeland which we were born and raised in, but no one spoke in the open about their plans, including the Muslim families who were sitting in the bus amongst us. Then suddenly, some started to sing songs that we had heard before to diffuse the impact of the fear factor which had overtaken us. After all, not everyone on the bus was trustworthy; especially row number six where two men were sitting together. All along the way we didn't hear any word exchanged by them, but occasionally they would turn around and look at all of us. Their action created some additional fear, because there's a saying in Arabic, "Walls could have ears; it can listen," so in everyone's mind there were these thoughts about these two men. We suspected them as being spies, and that they were planted by the regime inside our bus? This type of action, at the time, was a common routine by the Baath regime, and they were occurring everywhere and every day.

At this point, we were three hours away from the border. Our freedom depended on crossing the border into Syria at the checkpoint called Rootba at any cost. Rootba was located on the western border of Iraq. As I remember, in the last three hours of our journey silence took over the bus; no talk and no laughter. It seemed like you were going to enter the twilight zone. The fear of entering an unfamiliar territory was causing me a great deal of stress and panic. But like everyone else I tried to sleep, but I couldn't. How could I sleep? The air inside the bus started to get gradually heavier and heavier with cigarette smoke as everyone started to smoke from their nervousness. The desert heat was a smashing 120 degrees Fahrenheit as the bus driver had announced. The bus's air conditioning was giving out, and the driver managed to turn it off and left the regular air to circulate only. No windows were to be opened because of the dust and the heat. It was a horrible situation. The bus driver said he had to turn off the air conditioning while crossing this section of the desert, so we wouldn't get stuck with a broken bus in the middle of the western Iraqi hot and unforgiving desert.

After a forty-five minute drive into our last three hours of our journey to reach the border, suddenly our bus came to a halt in the middle of the desert, and we saw this Iraqi soldier in uniform with a large brown bag in his hand enter the bus as the driver had decided to stop for him. After the brown bag was placed behind the driver's seat, both the bus driver and this soldier went outside the bus for a few moments, and when they returned to the bus, the soldier went all the way to the back of the bus and laid down to sleep. We were all puzzled, but it was, as usual, no one's business to know who he was and what was he doing in the middle of the desert, and why he got on the bus. No one asked any questions. The bus rolled away again, continuing the journey toward the border. The heat was unbearable. My grandmother, God bless her soul, managed to wet small towels by using the water from the glass bottle in her hand and giving it to us, her grandchildren, so we could rub our faces and hands with it to cool off.

This trip reminded her of her own childhood days and told us her story of when the Turkish soldiers killed and pushed everyone toward the desert to exterminate the Armenian race from the face of the earth in the Twentieth Century's first genocide that was committed against humanity. She remembered her own mother named Kishmo when she was doing the same thing to her as they marched and survived the desert and the long walks from Turkey to enter the Iraqi northern border as refugees in 1915. My grandmother was a smart lady and had a lot of common sense. She was trying to calm us down and divert our attention toward her past, so it wouldn't be so painful for us brothers to handle these horrible conditions inside the bus. Her love for her grandchildren was greater than loving herself. We were three boys and grandchildren from her only son, and the rest didn't matter to her at all. Her stories caused a great deal of comfort in me.

Finally, we were in the final miles of reaching the western Iraqi border of Rootba. The bus started to slow down in the border's traffic jam, and as we witnessed, it was like a zoo. The camels and the dessert Bedouins along with their families as well as other buses and taxies full of people that were ahead of us were also trying to cross the same border at the same time. We could all see the border from a short distance from within our bus, but it was like a slow-motion movie. We were so close, yet it seemed so far away. The anxiety was getting high. At one point, the driver was smart. He felt our anxiety and decided to stop the bus and ordered us out to stretch out until the big caravan of camels and their owners and the small taxies with individuals could make headway in their crossing, so we could move on shortly after them. This action didn't help much other than we were all outside the bus and we could all move and breathe the air because we all wanted to flee Iraq a minute sooner rather than later. It was a little bit cooler on the border than three hours ago. It felt like 85 degrees Fahrenheit instead of 120 degrees. I enjoyed looking and being in this part of the Iraqi dessert, which I had never been in before. It was all tan in color on our side and just a little bit reddish across the border on Syria's side. The sky was so clear and blue. The land in this region was so flat you could see miles away in one direction, but the mirage of the dessert can fool you as well if you're not paying any attention. From a distance the mirage might resemble a lake or an ocean as much as your eyes can aim and see in the far horizon, which did not really exist.

After approximately twenty minutes of layover the call was for all of us to get back on the bus, which we all did. The bus drove away, and we reached a point where the bus was passing across a long-fenced gate where you could notice the border patrol or soldiers. The Syrian patrol only stopped us to check our valid passports and visas for the last time before entering their country. It was another ordeal we all had to go through. Aamo and his family were questioned again, and, at one point, we all had to open our suitcases at random for a final search. Our suitcases were passed, and after that my grandmother managed to put the bag which contained the gold items that belonged to Aamo's family into one of our already searched suitcases while the border soldiers were not paying attention. All the time we were getting in or out of the bus, my grandmother kept sitting inside the bus and guarding the gold, which was put between her legs. Then they opened Aamo's suitcases, and, again, the bus driver was kind enough to explain for the last time about Aamo's bloody shirt. The soldiers made another phone call to other stations and the path was finally clear for Aamo to go on and ride the bus with his family. But a question was always on my mind to ask. After several inspections, why didn't Aamo get rid of his bloody shirt for good to avoid all the questioning? It beats me, I had no clue. Now the two men in row six that we were all watching with fear throughout our journey were nowhere to be found after the border crossing check-point. We didn't know why, but as the bus started to enter Syria, I saw both men were already on the Syrian side away from the Iraqi border fence, and they were cheering and jumping up and down from happiness. We found out they were not spies after all, but a couple of Iraqi elementary school teachers. At that time, it was a crime for a teacher or doctor or any engineer to travel and leave the country. It was not allowed because the regime needed them supposedly. These two men somehow managed to do whatever it would take and get out of the country to flee it for good. Who knows how many bribes were paid and sacrifices were taken to accomplish their goal of leaving the country. It was a pleasant moment for me to see two people happy and singing for their freedom.

On the afternoon of July 2, 1973, our bus drove away toward Damascus, the capital of Syria, where we planned to go at first and then catch a taxicab the next day in order to reach our planned destination, which was Beirut, Lebanon. It was very necessary for us to reach Beirut in order to get registered with the World Council of Churches where they were helping all Christians and Christian Armenians to be registered with their office as refugees, and then all of us could travel to our final destination to the land of the free and freedom, the United States of America. It was my father's biggest dream from his childhood days to be there and pursue his acting career even though he was in his mid-forties. A dream like this was considered a mistake by some of our relatives who stayed behind in Baghdad assuming things will get better and better in time. What was called a mistake by our relatives back home saved the lives of all three of us brothers from being a part of Saddam's future war machine and serving his army, and the objective of refusing to join his armed forces in the future was accomplished?

I would like to give my thanks and appreciation to my parent's decision to escape Iraq. The so-called "mistake" by our relatives was well paid off at the end.

CHAPTER

5

Living in Syria, Lebanon, and the Road to America

The bus had dropped us off in the middle of the city of Damascus, the capital of Syria, as it was its destination for that day. All of the passengers picked up their suitcases after the bus driver had put them on the curb, so they could move on to hotels and elsewhere. Some of us, including Aamo's family, decided to stay together and find a hotel that could accommodate all of us in the same place so we all could keep a close eye on each other, to be with each other, and to be in touch with each other. Damascus, Syria was no Iraq to me. The Arabic language was spoken in a different dialect, and it was not easy to comprehend. I was the person who spoke the Arabic language the best among all my family at the time. What I knew was not good enough, even to communicate and get by with. I couldn't understand some of the words that the Syrians were using. I felt strange, and it was known by the natives that we were from a different Arab country. Often, whoever we spoke to asked us right away if we were from the Gulf region, meaning the Persian or Arabian Gulf, but our answer was always no and that we were from Iraq. And, for the first time in my life I felt proud to say I am an Iraqi. I felt I had a country. It was a strange feeling I couldn't explain, but I felt good finding my identity in a strange way, and as an Iraqi citizen in Syria. We asked around and were directed toward a hotel at the other end of the city. We got there by taxicab, but we were cautious not to speak out about our plans to anyone. While Syria was a better place for the time being, it was not any less brutal in treating their people than Iraq. After all, the same Baath party was governing Syria with one fundamental difference. One was the rightist party, the other was the leftist side of the Baath party, but I must be fair toward the Syrians. They treated us well knowing we were all victims of the Iraqi regime.

At last, we were assigned to hotel rooms with several Iraqi Christian families who were on the bus with us along the way. We all knew each other's intentions for leaving Iraq after we had chatted freely. Apparently, we were all going to do the same thing, which was to go to Beirut Lebanon and register with the World Council of Churches to immigrate to America. They all kept this information secret to avoid difficulties and dangers. After we had all settled down, we tried to take a hot shower, but the water supply inside the hotel was limited to so many gallons per room. I don't know if that was done on purpose just to make us pay more money, but, nevertheless, we managed again to live like the homeless in an acceptable Syrian hotel. We had to use a bucket and a plastic cup to pour water on ourselves while trying to clean up, or if you can call it a bath. Another words, we used the bucket to collect and mix the hot and cold water in it. Then whoever wanted to clean up must rinse themselves first by using the water in the bucket and by dipping the plastic picnic cup into the bucket and getting the mixed water out to pour it on oneself. This way, we could conserve and use the limited water supply that we had collected inside the hotel bathroom. It didn't bother any of us since we knew we would find difficulties along the way, and we were like one for all and all for one mentality in order to survive and to reach our final destination, which was the land of the free and the land of opportunity; America.

We were all exhausted after taking our baths or showers. The hotel rooms were very small, and there were not enough beds or blankets available. We had to pay for any extra services or needs. Luckily, my grandmother and my mom thought about these kinds of things ahead of time, and they brought all our blankets from home with them and were put in our luggage We used the blankets as covers. We folded some of them to make it bulky, and we were using them as pillows as well. My parents slept on one of the beds and the other bed was used by my grandmother. The rest of us were sleeping on the floor like pets, but we didn't care because the smell or the taste of a much safer and peaceful mind for the time being was sweet.

What about Lebanon or America? When were we going to reach it? All these thoughts were rushing into my mind as I was falling asleep. Before we slept, I saw my grandmother as usual praying for all us from her bedside. For our first night, it really comforted me very much to sleep across the border in a hotel in Damascus, Syria. Somehow, I felt I was still sleeping on the living room floor at home. I felt good for a change, and I felt we were important. I could breathe a little bit better that night being in Syria. For me this was not the first time traveling into Syria. You see, I had been here before on a trip with my aunt Sofina's family for a summer vacation. I was used to it somewhat, but it was special for me this time around because I had my entire immediate family with me. Then I fell asleep with all these thoughts.

On the morning of July 3, 1973, we woke up and lined up at the doorstep of the only bathroom inside our hotel room in order to wash up. Then my dad and I went to find a restaurant or a market where we could get some food to bring to the hotel, so we could have breakfast together. We didn't go too far since we didn't want to get lost walking around. We found a market and bought some bread, cheese and olives as well as some butter and jam. Then we purchased some ice along with some sugar and loose tea to take back to the hotel room. We had to use this dirty and rusted trash can as an icebox inside our hotel room. We put the ice in a plastic bag and inserted into the trash can, then the butter and the cheese were placed inside the trash can on the ice. We used the teapot, which we brought with us from Iraq, to get the hot burning water from the bathroom to make some tea to drink with our breakfast. We didn't have a portable stove, so we had to use the water heater or the boiled water from the tub faucet. We didn't know any better that this water couldn't be healthy. We were not that sophisticated yet. It was not the best accommodations, but there's no gain without any pain. I learned this at a very young age. At lunch time we only ate bread and tea, and around dinner time we managed to go across the hotel to get some shish kebob (barbecued beef on skewer). It was not much, but enough for all six of us to have some meat as a supply of protein. Unfortunately, the eating pattern and the meals were not the same every day due to lack of finances and shortage of money. We were not allowed to work. We didn't have any legal status to be hired anywhere, plus our stay in Damascus was for a short period of time; only until we could find a way to get across the Syrian border to reach Beirut, Lebanon.

On the third day of our stay in Damascus on July 4, 1973, and after being stuck in the hotel room for the last forty-eight hours due to our worries that someone could break into our hotel room and steal our luggage and belongings, we decided to get out of the hotel room. The last forty-eight hours had taught us not to worry much and live life a day at a time. We all went downstairs and out of the hotel. But before doing that, we informed the other families about our destination, and whoever was left behind in the rooms he/she would be put in charge of watching our luggage. At times, we had to transfer our suitcases into the room where that person was staying in order so that that individual could watch over them. We all took turns to help each other every day. Folks, fear was not a pleasant thing to carry in your mind daily, but it was there very often. We walked into this Syrian famous market place called Soog El-Sirsoog. It was like a street mall; a big Arabian-style marketplace with stores lined up next to each other on ground level and covered with one common, old galvanized metal roofing. It's like a half dome or an arch. The roof wouldn't hold much weight other than minimizing the impact of the direct hot sun light. It was hot and humid, and people were walking along the middle path of this marketplace. It was shoulder-to-shoulder traffic, and every now and then everyone's shoulders were getting hit against each other. I noticed that most of the Syrian women had their black veils covering their faces, and the men were wearing their long Arabian dress-like costume with their head pieces on their heads, but some had regular pants and shirts on along with their Arabian headpieces. The smell of sweating bodies was everywhere in this typical Middle Eastern marketplace in the 1970's. To be honest, there were some store owners and customers who were very well groomed. You could spot women or men passing by us due to their perfume or cologne smell. You could tell not everyone had the same lifestyle in this city. At this famous marketplace you could find everything you wanted, but we were not the ones who were going to purchase any unnecessary goods. We were only going window shopping because we were not there as tourists to begin with. We passed by a pastry shop. I love sweets, but I had to quench my desires as there was no money in my pocket whatsoever to buy any sweets. My dad was the head of the family and he made the financial decisions. For example, if he wanted us to eat sweets, he would call the shot and vice versa. It was hard for me to accept this fact as a teenager, but I had no choice, and those days had taught me some hard lessons. Then I promised myself I would never be poor, that I would always have or try to have money in my pocket no matter what it would take. I would work hard and not let anyone tell me how I should live my life or what to eat or what not to eat. All these thoughts were passing through my mind as I was passing by this bakery. I had no choice but to watch and wish to have something sweet in my mouth to eat, but my wishes were not granted that day.

We finished exploring the marketplace and began to return to the hotel. We saw a man carrying a big leather-like bag full of liquid on his back, and at the end of the bag there was this tiny brass nozzle which was used to dispense the liquid. This turned out to be a famous Syrian drink called "soos". It was made of some natural herbs and water and tasted very weird, but everyone in Syria loved it, and it was a refreshing cold summer drink. My dad decided we could buy some of this drink because the weather was hot, and we needed to consume something to get refreshed before the long walk back to the hotel. The way to drink this item is to get a sip of the whole cup all at once; otherwise, it would make you not want to finish the rest of it due to its grass-like taste. Well, at least that's how I experienced it. My mom and grandmother did the same, but my dad and I managed to drink it anyway. After all, we weren't going to waste the drinks.

That afternoon when we got back to the hotel, we witnessed some of the Iraqi refugees like us who were staying at the same hotel were going back and forth to the border between Syria and Lebanon just to check the status of the border crossing into Lebanon because most of us, especially the men over eighteen years of age and whoever didn't serve the Iraqi armed forces, didn't have any visas or permission in our passports to enter Lebanon including my father and me. That's how our Iraqi passports were stamped by the Iraqi passport agency and it read like this, "The bearer of this passport is allowed to enter all the Arab countries and Turkey only, except Iran and Lebanon." You could see the stamp inside the passports for males that they had scratched out the word Iran. In addition, they had carved out the word Lebanon from the stamp pad which was being used at the passport agency to prevent the Iraqi males to travel to either Iran or Lebanon. But it was the opposite for the females and males under the age of eighteen. Both gender groups had the permission to enter Iran and Lebanon. You could see the mentality of the Iraqi Baath government. In other words, to have your Iraqi passport as a male individual was one thing, and to get the right visas to travel to certain countries was quite another. This resembled Saddam's Baath mentality toward his own people and ethnic minorities. I'm not sure if this was a coincidence, but possibly a calculated agenda. The Iraqi government was trying to divide the unity of the family into male and female groups, disregarding the ties among them and not paying attention to the word family where that's what the word exactly means, "unity and bond" by planting fear among us. I'm not surprised because the head of it all was General Saddam Hussein, who was in charge of the Iraqi Security

Department. He didn't have a unified family life or a concerned father to look after him as he was growing up. He lived a life of a thief as a child, and a murderer as an adult.

Money talks in Iraq as well as all around the world, and there were people who you could pay a great deal of money to as a bribe to alter your passport and to show the word Lebanon stamped into your passport in those days as if it was done originally with the original stamp by the agency. Some people paid top money and got away with it. They got themselves a visa to enter Lebanon without the hassle of staying in Syrian hotels and the hassle of the lifestyle changes that we had to encounter for many days. But my father was not going to bribe anyone. He was against that type of idea. He had his share of misfortunes because he was jailed and tortured in Iraq before, and he was not about to take any risks like that for all of us for one; and, second, the issue of lack of finances to pay for travel was just another. I agreed with him on these points.

The Lebanese government opened the borders willingly to help Iraqi's enter on particular days regardless what their passports were stamped with because they knew why we headed toward their country, in addition to solving refugee congestion at their borders. As refugees, we had one positive impact by staying in Beirut in that we were all going to spend our life savings in their territory, which was a good enough reason that could contribute in boosting their economy. In relation to their action at the border in letting people in without checking every one's passports at times, this was to ease up the traffic travelling on their borders from Syria into Lebanon and knowing that all were fleeing Iraq and escaping Saddam and the Baath regime. By opening their borders willingly, and at random, the Lebanese government's action created some hope and encouragement for all of us to endure.

July 5, 1973. I remember this day very well. It was a Thursday, early in the morning. Two young men who were brothers were living in the same hotel with us and who had left both of their parents in Iraq fled the country with us on the same bus at the same time. Somehow, they decided that morning not to stay behind in Syria at this hotel for too long due to their fear that Syrian secret services may spot them as fugitives from Iraqi armed forces where this could lead to their capture and handing them over to Iraqi authorities. These two young men had informed all of us that they were going to pay a visit to the border, and they would be back to inform us if the coast is clear and it would be okay to travel to reach Lebanon that day. They were both very brave individuals who cared to help out. These brothers, named Kirk and Harry, were from a very good family in terms of their values, and they would give their shirts to you if you needed them. We had seen them doing so along the entire journey since the bus had left Iraq, and they must have had some type of permission papers that did the trick for them to cross the borders along with all of us on the same bus into Syria a few days ago. We and all the other families had decided to pack everything up that day and wait for these two brothers to come back with positive news. There were no emails and cell phones around those days to get things moving fast and effectively.

The border was not too far, and it was about a one and a half or two-hour drive one way from where were all staying. The two brothers left early so they could have enough time to come back and direct us to follow them with taxicabs perhaps to this new destination, which was the Lebanese border. It was almost noon time when we heard that the two brothers had just gotten back and told us it was clear to go ahead and check out from the hotel. We all rushed to the front desk to check out and follow them to the border because they said they witnessed that most of the families were crossing the border without too much trouble, and all had done it legally through the Lebanese border checkpoints. This border checkpoint area was called El Massnaa, which was set between the western border of Syria and the eastern border of Lebanon. This was very exciting for all of us to hear, and we did what we had to do by getting a taxicab large enough for six members of our family. The two brothers got in a cab with another family and sat in the front seats of the taxicab. We were behind them in another taxicab, and Aamo's family was following behind us. A total of five taxicabs in all were following each other. After a long two and half hours of slow driven cabs, we had reached the border. We were all drained from energy due to the hot humid weather. Throughout the trip the cab driver didn't use any air conditioning for the last two and half hours of traveling. The scenery was very exciting. The mountains were green and full of pine trees which had re- energized us to move on. When we reached the border, all five taxicabs were stopped including the cab the two brothers were in when the Lebanese border soldiers began the passport search. Well, so much for the coast being clear as we were informed by our two scouts. Meaning passing the border was not going to be a free passage at this time. Some of the other families were passing through without any problems, and some were getting rejected and on temporary hold. The rejected families ended up taking taxicabs back to Damascus, Syria to find hotel rooms again. This had created a big anxiety amongst us all and the fear of rejection as Iraqi citizens once more. Now the time had come for our taxicab to pull forward to the checkpoint. All the guards were in their military uniforms with machine guns and pistols in their side holsters. Also, a few Lebanese military armored tanks and trucks were parked on one side of the road next to a building that was totally constructed by stone material, which was serving as border offices and possibly a border jail or prison quarters.

Our taxicab driver pulled forward as he was directed by the soldiers and lowered his window and spoke to them in Arabic. The cab driver tried to help us but the guard told him to step out and leave him alone to investigate the passengers in his cab, which was all of us in our family. By then, I was used to this kind of pain. I didn't care about anything anymore, and I was ready to die if needed, so to speak, in order to save my family's situation. But the circumstances were different. The guard started to check my mother's, my grandmother's and my brothers' passports, and when he was done checking, he said they were okay. I had a smile on my face. I knew that the passports for four of our family members were checked, okayed and stamped with visas to enter Lebanon. The time had come to check both my dad's and my passports. The guard pointed with his finger to me and to my dad and said with a loud tone of voice like he was dealing with cattle, "Hey, both of you step out of the car." Fear overtook us again. I saw it on my dad's face. Then both of us stepped out of the taxicab, and we were taken to the border office inside the stone building where all the armored tanks and the army trucks were parked outside as I had mentioned earlier. We were both told we couldn't enter their country, Lebanon, for not having the word "Lebanon" stamped in our passports by the Iraqi passport agency as an authorized destination to visit. My dad tried to explain to the officers as I was listening and following his tone of voice, which had just started to fade out. The guard yelled at us to go back and say goodbye to the rest of the family, if it was our wish for them to continue entering Lebanon, or we could all go back to Syria, he said. There was not much time to react or have a choice in the matter. It felt like I was getting drowned in the ocean, but I had a few more breaths to take yet. My chest was getting smaller and smaller. I felt like dying, but I kept it to myself, so my mom wouldn't see the pain on my face.

We walked back to the taxi driver and told my mom the bad news. My mom broke down in tears, and I could see the fear on her face. She said, "I can't believe this! Both of you, the two men in my family, are going to be staying behind and away from me."

By now, my dad started to collect himself and assured her that it was only on a temporary basis. We knew we had to change our way of thinking and dealing with situations like this. Our new challenges had just begun. My father, Mike, tried to comfort his family and encourage them to move on. Our situation reflected that we couldn't legally enter Lebanon, but my dad also knew there were other methods to follow to overcome this unwanted ordeal, some methods which he didn't have faith in, nor would he approve of. My dad told my mom to go ahead and continue the journey into Lebanon without both of us for the time being. He told the driver to take his family to Beirut and to a hotel called "Lux" where all the Iraqi Armenian refugees were residing at their first entry until they find housing and possibly jobs. My dad and I opened our suitcases and took some of our clothes, two blankets, and one shirt for each. Then my dad took some money out of his travel checkbook and handed the rest of the money to my mom and told the taxi driver to go. The separation was hard. All of us were crying as I looked at the back of the taxi-cab as it drove away. Our family suffered a great deal leaving Iraq and reaching Syria where we managed to pull our lives together with all its challenges in a tiny hotel room because we cared about each other. Now we were getting separated from each other once more; into what fate, I just don't know. It was very tough on both of us to encounter this. The sadness once again started to enter my heart. My mind went back again to the time when they took my dad away to prison. Although this was a different kind of fear and anger; nevertheless, it would leave a scar in my heart. When my dad was taken away from our home, there was some control that I had over the situation. I helped others in my family, so I could forget the pain and the confusion. Now the separation from my family was much harder.

We were both going to sleep at the border tonight for sure, and there was no two ways about it. We found a place to sleep. It was inside a storage room, which was attached to and belonged to the border grocery market, which was located across from the border passport offices. In other words, both buildings were facing each other with a main road passing through them. This store was selling food and goods on the border. We quickly learned to pay a fee to the market owner in order to reserve a sleeping spot for both of us inside the storage room rather than sleeping hopelessly in the cold on the front porch of this market. We had to ask the owner's permission before others could get these spots. It was impossible to bare the cold weather at nightfall outdoors.

I know, you're puzzled now and asking, "Cold nights in July?" The answer is yes, cold nights in July. The Lebanese border was on high elevation in this area, and it was very cold during the nights. Well, it was for us anyway. If you didn't seek shelter for yourself, you would be frozen until the morning when the sun comes up. This obstacle was solved. But this situation was completely different than my father's imprisonment. I had no control over what would happen next, or what we were waiting for, or how we were going to solve it. The border soldiers and officers made up their minds not to let us into their country. What was next for both of us, and when? Just in case you're wondering what the heck happened to the two brave brothers, Kirk and Harry, well they had just gotten to cross the border in time ahead of us when the border barrier was open, and the cabs moved freely. Suddenly, the barrier was closed once more and without any advance notice from the Lebanese. This provided them with better control over their security measures. I was told this much later.

CHAPTER

6

The Lebanese Border, and the Betrayal

The next thing my dad said was, "Let's go, son, and sit down on the front porch of the market to wait and hope for the best."

I carried the two blankets which were full of clothing, which I had used like a duffle bag, and they were on my right shoulder. I followed my dad to the porch. Hours and hours went by, and hundreds and hundreds of people went in and out of Lebanon into Syria and vice versa. I started talking to myself and to God at the same time and asked why I couldn't be like one of these border-crossing citizens. Why was the Iraqi regime's curse or bad luck still following us? When were we going to be considered free human beings and live life like other nations? My mind was flooded with anger and confusion. Then, soon enough, the night started to fall and the weather started to change into a cooler mode. You could see the beautiful moon starting to take over the sky with a very wide smile; it was very shiny and bright. A few clouds with some winds started to blow its draft through the porch. It was summer, but the border area was on a higher elevation than the rest of the city. The mountain cold breeze started to settle in. I had to open my blanket in order to take out warm clothing and to put it on. Being cold was one thing, but I was also hungry at the same time. I asked my dad if he was hungry too, and if we should eat before the market closes. He said it was a good idea, and we went in and got some sandwiches for both of us, and plenty of bottles of water. It was enough to get us by through the night. We also got some Lebanese alcohol called arak. It's a colorless liquid just like water or vodka made from grapes and has some additives and anise seeds for flavoring. My dad looked at the bottle to see what the level of the alcohol content was. It was 100 proof. Meaning 50 percent of it was real alcohol as he had explained to me. We had no first aid kit or any medicine with us and the alcohol was to help solve some emergencies like tooth pain, stomach pain, cuts, wounds, etc.

We hid the bottle inside our clothes so whoever was going to sleep inside the storage room besides us wouldn't steal it away at night. We were like the homeless in a shelter. The storage room was big, and with concrete slab flooring. In order to get in, you had to step down from the market porch into the storage room using concrete steps going down. The very first thing you faced was the dirty and smelly bathrooms. Also, this storage had no windows whatsoever. The original idea was to keep the mountain wild life outside of it, but in order to sleep inside, we needed to have air circulation to breath. What my dad and I had to do was to sleep right next to the bathroom on the cold concrete floor where we had to place some cardboards underneath us just like two homeless people would do in any city street at nights. In reality, we were two homeless people at that moment, no less. Then both of us hugged each other and wrapped ourselves with one blanket to keep the air tight around us so we didn't have to lose much body heat at night. The room didn't have any heater, but we had to manage. The storage room was full of canned foods, bags of potatoes and onions. In order to breathe, we had to leave the storage room door open with a tiny opening while we piled some boxes full of canned foods behind the door. We used the boxes of canned foods as substitution for weight as a door stop at night so no one could open the door while we were sleeping, or to block it from any mountain lion from entering. The tiny three-inch door opening was enough to enjoy the breeze from the outside and have some circulation going inside the room. The other concern we had was the Lebanese mountain rats. The rats were brown in color, fat, and eight inches in length. They could enter through the three-inch opening, but at that point you couldn't win them all. We had to take our chances to survive. We would rather have seen a rat than a mountain lion entering. The latter is not manageable because we were both defenseless. We managed to sleep inside the storage room for the first night as I mentioned, and without much hassle. It was okay and not too bad.

The next morning was July 6, 1973. We got up and went to the market to have something to eat. We used the market phone by paying, of course, because nothing is free to call Hotel Lux where the rest of our family was residing at the time. My dad managed to talk to my mom and tell her that we were okay so far. My mom said that she heard from some of the refugees who had experienced a similar situation like us where they had to sleep on the border for a few days as well due to lack of the Lebanese entry visa being stamped inside their passports by the Iraqi authorities. She told him that in order for both of us to enter Lebanon, we had to visit and consult with a Christian Assyrian priest to resolve the matter. The priest knew some officers with high ranking authority in Beirut where they could help us get into Beirut. In other words, she told my dad, she had to bribe the authorities, so they could release both of us to cross the border to reach Beirut. My dad was not too sure of this. He said to my mom, "Let's wait a few more days and find some other ways to solve this problem." He didn't like to hear about illegal bribes and deals. He never did such a thing in his entire life, and he was not too comfortable with the idea. Then my mother added by reminding my dad about his friend who, at one point in the past, my dad trusted so he could smuggle me outside Iraq while we were living there. My mom told my dad that his so-called trustworthy friend informed my mother that he was going to come and visit us on the border and keep us company. My dad's friend had lived in Beirut for years and he knew an alternative way where he could help us to get into Beirut. What I had seen this man doing was mostly done illegally and not through honesty. My dad said he would like to hear what his friend wanted to tell him first, and then advised my mom by saying, "You can't discuss things in this fashion over the phone, so please be careful" due to his fears and remembering our landline phone back home where the Baath regime had bugged it for a period of time after he had left the prison.

After hearing all the updated news from my mom, I was somewhat relieved knowing that the rest of my family was okay. I missed my brothers, their jokes and our playing time. I knew there was some hope for us as we were not going to stay on the border forever and die here.

Time was passing by very slowly, and I noticed a lot of Iraqi Christians were entering Lebanon. Most of them were getting stopped for passport and visa validity and observations. Some of them were coming to the store to buy food for the road. Then all of them were asking, why both of us were stuck here? Our answer was always honest and simple by saying, "In our passports, we don't have permission as male Iraqi citizens to enter Lebanon." In order for the people that I had encountered to enter Lebanon, there was some simple paperwork to be filed. Some of the Christian Armenians and other Christian families who were asking us about our situation couldn't read and write in Arabic. They asked me to help them with their visa applications, and, as usual, I offered to help them by filling out their paperwork in Arabic at no cost. They could submit their paperwork to the Lebanese border's immigration office and get their entry visas. I was not wise, or business minded at the time. I could have made a lot of money by doing this process. Some offered me money, but I didn't want any money from them as they were refugees like us. I was doing it because it was my nature to endlessly help anyone that asked and needed help. After all, their situation was not any better than ours. We all had to leave behind everything we owned in Baghdad and leave the country empty handed.

On the afternoon of July 6, 1973 around four o'clock, we noticed a taxicab had stopped at the front porch of the market on the border, and my dad's friend came out of the cab and walked toward us. I never liked this man before, and I wasn't about to like him now. He started to talk to my dad about how he knew of a way to get us to enter Lebanon. My dad trusted his so-called friend very much once again. He was the same individual who previously tried to smuggle me out of Iraq, and we ended up rejecting his risky plan. And now he was planning for us once more. His plan was for that same night around midnight when the border guards would be changing their shifts and positions, there would be new guards coming to work during the night shift. The guard changing process was going to take fifteen minutes. And before they did their routine check or count for who was staying at the border and who was in jail, etc. and while their attention was shifted, my dad and I were to take advantage of this situation and escape. My dad's friend was going to come to our location and have us follow him and walk on a dark road leading towards the first Lebanese village inside Lebanon. He knew a safe house where we could spend the night and then he was going to go away and come back in the early morning to pick us up and drive us into Beirut illegally, so we could register with the World Council of Churches office as refugees, which was our objective to begin with. They were to protect us from being expelled out of Lebanon until our case was settled to reside elsewhere around the world permanently. He said he had done this before for others, and he told my dad not to worry much.

There was a big pause from me. How in the world did my father not listen to my mom's advice about the bribe deal yesterday, and now we were going to walk into fire, so to speak. Then my dad asked my opinion about his friend's plan. I got up and walked away. I didn't want to hear anymore. I never trusted his friend at all, and my heart was telling me something bad was going to happen. Then my dad came to talk to me and said, "Son, I believe we have no choice. We have to take his plan." I replied, "What about what mom said? She never lies, and she must have known something when she told us about the Christian priest in Beirut. Dad let's pay some money and go with the plan she explained to you over the phone. After all, there is proof because some of the people who had paid their share are already inside the city of Beirut and inside the very same hotel where the rest of our family is staying." I said to him, "I never trusted your friend because he was selfish and had nothing to lose. He lived in Beirut illegally for five years in the shipyards according to what he told me before. Why did the Iraqi regime not put him in prison with all of you? Wasn't he also a part of the very same organization? Why were you and your other friends captured and tortured for it? How come he was free at that time?" Well, my father was not about to put his friend's idea away easily. After all, he was my old man, and an authority over me. He decided to go with his friend's plan. His friend disappeared for a good several hours, and we didn't ask him where he was going or where he was going to stay. Then around 11:55 p.m. he showed up again. My dad and I were ready and waiting to execute his plan. Somehow that night, the winds started to get stronger and got colder than the nights before. I wore several wool sweaters and doubled up on wearing my socks. At exactly 12:05 a.m., we started walking to escape from the Lebanese border toward the safe house, and, for a moment, it felt good that we were walking on the road in the dark trying to improve our situation. But the fear of wrongdoing never left my mind. After a good three-hour walk, we reached the safe house in the middle of nowhere, but it was a long distance from the border, which his friend called Eshtorra. Then my dad's friend directed us inside this safe house and spoke with a man called Abu Sherbel (to the best of my recollection after 43 years). Abu Sherbel talked to us in his native Arabic dialect and directed us to a room inside this house. The walls were all made from mud and bricks. There were two wooden beds, which were all possibly handmade from tree branches and were not much, but it would do for the night. The safe house was full of odors, but it was warmer than the storage room and the concrete floors where we slept last night. Both of us were very exhausted from walking. Then my dad's friend and Abu Sherbel left us alone to sleep in the dark where no lights were allowed in order to conceal ourselves inside this dump. We went to bed, so we could wake up early around 6:00 a.m. His friend was to come back and take us with him through another route through the back side of Lebanon's mountainous roads and head toward the capitol city of Beirut by cab, of course, and not on foot as was his plan. We went to bed around almost 3:00 a.m. We had to sleep three hours before we would be up again and run away illegally.

Right away, I fell asleep and was into my dreams already but, unfortunately, I was woken up by this big bang on the door a short time later, which I thought was the wind banging on the door. My eyes were shut, but my ears were somewhat listening. I didn't know if it was a dream or reality. I fell asleep again, but suddenly I felt a big pain; a big kick into my stomach. It was the wooden end of a soldier's rifle. He had hit me in my sleep, so I could wake up. I woke up with a big pain and panic in the dark, and then I started to shout, "Dad, dad? Where are you? What happened?" There was no sign of my dad. Then the small flash-light beam started to make me realize this is not a dream, and the light was directed at my face by the Lebanese soldiers. They held my arms towards my back and led me towards the outside of the safe house. I saw my dad's hands also cuffed. Their armored tank was waiting outside the safe house. They had my dad sit in the front of the armored tank and right on top of the cold metal body of this armored tank and about several inches away from the machine gun nozzle. We were both getting arrested by the Lebanese border patrol at this point. They made me ride in the front next to my dad on the opposite side of the machine gun nozzle, which was the only thing that was separating us. They drove us back to the border. The cold was like a sharp knife cutting through our chilled chests and leg bones, and our confused brains were shaken from waking up by their hostility. It's very hard to explain, and I don't wish my closest enemy to experience this kind of abuse. But we both deserved it because we had entered Lebanon illegally. I looked back while the armored tank was moving forward, and there was no sign of either one of the men at the safe house where we were staying. This seemed to me that it was a setup. We were supposed to be watched throughout the night by the owner of the safe house, and we were to be warned if such a thing was to happen, but he failed to do so. My dad failed in making a right decision again. I warned him about such a possibility, and all these thoughts were making my frozen brain stay alert and to think fast, but the unforgiving cold was a horrible thing to accept. We didn't have anything with us like food or drink or any alcohol as a savior anymore. They were all left behind in the safe house along with our clothes. We didn't know what our fate was going to be next. I started to cry and pray knowing this was the end for both of us. Lebanon was not a western country where laws and rules were practiced based on democratic values. An individual's fate was decided by the military officer who would be judging and possibly punishing us. We were basically at the immigration officer's mercy, hoping they would understand and forgive us; and that's only if he was feeling okay. If not, then God knows. Maybe we would be jailed here forever or be sent back to the Iraqi border.

The Lebanese border patrol took us back to the border immigration office by riding on their armored tank. They removed the almost half-frozen handcuffs from our hands. As we entered inside the immigration office, it took me at least fifteen minutes to gain my strength so I could talk. We were shouted and cussed at by the night immigration officer who was in charge. I told him it was not our fault. Then when I started to say the words "My dad's friend…," my father turned around and was just about to slap me, but he didn't, so I stopped from saying anything anymore. The officer asked my father why he did such a thing knowing that he was not allowed in their country legally. My father replied by saying he was worried that we were going to die by staying at the border forever, and he would never have a chance to see his wife and his other children again. The officer didn't buy that, and he kept shouting at us. After a half hour of harsh questioning and interrogation, we were left in his office unattended for another fifteen minutes. Then he came back and said that if we were ever caught doing such a thing again, he was going to ship us directly to the Iraqi and Syrian border instead. We tried to ask for forgiveness, but with no use. As my dad was answering a few more questions asked by the officer, the officer got angrier and raised his hand to slap my dad on his face, but then suddenly something happened within him. I don't know what, but maybe it was my prayers. The officer backed down from slapping my father. He pulled his hand down in a hurry and in such a manner as if someone invisible had pulled his arm down. Then he looked at his arm briefly, shook his head and shouted again in our faces saying, "Both of you get the hell out of my office now and back to the porch of the market!"

Time passed, and it was already in the early morning hours before sunrise. We ran in a hurry to leave the office and go across the street toward the market storage room in order to get some sleep, but, unfortunately, the storage room was taken over by three other men by that time. We knocked on the door, and they were kind enough to let us in. We went in and found two blankets that were left on the floor, and they were smelly. We wrapped our- selves with these blankets because it was very cold, and we had no other choice. We tried to sleep while sitting on the concrete floor in the storage room by resting our backs against the bathroom walls. Suddenly, we noticed water started to overflow out of the toilets and onto the concrete floors. Regardless of how tired and sleepy we were, we had to pull a wooden crate quickly from the corner of the storage room and put it under us to avoid the leakage of the toilet bowl water from getting onto our clothes. Our situation was horrible. Before we knew it, the sun was up, and everyone was going out of the storage room. The day had started as usual at the market store on the border. We went out of the storage room like zombies because our bodies were weak from lack of sleep and shock. We went outside and sat on the porch in the sun. Oh boy, that felt good! The heat from the sun was so nice I felt as if I was sitting inside a hot tub. I couldn't help it. I quickly fell asleep and didn't care what was happening around me. I woke up that afternoon hungry. My dad told me he had already made a phone call and had spoken with mom regarding the bribery plan as she had explained to him yesterday. I was happy for once that his brain started to work in the right direction. Even though bribery was not what we should encourage in life, but it was safe and was done quietly where we didn't have to know how or what they did with the bribe money. All what we cared about that day was to be with our family again. The experience of the previous night was a wakeup call for me telling me that I could no longer depend on my father's decisions and that he can't make correct judgments anymore, which was obvious. It was possible that the torture he had received and faced in the Iraqi prison had changed him mentally somewhat, especially since there was no psychiatric help that he should have received after he left the prison. He may have been facing some type of trauma and wanted to be a hero by always taking control of everything. He had very poor judgment most of the time, so I decided if we reach our destination, which was Beirut, from then on, I would find a job, and I would make my own decisions without endangering anyone in the family. His so-called untrustworthy friend was nowhere to be found to guide us or help us anymore. I knew this was going to happen. I saw it in my heart before it took place, and I believe God was talking to me somehow, but I didn't know where all these feelings and warning signs were coming from at the time.

We stayed three full days on the Lebanese border. On July 7, 1973, around 11:00 a.m., one of the immigration officers alerted us by calling both of our names with his paging system from across the street. At first, we were worried if this was for punishment or for good news. We couldn't afford not to respond to his call. After all, they were the ones who were controlling the border. My dad and I went to the building across the street. The officer yelled for us to hurry and to give him our passports. I replied that our passports were in their pos-session. Then with a very low voice, and because our hearts were full of fear, my dad asked him, "What are you going to do with us?"

He smiled and said, "Both of you are going to Beirut. I'm giving you a visitor's visa to enter Lebanon."

Well, thank you, Lord, and thank you Mom for a job well done! Money can move mountains, especially in this region of the world. Bribery was a daily life in the 1970's while we were in Lebanon due to a lot of refugees and visitors in the same region. I was looking at the officer's face, the very same one who almost put us in jail and was going to ship us back. Now, it must have been that his bank account was getting fat. We didn't know, and we didn't care because we came to Lebanon after we had sold all our belongings back home only for one reason and that was to continue our journey going to the westernized countries like America. It took this officer exactly ten minutes to stamp our passports. Then he offered his help, if we should need a taxicab. Wow! How much money did my mom have to pay so we could be treated nicely like kings? My dad replied to the officer with a great deal of confidence this time and said, "Yes, it would be good if you could arrange a taxicab for us." We also told the officer that we didn't have any money left with us, and that we would pay the taxi driver when we get to our destination. He told us it would be no problem, and that he would arrange that as well. I knew one thing for a fact in life, and I learned this from my uncle, Sofina's husband, in the past, and that was when I visited Lebanon with them as a tourist on one of the summer vacations. It's a fact that Lebanon's economy was based on tourism, and the people were not like Iraqi people. Their society classes were an obvious thing; the poor were very poor, and the rich were very rich. There was no middle class, and everyone knew everyone. They were accustomed to using their hospitality and helping tourists to go around and taking advantage of them by making commissions behind their backs. I'm not referring to the whole Lebanese population, but referring to my unpleasant experiences. I also witnessed that there were a lot of good people inside the Lebanese society, just like us Iraqis, who help others without any financial gains. Acknowledging this, the question that comes to one's mind is this. Why would a rotten officer like the one we were dealing with on the border do us a favor at the last minute? He must have some sort of profit from it all, especially since he was controlling the border traffic. It was a fact that he was a Lebanese soldier. But was he abusing the power which was given to him? Like they say money talks and bullshit walks. I learned this at an early age from my uncle's wine business, and, as matter of fact, he told me that every deal you make in life or for any good you do to people, you should be awarded for it. And, he told me that in his business world it was called a commission. I disagreed with him, and I told him that I'm one of those people who can't use others for my own profit or gain. If anyone needed my help, I would give the shirt off my back to them because life for me is not just about money only, at least I was not built and raised that way in Iraq by my parents. My uncle looked at me and smiled, and said, "You will do well in life, but you will never be wealthy if you think this way." In fact, I hate the word commission to this very day in my life. By remembering this incident from the past, it just made me cautious when the border officer said he would take care of the taxicab for us with a smile.

Anyhow, he gave us our passports back, and, to our surprise, another solider handed us our belongings, which were left behind in the safe house on the night they picked us up. We went quickly to pick up our blankets and our dirty clothing. We left the Immigration building and walked across the street to find a place to change and wash up. We managed to change our underwear and socks inside the storage room, and we only rinsed and wiped ourselves with a wash cloth and cold water by using the faucet that was behind the market building because there was no place to take a shower. All these discomforts didn't matter to me or to my dad. Our focus was that in a few hours, with God's help, both of us would be at Hotel Lux in Beirut and joined with the rest of our family members, and then we could really rest and take our showers.

As we were waiting, a taxicab arrived and dropped off people on the border who were going to take another cab and travel to Syria. The driver had parked his car next to the market porch where we were sitting to purchase food for the road and to pick up passengers from the border to go back to Beirut. My father approached him and asked him if he was responding to the border officer's call to pick us up and take us to Beirut as was promised by the border officer for this arrangement. The driver looked at us and said, "No, there was no such arrangement," and he walked into the market. Right away I told my dad that it was ok, and we didn't need the officer's help. Let's ask this driver ourselves and see if he would be able to take us with him and get paid on arrival at the hotel, rather than now. When the driver walked out of the market and as he was putting his stuff in his cab, my father did just that and asked him if he could take us and get paid later at the hotel when we arrive. Could you imagine for a moment how difficult it was for both of us to have no help and money and feel as hopeless as refugees on another country's border? My faith in people had not failed me yet, and I was sure in my heart that he would do this for us. The cab driver took a moment to think. He nodded his head and agreed. Ten minutes later both of us got inside the cab, and we were on our way to Beirut.

As I mentioned, the border was on a higher ground with hillside elevation, and the driver drove down the hill toward an agricultural region. It was all divided in rectangular shapes. Some were green in color from a distance and were full of vegetation, and others were just flat seeded soil and red and tan in color. It was so beautiful. I was already falling in love with Lebanon. We never had such a geographical region back home in Iraq, or at least I hadn't seen it throughout my years growing up. Most of the agricultural regions back in Iraq were in the southern and in the northern part of the country, which was controlled by farmers who were all Muslim Arabs in the southern region, and Muslim Kurds in the north-ern region.

I noticed the taxi driver was passing through a village where in the past I had visited there with Aunt Sofina's family on a summer vacation. I started acting like a tour guide and telling my dad about this village and the region. Then the taxi driver noticed we were speaking Armenian, and he started to talk to us in the same language. He was an Armenian as well. We were happy to hear him, and we let him take over being the tour guide. A short drive later he stopped his car beside a fruit stand on the side of the road. It was the first village we encountered, and it was the village that we had walked to on foot a day ago where we tried to stay at the safe house for that one night. What an experience that was! Both of us didn't want to mention this to the cab driver in order to maintain his trust. The taxi driver purchased some large green and red apples, and some large tomatoes. All these fruits were grown in this valley. He gave us some to eat, and said, "I know you are both hungry. Please have some fruit. We should be in Beirut by the time you finish eating your apples." And then he laughed. We thanked him for his kindness. I had never tasted apples like these before. They were juicy, sweet, and fresh. The driver said, "I know both of you are refugees in my country. We Armenians and Christians do help each other very much in Beirut." He added that 50 percent of the government is Christian, and the other 50 percent is Muslim. But he told us Lebanon was nothing like the country we were coming from, and we would enjoy living there. And there was a lot of work to go around for everyone. He added that his people are generally kind. He also told us the ocean and the mountains were a half hour driving distance from each other, and in the summer, he had a lot of tourists from all over the world come and enjoy the beaches and the Lebanese hospitality. I replied by saying, "I know that." The driver asked how I knew. I told him I had been in Beirut when I was fourteen and fifteen years old, two years in a row around the summertime with my aunt's family for summer vacation. He was happy to hear that. Then before you knew it, there was the city of Beirut, "the Las Vegas of the Middle East," as it was called around those years, lying around the Mediterranean Sea. My dad was amazed at what all he had been seeing and was speech-less, for once.

My family had left Baghdad and headed toward Lebanon on July 1, 1973 (I was at the age of seventeen and a half) to escape Iraq and seek freedom elsewhere in the world.

CHAPTER
7

The Reunion with My Family and Prayers Do Works

My father and I entered Lebanon on the morning of July 7, 1973 and headed toward Hotel Lux located in downtown Beirut. We had just arrived there, and I couldn't wait to see my family. I got out of the taxicab, and I ran up the hotel staircase in a hurry and my dad used the elevator to get to the hotel rooftop recreation area. My whole family was sitting and waiting for us there. I hugged my brothers, my mom, and my grandmother who were all waiting for our arrival that day. They were very happy to see us both. My grandmother hugged me and said, "I knew I would see you again." Then she hugged her only son, my father. After my dad picked up some money from my mom, we rushed down to pay the taxi driver. At my father's surprise the taxi driver charged us half the price what he would usually charge. He said, "Welcome to my home, Beirut, Lebanon." We thanked him profusely, and he went on his way. We got up to the rooftop recreation area again, but this time we both took the elevator; it was much faster. My dad and I rushed to go to our rooms to clean up and take our showers. It was such a relief. We left our rooms to join the refugees who sympathized with us at the hotel. They were very happy to see our arrival and that we were freed. They had been counting the days along with my mom and grandmother and praying for us to be freed soon. Their prayers worked, and prayers do work. Keep that in mind. All you have to do is ask with all your heart.

When we woke up the next morning, it was just like waking up from a bad dream. I was happy to see myself inside a hotel room along with my family. There was no more sleeping on concrete floors, no more bad toilet smells and water leaks in the middle of the night, no more hunger or thirst, and no more army harassments. These were the thoughts on my mind as I woke up in the morning.

Hotel Lux was a walking distance from the beach in the middle of downtown Beirut. After a good, hot breakfast meal, I went down with my friend who I had met in the hotel and who had been residing in the hotel with his family for over two months. I went out with him because he knew his way around the city. He took me to the free and peaceful Mediterranean

Lebanese beach front where all the tourists and the beach houses were located. We walked and walked, and every now and then I had to turn and look back, thinking that we were being followed. The fear of not being free at will all your life was not going to go away just overnight. But I always felt that nothing bad will happen, and with a little bit of courage we can make it and live for the time being among these new people and this new country.

I love both nature and the ocean. I love nature because it comforts my soul, and I love the ocean because it relaxes my mind. I could have a daily dose of both nature and the beach without being bored. When I saw the nature and the beauty of this beach, which we were exploring, I was thoroughly speechless, something told me that all we had gone through was going to fade away, and to go ahead and enjoy it for now. I am very appreciative of the beauty in people, especially the beauty of the women I was encountering around this beach site. The freedom of observing a woman in public was taboo in my country. The society in Iraq back in the 1970's was very closed and conservative under Islamic rule in every way. We couldn't express ourselves openly and freely to talk and discuss anything about women. We couldn't even see the beauty of a woman because most of them were covered by black veils or robes. But I always knew my limits as a young man and respected women in general; no games or fouling around. It didn't matter. I was going to be the same person in Lebanon because even though Lebanon was an open society, it was still an Arab country with the majority of them being of Muslim faith. They practiced the same religion and the same cultural values based on their Islamic rules as a way of life. There was nothing wrong with that. It was only the way I was brought up as a Christian, and it was a totally different observation about life. I felt that walking around the beach was very pleasant except we were not equipped yet with beach gear. We were refugees with long pants, leather shoes, long hair, no hats or sun glasses and long-sleeved shirts resembling nerds. But everyone else was in their shorts and swimming trunks as well as sun glasses and so on. Our looks were like a person who just got out of the jungle compared to the Lebanese or the tourists who were around the beach.

Coming to a new world of European style living was not easy to blend with, and to see all this and not want to be like the locals was difficult to accept. Being young and eighteen at the time, we were confused and whatever we saw, we wanted.

My friend and I got tired of the sun fast, and the ocean was not something he cared for, so he wanted to go back to the hotel. We cut the day short and walked back to the hotel. I couldn't help myself not to turn around and look back at the waves and the people along the way. I told myself one day I will have to get a home for all of us on the beach, and it should happen in the future because America was our final destination, and not Lebanon. I assumed there were many miles to go and obstacles to overcome in life for us, even before we would reach the shores of the United States of America.

My family didn't stay in the Lux hotel for too long. The hotel was an expensive place to stay, and we needed to find work first, so we started to look for a job and then we started to look for an apartment to live in. We met people who were relatives on my mom's sister-in-law's side, and it was their turn to help us get our feet wet to find some work and to guide us to find living quarters. To explain how and where my family had met these people, I must take you back to the year 1967.

I remember watching TV at home in Baghdad at the age of 11 and seeing the Israeli and Palestinian war breaking out. My mom's brother (my older uncle, Armo) was a caterpillar equipment repair supervisor in Jordan. He was working for a British company, and they were building the Jordanian dam. My uncle moved his wife and her brother's family with him to Jordan where he found a new job for his brother-in-law to work at the same company with him, but the 1967 Israeli and Palestinian war had suddenly started while everyone was at work. Both my uncle and his brother-in-law had to flee and run away along with their families. They were jammed into one Land Rover truck that belonged to the British company who employed them. They drove fast and were trying to make it across the Israeli and Jordanian borders into Jordan then continue driving to reach Baghdad, Iraq. They told us they had to drive over all the dead bodies of war casualties which were lying in the streets. They said the Israelis had bombed that region, so they drove day and night non-stop and reached our house in the suburbs of Baghdad in the middle of the night. They had no clothes, no money, and nowhere to go. My parents took all of them into our house to stay with us as long as it took until things were settled at the war site. I mentioned to you previously that I had very caring parents. Our guests had stayed almost two months with us, all six of them, including their children before they received a call from the British company who they were working for stating that the company had special permission from the Israeli government to go into the war zone where their employees' homes were and pick up all their household furniture and belongings in order to ship them back wherever the employee wished to have them. After the phone call, both my uncle and his brother-in-law decided to have my uncle's belongings shipped to Baghdad and his brother-in-law's belongings to Beirut, Lebanon where he resided originally and had lived there before he had taken the job offer at the Jordanian dam project.

I had mentioned here in this chapter in reference to how we helped my uncle and his brother-in-law's family in the past. Now the time had come for his brother-in-law to help us in his own country in terms of finding a job and a new place to live so that we could leave the hotel. We met with my uncle's relatives, and they told my dad they would do everything within their power to help us finding a job and new living quarters. We had to extend our stay another week at the hotel. Then one week later, we were contacted by these relatives who had not stopped looking determinedly to help us find an apartment and jobs. They informed my parents that they found this new place for us, and they asked my parents to go and see the place. It was a new apartment building that was being built in an area called Sid El Boosharia, a half hour ride by taxicab from the hotel where we were staying. The apartments were three bedrooms and two baths in a five-story building and ten units in total. It was designed to be two units per each floor with an elevator in the middle of the building and a rooftop that was going to be used as community space (meaning we all could use the roof space for recreation). After they had explored this place my parents liked it, but it was not cheap to rent in those days. It was a brand-new building. My parents came up with this unique idea. They said that since we were not going to live in Beirut forever, and it was only a matter of months, they decided to share this apartment with another family in order to share the rent and the expenses. Hmm, this was not a bad idea. The decision was made that the first thing to do, and a must, and before even thinking to rent any space, was to go and get registered with the World Council of Churches (WCOC) as refugees. It was possible that we couldn't be qualified and considered for refugee status. Then renting an apartment would be useless. I remember mentioning this in an earlier chapter that the WCOC was a Christian organization, which was affiliated with the United Nations as we were told by their authorities. The WCOC's job was to accept and register Christian refugees fleeing Iraq due to fear for their lives and lack of practicing religious freedom. It would take the WCOC's office in Beirut a good several weeks to work on the paperwork before we could even be accepted by their organization as refugees. After the approval period, and if our applications were accepted, then all of us would be issued a refugee status which would enable us to stay in Beirut for a certain time until we could continue our journey to our destination, which was the United States of America. But not until an official interview was to be conducted by their office to meet with each individual or family member to see if we had a just cause for our fears for not being able to live in our own country, Iraq. At this point, if you really had a just cause, you would be accepted as a refugee, and you would be granted a status after a few weeks. Now if all went well, then the time frame, which was designated to accomplish this task, was to be a maximum of four to six months for each family to travel to America. Our stay in Beirut was going to be only for a half a year at the most, as we had heard and seen from others with experiences, which was showing us that this is a systematic process, and which was designed to send everyone to the United States soon. But the WCOC's office had their own rules to enforce for all refugees.

Rule number one was, once you enter Lebanon and register with their office, you could no longer travel outside this country. You had to stay to finish the process in order to get your immigrant visa. Rule number two was, all personnel should maintain good behavior with the local law enforcement agencies and not get involved with any crime, unlawful activities, or get arrested by the local Lebanese police force. If anyone couldn't follow these simple rules and couldn't obey them, they would face the organization's refusal for granting him/her/ them the status of refugee. Now with that being said, and regardless of all the warnings from the WCOC's committee or the administration office, there were some people who were causing lots of fear and trouble who were living among us. And, if you were not alert and were naïve, you could fall for their fraudulent games. For example, some men among us refugees would meet with you and they would ask you if you could help them with this one problem as humanly as possible. They would ask you "Can you take my son or daughter to stay with you for several days?" because they had an emergency and must go visit their mom or whoever they said they were going to visit. They would make you believe that they don't have any money to take their children with them, and it was an urgent matter for them to visit their relatives who happened to be residing and living in a different part of Lebanon. On the contrary, by doing this kind of favor for those people, you already endangered yourself by breaking the law. Accommodating these people made you believe they were honest, and you should help them. It turned out that these were not their children, and these people were smugglers or human traffickers. They got paid for smuggling these kids in the first place, and they wanted to plant them among a refugee family in a time and moment when we were living our lives with a disrupted routine. We were very vulnerable due to our lifestyle changes. They tried to play with our emotions and out of our pity for these children, we would try to take care of them for a short while. The idea of the smugglers was to leave the children behind with you once you decided to accept and accommodate them prior to your registration with the WCOC's office, unless you had been registered already and had an application filed with their office. Then that would defeat the smuggler's purpose to approach you with such a request. By agreeing with their requests and being uninformed, suddenly you have a few more people inside your household to feed and care for just like your own. But, if you had not filed an application with the WCOC yet and by agreeing with their request, then this unknown new child could be registered with you as part of your own family to immigrate to America. At times, these smugglers paid families some money to do this kind of work and only if they trusted that chosen family who would pursue it. In terms of these children's legal paperwork, the smugglers would usually tell you that the children had lost them in Lebanon. This is what happened on occasion in order to get more people registered to go to America or elsewhere. But it was not that easy for what they were thinking to accomplish, and it was almost impossible because the WCOC's office had a very effective system in place where you could get caught doing so, and if they ever caught you for wrongdoing, your whole family got dropped from their list, and you would never get your status or see America ever. Now, I don't know if this was designed on purpose by the local authorities in cooperation with these kinds of con artist activities so that the local police could make some money from the refugees by arresting them first, then getting people out based on bail money in cash. We knew this type of operation existed, but we knew of none that was accomplished.

Going back to the matter of renting the new apartment that my uncle's brother-in-law had found for us, we couldn't afford to rent it yet. My mom suggested to my dad to rent the three- bedroom, two-bathroom apartment rented and then share the cost with another family living with us for the time being. Ultimately both families could share the rent and other expenses by sharing the space and the shopping cost. My parents had a very good idea about whom we should share our life with in this apartment for a short time. Both my parents went ahead and signed the lease, and when they came back to the hotel that evening, we were told the good news, and we were excited about moving out from the hotel. Since these apartments were still under construction, and because the paint job was not done, the place was not going to be ready for another week. I admired my parents very much for their courage and determination. They always put their children first and were never selfish in thinking or doing, but, at times, they were over protective of us, which stayed with us throughout our lives. I am somewhat doing the same things dealing with my own children today.

On Monday, July 30, 1973, the apartment was ready, but what we needed was furniture. Let's remember that my aunt Sofina's husband was a rich man who owned a winery in the northern part of Iraq, and, as I mentioned it in the past chapters. When they had visited Lebanon in 1971 for the last time on their summer vacation (I remember it because I was with them that year on that vacation), Sofina's husband went and rented a home in the mountains of Lebanon approximately forty-five minutes from the capital city of Beirut in a town called Baabdat. He arrived early in Beirut that summer about a week ahead of his family, so he could arrange a permanent vacation home with a complete set of furniture. This rented property was designed as a furnished vacation home to be used year-after-year. Later on, in 1971 when we got there, the vacation home was nicely set up with furniture enough to cover all the space for three bedrooms, two baths, living room, dining room, a TV set, etc., for his own family's use. Now we needed all this furniture to put them in our newly rented apartment and use them until we depart. My father made a phone call to his brother-in-law's office in Baghdad that year and asked his brother-in-law's (Sofina's husband) permission to use their furniture. We ended up getting them all. Sofina's husband didn't mind one bit, and in this way our problem was solved. Whoever shared the apartment to split the rent with us had a chance to use the same furniture as well. After all, they were refugees like us who had left their homes in Iraq with their suitcases only as belongings.

We didn't want to raise any red flags, and we tried to avoid trouble by keeping a low profile about the furniture. Also, knowing that most refugee families had developed a habit of using their suitcases as pillows and their blankets as mattresses to sleep on at nights, and since they had no kitchenware, etc., having all these items in our apartment was going to be a privilege to anyone who wanted to pay and share the rent for this apartment. They wouldn't miss out on normal life routines by living in full furnished quarters. However, this didn't stop people from envying us throughout the time we lived there, and the rumors got out that we had a lot of money and gold, which we had smuggled out with us and was echoing the idea among refugees, stating that's why we can afford all these items. Boy, I wish we had what people claimed we had; the money and the gold. We would have had a blast and a good life without worrying about work and winning the daily bread. Due to this latter painted picture of us living comfortably at this apartment, it created the belief among others where every-one was saying that my family was here to stay in Beirut, and not to immigrate to America. Luckily, they were wrong, and it was only a rumor.

CHAPTER

8

Christians and Muslims Working in Beirut

Work was a must in order to survive, pay rent, eat, live, etc. There were no worries about health or medical expenses. We took it for granted that no one would get sick. We didn't want to think about going to the doctors or hospitals. These were every refugee's greatest fears, including my family's. We were all raised up hating doctors and hospitals. Most Iraqi doctors that I had encountered back in the sixties, were not so professional and I state this in general terms about most, and not all, doctors and hospitals with their treatments. The Iraqi regime, or the system, was a socialist one, and you could receive medical services for free, but it was zero to none. Any person who had the skill for injecting a needle in your arm was respected by the society very much due to ignorance, and people used to call them doctors as well.

As far as getting an education, I wanted to be an electrical engineer. I liked working and designing electricity and electrical systems. Electricity as a subject was a big interest of mine, but our situation had changed by living in Beirut, and all my visions for the engineering field had to take a dive for the time being. I had to look after my family and consider them first before I could consider myself or follow my dreams or my visionary goals. I had to put my ambitions in life on hold. I needed to work and take care of them. There was no time for school and education. My mother's older brother, my older uncle, who left Baghdad a short time after we did, had gotten a job already. He was working at an aluminum factory. This factory was making and producing wall mount grills for air conditioning and heating by using raw aluminum bars and materials. I asked him if he could talk to the factory foreman, and if there was any work for me there to start working alongside of him. One fact we should realize here is that the Lebanese authorities at the Lebanese border had stamped all the refugees' passports with visitor visas. We didn't have the authorization to work. What this means is that none of us were authorized to have work permits no matter how bad our living status was, unless you do it illegally. We were to just stay there as visitors for the next three to six months. Well, I didn't care about the outcome and what could happen to me if I got caught working without a work permit and illegally in order to survive. I noticed the reality that everyone else was bending the law to work and not breaking it. I came to the realization that my family needed me to feed them because I couldn't depend on my father to do this task. He had no skills or education, he was in his late forties and his chances of getting hired were slim because of his demeanor.

Two weeks later I got an answer from my uncle. He said he talked to his boss, Mr. James, regarding my employment, and his boss would like to conduct a panel interview with me along with one of the factory owners, as well as by my uncle's brother-in-law who was also the department supervisor in the factory at that time. I was very happy to hear this at the age of seventeen because I knew his brother-in-law from the past when both his family and my uncle's family fled from Israel through Jordon in 1967 to avoid Israeli and Arab war hardships while working for a British company to get the Jordanian dam built. They all came to Iraq and stayed with us for a few months. I was happy to know that he was going to be our supervisor. Of course, that is if I had the chance to get hired and work at this factory. The factory was owned by two Lebanese Christian partners, and the factory was called Yuma aluminum factory, which was in an area called Dekwaynee.

The next morning, I went to the factory for the interview. I was very early that morning arriving around 7:30 a.m. My interview was done in five minutes by my uncle's boss along with one of the owners of the factory. They looked at me like they were staring at a new creature from space. I didn't understand what they were looking at. I was nervous at first and then they asked me if I knew anyone working inside the factory. I said, "Yes, my uncle and his brother-in-law, the supervisor. They said okay. I was puzzled at first and nervous again. This job was going to be my very first paying job in my life. The boss and the factory owner didn't mind me being an illegal alien and with no work permit. They wanted to help Iraqi refugees by giving them jobs for sake of surviving. They told me they would pay me eight liras (Lebanese currency was called lira and each lira was equal to thirty to forty American cents back in 1973), and 8 liras was my daily pay rate equal to two and a half American dollars per day. I didn't care about the rate much, and, to be honest, it was better than nothing because I didn't have any experience knowing what the labor rates in Lebanon were. After all, I didn't have a work permit either, and I couldn't work legally.

Right after the interview, naturally, I said thank you, and then I asked when I could start. They asked me if I wanted to start right then and there. I looked at my clothes first. They were not factory working clothes. And, I was wearing some fine shoes, but I didn't want to lose my chances of working there, so I said, "Yes, I can start now." The very first thing they did was send me to the accounting office and handed me to this heavy-bearded young man who was the bookkeeper. Then they made a copy of my passport, and they told me they would put it in a special file and aside from the rest of the employee files. Well, I don't know what they were implying here, but, again, it was not my business to ask. I just wanted the job. My name got registered in their cash ledger books and not in their regular payroll books. I knew this as I was listening to their conversation among the finance people while I was waiting inside the accounting office. I also learned the reasons why they wanted a copy of my passport. I learned this later when I asked the other illegals who had been working in this factory already, and they told me that the reason was if something goes wrong and if I steal any tools or materials, the employer could give your name to the authorities regardless if they were violating labor laws at the time. The factory owners were very powerful men, and you would fear them when they walked around the work place at times. They already had their cash money set to bypass the system. Well, again, to be honest, it was not my concern to worry about it. They hired me to work for them, and it was their problem to worry about it as long as I was doing my job and getting paid for it.

One must be smart about this entire process, and, also, one must try to avoid any conflicts or troubles throughout. It was not easy to work under all these conditions as a human being, but it was a must for me. After the registration process, I was given a half hour instruction about the factory working conditions and its rules by my boss inside the accounting office. My boss told me to follow him back to the factory floor, and I was guided where to go from there on. At first, I was given a broom and a bucket to go and clean the floors around all the punch press machines, which were huge and very noisy equipment. A few days of observations and doing this task made me learn how these machines operated. The heavy machine arm was weighing an approximate weight of more than a ton, which was getting lifted and dropped down in a certain rhythm, and you could see the ground around the machines shaking like in an earthquake. The shake was occurring every ten seconds throughout the whole eight-hour day shift, which could be calculated at the rate of six times per minute and 360 times per hour. My job was to clean all metal particles and metal materials disposed from around these monster machines. Every time a cut was made on the sheet metals there were some big sparks of fire that were flying out of these machines. The sparks of fire were hot, and I was to clean around these machines without getting hurt or burned. Well, I didn't know any better, because I was a bit green behind the ears, so to speak, working as labor in an industrial factory environment, but I learned fast how to clean around these machines and without getting hurt. I started to spray some water first on the floors so that it didn't create much dust, and then I swept the floors. But there was one thing I didn't know, which was that the equipment's electrical powers were supplied through the ground level. Then a nice fellow and a co-worker who was operating one of these big punch press machines stopped his machine from running when he saw me working around it and warned me from spreading any water on the floors before sweeping. I asked him why at first, and then I explained to him the reason for me doing it in that fashion, which was to avoid getting the floor dust in the air. He replied, "Well, you'll be causing damage and harm to yourself by spreading water on the floors. Then he added that a year ago someone was hurt due to a big electrical shock because he was spraying water on the ground just like me, and the water had gotten inside the electrical boxes on the ground while that employee was standing in the middle of a puddle of water and he got electrocuted very badly. Then he added more by saying, "Don't you see the wooden crates where all machine operators are standing on them?" I said, "Yes." He said, "This has been our only insulation from the wet floors." Wow! I told this man that my instructions were to do just that, and I was to spray water on the ground before and after sweeping. After a few moments while he thought to himself, he smiled and said, "Listen, I tried to warn you. They don't care if you die or live. "Remember," he said, "you are wearing shoes with leather soles, you are not isolated from the ground like us and electricity could get you too, because electricity and water is not a good mix. You decide what you want to do, kid." Hum, these new instructions and word of caution from this co-worker had opened my eyes to work smart and not just hard. He left me alone and went back and turned his machine on to continue working. This must have taken him two to three minutes at the most to tell me all this, and before I had the chance to ask him who didn't care if I live or die, the floor foreman saw all this happening, and he came walking toward me. He started to push his weight around as any boss would do. Then he said, "When we work, we don't have to stop and talk to others. Do you understand? Just do your damn work." With my head half-way bowed down I said, "Yes, sir. It will not happen again." I continued to do what I was doing, but I remembered the machine operator's advice. He said no water to be sprayed on the ground, so this time I stopped throwing water on the ground.

My first day at work was going fast. I was very hungry, but I didn't have any money in my pocket to buy food that day. The lunch siren went off and was very loud, and I went off guard and jumped from the noise. Everyone around me laughed because they were used to it. It was my first time encountering such a sudden and loud noise. I saw my uncle and his brother-in-law both coming down the stairs from the third floor they were happy that I got hired, and they both treated me for lunch. Oh boy, that was a life saver! At lunchtime they asked me what I was doing downstairs with clean clothes, and have I been hired yet?

I asked, "You don't know?"

They both answered me with a no. I explained what happened, and then my uncle's brother-in-law, our supervisor, got upset. He asked me who gave me the broom and the bucket. Well, I told him the bookkeeper, and right away after the lunch break both the supervisor and his boss went to the Accounting office. All I could see and hear was a loud and angry argument and body pushing in the Accounting office between the bookkeeper and my uncle's brother-in-law, the supervisor. At first, I was scared to lose my job because I didn't know what was going on and why. Earlier that day I was asked by Mr. James, the main boss, to go see him after lunch. I went to his office, which was in one of the corners of the factory. A noticeable fear had covered my face, and I met the boss again that day. He said, "Listen, I'm going to send you home today." Here was where I got angry due to my fear of possibly getting fired even before starting a full day's work on my first day at the factory. I had to cut my boss's conversation off to defend myself by telling him, "Mr. James, I didn't do anything wrong." My boss understood the pressure that I was under, and he calmed me down. He said, "Listen, son, you're not going to lose your job as long as I'm the boss. You have my promise. But there are some local issues within the factory and maybe this will be new to you to understand them. What I'm going to tell you is that here in Lebanon we have divisions in our society and as a result of that, Muslim fanatics and Christians or Armenians don't mix together. That's all I can tell you for now. From now on if anyone asks you to do anything, you run it by me first. Is that clear?"

I said, "Yes" knowing I still have my job. He said, "Go home and tomorrow wear some work clothes, and when you get here in the morning, stop by my office before you start work and don't worry about a thing."

Well, I thanked him very much, and then I left to go home. I didn't have any money on me, so I had to walk all the way home as I did earlier that morning coming to the factory for the interview. It took me one hour in that hot and humid summer heat to get home. As I walked into our apartment, my family panicked at my look. All my clothes were covered and stained, my nose was black, and my hands were all black from sweeping the black metal dust off the factory floors. They asked me what happened, and I had to explain, "Well, I have to clean up first, and then I can tell you." I explained to them later that afternoon about most of what had happened in the factory that day. My dad, being a good father, was never short of advising me in regard to how things should be handled. But the strange thing about it was that he was not even present in the factory to witness or hear what had happened. Through his assumptions, he tried to advise me that I shouldn't answer anyone back, and I should always listen to authority and obey their instructions. Well, it was all well said, but it had no merit.

I said, "Dad, don't worry. I still have a job, and I'll be working there tomorrow.

That evening I went and visited my uncle who was behind all these good deeds that happened. He was the reason for me being hired and working in the same factory. I asked him, "What happened after I left?" He said, "Mr. James had requested from the owners to fill an open position in the Assembly Department, and after you left, there was a lot of talk among the bosses and the owners because you were supposed to come and work with us in the Assembly Department, and not what the bookkeeper instructed you to do. I asked him to go on. Then he said the argument was that the bookkeeper had requested earlier from the owners to fill this position by hiring his cousin and not another Christian like me for some reason.

My uncle added by saying, "Do you remember back home when all of us were living among our Muslim neighbors?"

I answered, "Yes, I do remember."

"We didn't have any problems of this nature, but there were other kinds of problems to deal with, which was fanaticism toward Islam, compared to the relations between Christians and Muslims living in Iraq versus Lebanon. A civil war was fought because of it in this country, unlike Iraq. Something called hate is taking place here in Lebanon among their society, which is divided as you can see, and each group has their own political parties and views. Some have their own militia, even with arms, and often a civil war breaks out around here for nonsense reasons due to power gains among the minority groups. But mainly for territorial power."

I said, "I don't understand why you're telling me all this." My uncle replied by saying, "It's all connected." I asked, "How?"

He replied, "A week ago, the bookkeeper asked his boss, one of the factory owners, to hire his cousin, but his boss refused to comply with his wishes, so it has nothing to do with you being hired. In order to stay in business, the owners of the factory must hire from the other religious groups so that the government can permit them to have their factory. The owners don't like the bookkeeper, but they had no choice due to a deal they have with this bookkeeper to protect their factory from harm in this area of the city because the bookkeeper knows a militia group and could ask them to help protect the workplace during a civil war outbreak. Additionally, most of the factory money was controlled by the Accounting Department. This bookkeeper is the one who keeps the cash books where we illegals get paid, and he has a hold of some kind on the factory owners. All these things were going on since last week, even before they hired you. You see, there were three job openings since last week, and all the hiring choices went with the owner's wishes. They hired non-Muslim workers to balance the workforce. The bookkeeper was upset when you were hired instead of his cousin, and he tried to get back on the owners by misguiding you to clean the floors instead of directing you to the Assembly Department which upset all the bosses, including the factory owners."

Then my uncle said, "Son, don't worry much. I'm just telling you these things for your own information, and don't let them know you have knowledge of any of this." My uncle had learned all this information from his brother-in-law, the supervisor, because his brother-in-law lived in the same building where Mr. James, his boss resided as well, and they would meet in the evenings at times to put together the next day's work schedule for us, and they would discuss all these matters amongst themselves. I said, "Wow, that's good to know and understand about this situation. Thank you, uncle. I'll see you tomorrow." He said, "Listen, not a word of this to anyone, not even your family. You don't want to worry your dad; otherwise, he will never let you continue to work with us. Son, I know this job is good for you, and you could learn a lot of things and skills until we all go to America with God's will."

Being a refugee, your life is never easy anywhere in the world. You get confused living and breathing life in a country that is not your own. You feel everyone is against you, and you're treated like trash by every stranger around you. The only thing you should worry about is having a place to live, survive and live life daily without getting hurt or killed. As a refugee, you feel the lowest of the lowest among society, and most of the time you feel rejected. It's a true picture of what I am describing here for everyone to know about being an illegal working and surviving in another country, and what I had to go through with back then, 43 years ago.

I'm referring also to countries where refugee situations are created because of war. The only thing that will keep you going is by keeping your self-respect, and something called hope and faith, which works together. It's the only medicine which I found that will cure all troubles of this kind. Faith, not in mankind, but in God, and trust me on this one. I have been there and have experienced it.

I woke up early the next morning. I didn't sleep very well throughout the night because I was thinking about the new job. I got up early at around 6:00 a.m., made some breakfast and sat down to eat. Then I saw my mom going to the kitchen to prepare lunch for me to take to work. She handed me a few liras (Lebanese currency) and said she didn't want me to walk to work. Then she said that she had asked around about taxicab fees and the cost for a soda drink around lunch time. "Here," she said, "take this money. It'll be enough for a few days for you to pay for these expenses until you get paid." I didn't know what to say. I only kissed her on the cheek and said, "Thank you, Mom. I'll see you after work."

I went to the main street leading toward the factory, and I saw my uncle was waiting there as well. We said good morning to each other. My uncle said, "Listen, maybe there won't be much room for both of us in the same cab when these taxicabs get here. I want you to take the very first one that arrives, and then I'll follow."

I asked, "Why not you first, uncle?"

He replied, "Because you're a new employee, and you don't want to be late." I said, "Okay, I'll do that."

I took the first cab which had arrived to go to work, and, luckily, there were three places in the back seat that were unoccupied. We both took the ride together to work that day. He didn't let me pay the fare that morning and took care of it for both of us. I was thoroughly blessed to have an uncle like him. Unfortunately, he never had any kids of his own. Due to some medical problems his wife had, she couldn't have any children. We arrived at work, and my uncle went to the third floor, and I went to see the boss, Mr. James, in his office as I was instructed by him yesterday. He was late, so I waited for him for ten minutes outside his office. He came in and said, "Come on in, kid." For the first hour of the day he trained me and showed me all the raw materials which they were using to make the products. Then he gave me a mini tour of the factory showing me where everything is being made and how. He said, "Now you know where to go if you're short of any material to do your assembly work, or if there is any defective material that you can't use, and you need to replace them. You should know where to go and get them or return them, or who you should interact with or contact." We both went upstairs to the third floor where I was going to start work. It was a big floor and several rooms built on it. My workplace was along and among other groups of people who were mostly Christians, Armenians, Muslims, all mixed and one Jew who had converted to Christianity. We had to sit around a huge rectangular table. They all had one hammer and a pair of pliers in their hands to do the work. The supervisor's desk was inside the room with us as well, and next door to us was another room with three people working in it. They had masks made from fabric material, one that is used to make couches, and was put on their heads. There were no gloves. These three employees were spraying lacquer paint on the surfaces of the final products. In other words, the room next door was a paint booth and all the odors were passing all over and into our assembly room. There was not much we could do about it, and we had to suffer breathing these chemicals every time they sprayed the paint on the final products. The only ventilation we had was a side door leading to the outside rooftop that was always left open , and if you couldn't take the smell of the paint, then you would have to quit the job and possibly starve as a refugee.

The workload of assembled products was not light; just everything you could imagine from cutting, bending, twisting, carrying, etc., which was mostly physically demanding. We all used to take turns carrying the workload several floors up or down daily. I found out we were all illegal workers, and that's why our workload was so much to deal with, which was getting piled on us as a human workforce daily. That's why we were working on the third floor and not the first in order to hide our presence as illegals. The rest of the factory divisions were working regular shifts and with normal workloads unlike our department. Well, at this point, I had to do what I had to do, and that was to work and work hard for peanut pay with lira currency. For the first three months I got used to the workload. Then in the fourth month I noticed that the factory had added a new service to its final assembly line. That service was the chemical treatment process with several different chemicals before the product could go to the final stage, which was a paint job. This process was very dangerous for all of us to handle, and it was not clear as to how we should deal with or work with these chemicals. After two weeks of training by the department's supervisor we learned how we should conduct this chemical process. Then he asked for volunteers to do the job. This was the only logical thing the supervisor could afford to do; that is, to ask for volunteers. It was a smart strategy, so no one would quit. Well volunteering or not, the job was still dangerous, especially since there was no industrial safety commission involved in this, if they ever did exist in those years in the early 1970's in Lebanon. I wouldn't know.

I was very energetic as a young man, and I had very good common sense. I was told that I was the first to start working with these chemicals, followed by my uncle Armo, and then others like some illegal Syrian citizens who were just like us and were being forced to do the job. When we started protesting by asking why Christians are only involved in this process, we were called by the supervisor to go and see the big boss, Mr. James, about our complaints that day; all five of us. The boss said if we don't want to do the job as we were told, then we should quit. The boss was not happy with what he was telling us to do either, but we knew he was put up to it to tell us. That's the way it was, and we didn't have a choice in the matter. No thanks to my uncle Armo's brother-in-law, our supervisor, who was speechless and couldn't do anything for us. After fifteen minutes of meeting behind closed doors, we all said, "Okay, we'll do it, but we need more money to feed our families." The big boss was shocked by our demands because he never expected that we would ask this question. He said he would take our suggestions to the owners first, and he was happy to hear us with our reasons.

The boss used our proposition as a good reasoning tool to face his superiors with and tell them that paying us more money would do it knowing that his superiors could refuse to accommodate him for our demands. A noncompliance by his superiors was going to be a good enough reason for all of us to be off the hook from doing this dangerous process. This was part of Mr. James's plans to try to schedule the chemical work to be done by outside vendors instead. Well to our big surprise the owners agreed to accommodate us with a new raise, but the raise could only be paid on the days where there was chemical process work to be done. In other words, we still didn't get a fair deal, and our boss, James, couldn't succeed to divert this type of work away from the factory in order to minimize the impact on refugees and illegals. James got it right. He was a good man and cared for all of us. Now the raise would be in effect for us only on those days when we were involved working with the chemicals. That meant, for example, my daily pay was 8 liras on a regular basis. On the days that I would be working with chemicals, I was going to get paid 15 liras instead for the entire day. What a bummer! For the extra 7 liras that I was going to get paid, they were buying my blood for that amount. This was also true for the rest of the group who were assigned to do the chemical work.

I want to mention here about these chemicals, their kind, and the way we were supposed to work with it. The chemicals I had to work with were potassium chloride and sulfuric acid. We were given a long gown, a pair of rubber garden gloves, tall hats to wear on our heads. The hats had cutouts on the front for our eyes to see out of. The pair of regular rain rubber boots was not much to brag about, and there were no protective masks or goggles. All these were supposed to keep us from getting harmed, but they never mentioned anything about all the fumes that we were going to inhale. The work aspect of this deal was that the potassium chloride was to be placed in this rectangular shaped pan about ten to twelve inches deep. The pan was put on several burners to dissolve the potassium material, and as it boiled, we were to dip into it the air conditioning grills made of aluminum and the aluminum assemblies. Then the aluminum grills would be dipped inside the pan to get boiled like you would boil a chicken in hot water. This boiling potassium chloride created a great deal of white smoke for several minutes. We had no choice but to hold on tight and breathe the chemicals while standing inside this white cloud. "The most common side effect associated with potassium chloride is gastrointestinal distress. This can include stomach pain, nausea, vomiting, gas and diarrhea. And high dosages of potassium chloride can be lethal. Its symptoms can include muscle fatigue, weakness, abnormal heart beat and an upset stomach." (Baker, 2013)

The fumes alone were enough to plug your nose and cause difficulty in breathing. If you could take all that abuse, then the next step would be to use long hooks to pull out the aluminum grills out of the boiling pan and to place them into a tank full of sulfuric acid.

In order to transfer the aluminum grill from a boiling pan full of potassium, which was hot and dripping all over the floors where its foamy liquid created a very dangerous and slippery floor condition for us to step on, we had to be extremely cautious. It was just like walking on slippery ice with rubber boots. Not to mention as we were dipping the grill into the sulfuric acid tank, it caused some splash which had started to damage and puncture our clothes.

Again, what choice did an illegal refugee worker have but to accept these horrible working conditions? This was the reason we occupied the Lebanese factory's dirty jobs as illegals. Most of the locals didn't want to deal with such work, period. Either way, the locals were coming ahead in this game by refusing to work with such jobs, they stayed much healthier and maintained a safe working environment. Fortunately, this kind of dangerous work didn't happen every day. But every time I was involved with the chemicals, I used to go home in the evenings walking on foot because no taxicab wanted to give me a ride due to the smell of the chemicals that were emanating from my clothes. My hair was all messy and white from the frozen potassium fumes resting on it. I used to get home tired and out of breath. The very first thing for me was to get rid of my dirty clothes and jump in the shower. It took me exactly one hour of showering to get rid of the soapy chemicals out of my hair due to the characteristics of the potassium. When it gets in touch with water, it turns into a soap-like solution no matter how much water you run through your hair to try and get rid of the chemical effects. Your hair will still get stuck together. But I learned to use a different kind of soap for my hair by asking a pharmacist, so I could get rid of all the chemicals faster.

The word got around about these chemicals to the neighbors who were living not too far from the factory. One day we witnessed someone we didn't know or seen him before walking around the area where we were working with these chemicals. He observed the entire process closely. We learned later that he was a part of some sort of local chemical inspection body or group. A week later we received word that we should all be drinking milk immediately after using these chemicals as a protective measure; otherwise, the whole operation would be shut down. I didn't know at the time, or until today, what milk had to do with us and our bodies. Then I saw some big cases of canned powdered milk which had arrived in our assembly department and had gotten stored inside a metal cabinet and locked away. I still remember the brand name; it was called "Nido" made by Nestle Corporation. The powdered milk was for us to use after working with these chemicals, but, some of the cans were being stolen by others to take them home to feed their children. We were left with hardly enough powdered milk to use for all of us on some days. This was another type of abuse we were encountering which was being done by other workers, presumably reminding us that we were not welcomed to work with no permit in their country, and we should go away. This was a demonstration by workers to tell us that no one cared about us, even though we were only ten of us illegals. We were the important work force and part of this factory's productive team. Well, like I mentioned before, we had no choice in the matter but to accept these conditions and the not so humane treatments as well. We were getting paid cash once a week. We all had to work six days a week to make ends meet due to being paid very low wages.

The pay day for all of us was every Saturday. We illegals were lining up in order to get to the Accounting window and be paid. There was a lot of cash money in the cash box of this office as we all could see it from a distance, and it was separated into 1's, 5's, 10's, 25's, etc. (liras) placed in a wooden tray-like box. Every one of us was to present their weekly time card in order to get paid, but if you lost your timecard that week, then good luck in getting paid fully by the cashier clerk. Some of the timecards had a calculation with some small change in the total pay due to the hours that the person had worked that week. But the bookkeeper didn't care to pay the change. He pocketed the change and shorted the worker's pay and paid us in even amounts of liras (Lebanese currency) claiming that there was not enough money to go around. Well, no one dared to say anything, but we all waited in panic to receive our money and weekly pay to feed our families. Just like a bunch of dogs waiting for a piece of bone to be thrown at them. For me it was an awful feeling to see all this going on and being done by another human being. It created a lot of anger in me at the time and lots of hate toward them, I must admit.

CHAPTER

9

My Social Life, and Love at First Sight

During the evenings after work and after dinner, I sometimes spent my time watching people walking on the street below our apartment building from our living room balcony. Our neighborhood was called Sed al Boosheria. In the Arabic language, these words mean the dam of Boosheria (dam-like water dams). Most of the Iraqi refugees were Armenians and Assyrian Christians. We were all living in harmony as neighbors. I made some friends throughout the months that I was living in this suburban area of Beirut. And on some evenings my friends and I used to take the taxicab together and go to visit the Rodeo Drive-like street on the west side of Beirut, which was named Shareeh al Hamra, which in Arabic means the red street. You could see all kinds of luxurious restaurants, shops, buildings, clubs, and even strip places along the alleys. It was a fun place to be at, but you needed lots of money to enjoy these places. It was obvious that I was going to do window shopping only. There was not enough money in my pocket to even spend it on a bottle of Coca Cola at times. My friends and I didn't mind walking around and talking to people and girls, and sometimes we got lucky. One evening, I was with one of my friends and while I was walking, I saw this blonde, nice looking girl sitting by herself inside this pizza place. At first I didn't pay any attention to her due to my shyness and fear that she may call me to join her inside this restaurant. Then how in the world was I going to afford to pay for anything. But the scenario was the opposite in Beirut. If a girl liked you, then she would take care of paying for everything. I learned this the hard way through one experience. As I mentioned earlier by looking inside this pizza place and through the glass window, I was looking at this beautiful blonde who started waving to me to go inside. In my confusion, I turned around to see if she was calling me, or if she was calling someone else. Then my friend said, "she's calling you." My chest got heavy and my legs were weak. I had never dated anyone before in my life. I was only eighteen to nineteen years of age. Then thinking of what my parents had told me rushed into my brain, and before I could do anything about it, I felt a soft hand holding my right wrist. It was the blonde girl. She walked outside the pizza place to take me in. I guess she saw the confusion on my face, I don't know, but, anyhow, I started to say hello, then I turned around and I saw my friend was waving his hand to say good-bye to me from across the street. He was riding in a taxicab. I was alone to handle all this by myself. I had handled life situations very well with all its challenges, but this challenge was a new one for me. Well, the first thing I said to her was, "What's your name?"

She replied to me with a very low and soft voice, which would make you fall in love at first site. Then she said, "Gemela." It's an Arabic name, which means beautiful. Right away I asked her, "Are you Christian or Muslim?"

She said, "I'm Christian," then she asked me for my name. "My name is Mark. I'm also a Christian and an Armenian."

She knew right away and said her neighbors were Armenian also. I was relieved because my parents always told me never fall in love or date anyone other than your own kind. The evening was young, as they say. After we finished our pizza, she invited me to walk with her to another restaurant where the outside curb seating was very nice and appealing. We sat down by the entry, and then she asked the waiter if they had any arak (a Middle Eastern alcoholic drink made from white grapes). The waiter replied, "Yes, we do madam." Then she turned and asked me if I would drink with her. I was shy to say anything, and I was asking myself how I was going to pay for the drinks.

I think she could read minds because she said, "You don't have to worry about the bill. I'll pay for everything. You just have to go along with me."

Go along? What is that? What in the world did she mean? All these thoughts were going around and around in my mind. Then I said, "Okay, let's have one drink." Along with the drinks she ordered some more food. We ate and finished our plates, and we had more than one drink.

After two hours of being together and chatting about where I'm from, and what I'm doing as far as work, and what she was all about, she asked me if I cared to go to her place. She said she would be giving me a phone number for an employer who will help me to get hired right away and for a better paying job and conditions. Well, she knew my story already, and I didn't refuse her offer because I was young, and she was irresistible. I had to go along like she had told me from the beginning, but again I didn't know what I was getting myself into yet. Then she called a cab, and we went to a town called Ashrafia. She had an apartment where she was living on the fifth floor of this modern looking building. We took the elevator up and walked down the long hallway. My heart was pounding hard, and I was wondering about my friend who I had left behind hoping that he doesn't go and tell my parents by mistake about me dating tonight. After we reached her apartment, Gemela opened the door, and we went inside. Gemela's apartment was better furnished compared to mine and with less people living in it. She lived there by herself, and she had her privacy. She said, "Make yourself at home." I was somewhat dizzy already from the alcohol which I drank earlier that evening. I sat down on the living room sofa and watched all the city lights from the 5th floor through the living room window. It was a very nice view. Then I saw Gemela coming out of her room and noticed she had changed into see through veil-like clothing. You could see what God created in women in the form of a beautiful body. Indeed! Without any warning she rushed toward me and started taking off my clothes. I hesitated at first, and then one thing led to another. I was in bed with her for a good several hours before I fell asleep. Suddenly, I woke up. The time was almost 4:30 a.m. Sunday morning. When I rushed to put my clothes on, Gamela woke up and told me to let her call me a cab. I thanked her in a panic and with a worried look. Only one thing was on my mind, and that was how was I going to get home and what excuse could I give my parents, if they ever asked me why it took me so long to get home. They must have been up worried sick about me. I had never done such a thing before in my life; that is, staying out that late with a stranger, and a woman at that. Well sure enough, she called a cab and then gave me her friend's phone number (the new employer), along with some cash to pay for the cab. She said if I ever wanted to see her again, to call her at another number, and she wrote both numbers on a piece of paper and handed it to me. I was in a much-needed rush to leave her place. I thanked her but forgot to kiss her good-bye.

The cab ride was okay. I got home in a half hour. I took the stairs going up four floors because our building manager was shutting down the elevator's power after twelve o'clock midnight every morning in order to save electricity. This was a very common procedure in Beirut because there was not enough electricity being generated to go around to all the areas. I reached the front door to my apartment, and I opened it with a great deal of care so as not to wake anyone up. When I got in, my grandmother was awake and praying in the early morning hours. Wow, that was a relief! She was puzzled if I was coming in or going out. Then she asked me with a low voice, "Where are you going, son?"

I said, "Go to sleep, Grandma. I was at my friend's house." I had to lie so she wouldn't tell the others about my coming home late that morning. But I wasn't fooling anyone; just being cautious.

I changed my clothes and went to sleep with whatever time I had left that morning to catch up with my sleep. It was a very enjoyable life experience for me the night before, and, to be honest, it was a very, very pleasant one. One week later, I decided to call the number that Gemela had given me for the new workplace. When I called the number, the voice on the other end of the phone was not so pleasant and was harsh. I told the individual I was given this number by Madam Gemela to call you about work.

The man replied, "Oh, yes. How old are you, and what is your name?" I said, "I'm eighteen, almost nineteen, and my name is Mark."

He asked, "Are you Armenian?" I said, "Yes." He said, "I'm Armenian too."

I said, "That's nice," and right away I asked, "When could I come and meet with you." I also told him that I was not permitted to work because I was an illegal in his country and on a tourist visa only. He said we'll talk about that when we meet next week. He gave me an appointment for one of the weekdays, and then I insisted to see him around lunch time because I couldn't afford to take a day off just to visit him because my workplace wouldn't pay me for the time off. We both agreed to do it around lunch time.

Time flew by, and before you knew it, the day had arrived to visit this new workplace. I took the bus to go several miles out of the area to Gemela's friend's business place. To my surprise, it was a junkyard for heavy metal surplus equipment, old military tanks, chains, cars, empty explosive bomb shells, and all type of metal materials from iron, brass, copper, aluminum, etc. I walked in and both employers received me and asked me to sit down. They both talked to me about their junkyard business. The man liked what he saw in me as a young man for being ambitious and hard working. He said the job is mine, if I wanted it. I asked how much I was going to get paid. They said not to worry, and they'll tell me how much when I start. That was not much of an assurance for me to leave my other job yet, but he mentioned Gemela's name as well in the interview, and I was puzzled. They said along with their pay of my wages I had a bonus and it was that I get to visit Gemela as many times as I want, and that was if I decided to work for them.

I said, "Sir, I work for wages, not for fun. I understand, and I thank you for the offer." I also added and told them both that I needed some time to think about their offer, and I would decide and call them soon. The position was to supervise three labor employees inside the junkyard where the owners were suspicious that these workers were stealing goods from them. They fired the past supervisor because he was one of the thieves, the owners said.

Hmm, the junkyard's owners had an idea and a reason to hire me. Their idea was based on if there was anything suspicious at any time regarding their workers' activities, I was to come and inform them about it. In other words, the offer was a spying supervisory job. And, as a part of this entire paying package deal, I also got to enjoy myself with Gemela as well. I went back to the factory two hours late and continued working until the end of that day. I went home, and while at home, we received a phone call from my cousin Jack. The call was from back home from Baghdad, Iraq. We didn't have any phone service or lines in our apartment. The phone call came to the grocery shop, which was located under our building. All the people from our building used this store for their daily grocery needs as well as for their telephone service. It was convenient enough for everyone to do so, and the store owner knew most of us by our names and by our apartment numbers. Anytime there was a phone call for any of us, he would send his worker to knock on our door to inform us to go down and take the call. We paid a fee to use his business phone.

I picked up the phone and talked to my step cousin Jack, Sofina's stepson. He said he was going to come and stay in Beirut with his own cousin's family from his dad's side in the Ashrafia area. He wanted to stay as long as we were living in Beirut because he missed me and my family ever since we left Baghdad some time ago, which I had mentioned before. "Well," I said, "things are not the same here like they were back- home in Baghdad. I'm working, and I'm taking care of a family now. I don't have enough time other than the weekends to spend with you. He told me he didn't care, and, besides, the situation was get-ting worse in Iraq. His father, my aunt Sofina's husband, was worried that they would draft him by force into the Iraqi armed forces. Right away, I told him not to talk crazy over the phone, and that we would never know who is listening. He ignored my warnings, and he continued talking. He told me in one week's time, he would come and see us. I welcomed him to do so as soon as possible.

Our neighborhood in Sid el Boosharia in the Beirut suburbs was not all that safe. I knew this when I witnessed the riot that happened one afternoon when I was standing on the back balcony of our apartment. As I mentioned, our apartment had another balcony at the front of the building, which you could get to through the living room, and it overlooked the main street below. While I was at the back balcony, I saw a group of people with machine guns shooting in the air in our neighborhood in the middle of the day shouting in Arabic, "Down with the regime, down with the regime!" I didn't know which regime they were talking about, and some of them were carrying a wooden coffin on top of their shoulders.

Since our balcony was on the fifth floor of the building, I could see this dead man's body lying inside the coffin, which was open and in the air without any lid covering it. The dead person was wrapped with white fabric and a Lebanese flag was covering him. I assumed it was a Muslim funeral that I was witnessing and not a riot. But why were they shootings guns in the air? It seemed like it was a local habit. In the Muslim tradition I believe they must bury their dead in less than forty-eight hours or the next day. All the gunshots were in the person's honor. I learned this from the grocery store owner the next day. This being said, no one was thinking about the physics of the matter, which says, "What goes up must come down," and all these stray bullets will fall and kill someone else instead. Right away I ran inside for cover and away from the glass windows because my next-door neighbor's son was injured from a stray bullet that hit his leg while he was sleeping one night. He got over his injuries some months later. He was a fifteen-year-old boy, a refugee like us and was waiting for his fate to be determined in obtaining a visa to travel to America. He was lucky that he was safe and sound after that incident.

CHAPTER

10

Lebanese Authorities and Knowing the Barber

Beirut is a beautiful city and the people are very helpful. I liked living and staying there very much at one time, but it was not much of an assurance for my future to call it a permanent home. We had a choice and that was to be a registered refugee with the World Council of Churches (WCOC) to immigrate to America. What was not certain at all were our tourist visas. We had to renew them every three months in order to extend our stay in this new country. It was not easy to accomplish the visa renewals. In order to renew them, we first had to pay a visit to this nice barber, who my dad got to know recently, at his shop. He was a very good man, and he owned a barber shop in downtown Beirut. This barber had devoted his life to help all Armenian and Christian refugees who came to his country. He had some big connections with Lebanese high-ranking officials, police captains, as well as army officers. All these important people visited him in his shop to have a haircut.

My father knew him through some connections and friends who he had associated with in Beirut, and he had his hair cut done at this shop as well. My father and the barber got very close. I have to keep his identity a secret for his own protection, and I'm not sure if he's still alive after all these years because our communication had come to a halt after our departure. We have not communicated with him for the past forty years until now. He was in his forties when we last saw him back in 1975. One day the barber came and visited us at our home at my father's invitation. Our relations grew very close as families and friends. He mentioned to us and to my dad specifically, that if we ever need any help to extend our visas in order to stay in his country as visitors, we should contact him. He would do the favor of taking us to the security office for visa issuing in Beirut, and he would help us to get an extension or have our passports stamped with new visas until we depart from his country to our final destination. When I heard that, I said to myself finally we have someone who can protect us in a country where we are known only as strangers. Also, I was glad to see my dad had made friends with this barber, and not like the one who betrayed us on the Lebanese border and almost got us killed.

A few weeks later one evening, I was eating my dinner and my cousin who was visiting us named Pat went down to see some friends below our building in the lobby area. I finished my dinner then, as usual, I went to sit down in the front balcony area to relax and get some fresh air. I witnessed a large dark green Lebanese army truck rolling into our street, and then I saw everyone in the street running and screaming. I couldn't hear them from my balcony as high as the fifth floor. I couldn't understand why they were screaming or couldn't hear any of their words clearly. Then I saw my cousin Pat looking up at me from down below, and with his hands he was communicating through sign language and trying to make me understand something. I didn't know what he was implying. I started yelling from my balcony, "What's the matter, Pat?" I witnessed with my own eyes this Lebanese soldier, who had a wooden stick in his hand, started hitting my cousin on his knees with it. My cousin went down, and they grabbed him and put him on the army truck. My eyes couldn't believe what happened. I got disoriented. I forgot I was on the fifth floor. I was almost going to jump on the army truck from where I was. Just then from the next-door balcony, my neighbor yelled and alerted me with his loud voice, which was a call from heaven. That prevented me from jumping, and for a minute I had lost it. He said, "Don't worry too much. The soldiers are looking for illegals, and your cousin has his passport with him, I hope. If so, they'll let him go." He added, "The passport should have a stamp for a valid tourist visa; otherwise, they'll book him at the local station." My next-door neighbor had been living in this neighborhood a longer time than we had. He told me he had seen these kinds of raids before in our streets. He said, "This neighborhood has a heavy concentration of Iraqi refugees. Every now and then, the police do this for a reason, and that is to investigate our validity in the country and for security of the area.

Well, I didn't care what this whole deal was all about because my concern was my cousin's capture. I rushed to my dad's bedroom, and I called him out to see the problem. My dad rushed to the living room balcony to witness the entire ordeal for himself. Right away I went to their bedroom, and I checked inside their nightstand drawer where we kept all the passports. We were to carry our passports if we were to go outside the apartment, and my cousin was told several times previously by my parents to do exactly just that. Sure enough, my cousin's passport was not in his pocket; it was still in the night stand drawer in the bedroom. I picked up the passport and, along with my father, we rushed five floors down using the staircase and got to the street fast. We ran behind the truck waving to the driver to stop. But all our efforts failed. We got back to the store under our building. My father called his barber friend for a rescue and told him what had just happened. The barber was amazed that such a thing could happen, especially since we had gone with him to the visa office last week where the barber had managed to get new visa extensions for all my family members including my cousin Pat. Then he told my father to wait for him downstairs. He said he would make a few phone calls here and there, and he would be right over.

An hour later the barber was at our apartment doorstep with his car, and he asked my dad to ride along with him. I wanted to go, but my father said no and that he would take care of the matter, especially police matters, with his friend. He told me to stay behind to protect the family while he was out. It made sense for me to stay behind, but my heart was with my cousin Pat. Two hours later around midnight the barber arrived with his car and dropped off my dad below our building and drove away. I was impatiently waiting along with the rest of the family for my cousin's arrival. As all of us were looking down from the front balcony, my dad came up and said everything is okay. But due to the number of arrests the police had made tonight, he said, "Your cousin has to wait his turn for the routine paperwork to be filed at the police station." When I heard this, I got angry and started yelling at my father, "What do you mean routine paperwork? I can't trust anyone! How could you leave him like that?" Then I said, "I am going right now to the police station. I don't care."

My mom along with my grandmother rushed to block me to prevent me from going out the door. My dad was worried, but he said his assurance was the barber who went inside and talked to the police chief of our area, and it happened that the barber knew the chief as well. My dad explained further that the barber came out and informed him that he asked the chief to make Pat a priority along with a few others that the barber knew and was surprised to see at the same station. They were booked for the same reason as my cousin Pat that evening, and they were all in police custody. The barber told the police chief that he knew his superiors well and warned him not to do anything foolish to these men by harming them. The police chief told him not to worry. All they were doing was a routine check for the security of the area. Now all we had to do was wait and see what time Pat could come home. For sure, my dad didn't want me or his family to worry. I sat down on the balcony totally confused, praying some and blaming God for it like a hopeless human being. My mom asked me to come inside and go to bed so that I could wake up early and go to work the next day. "It's already late," she said. As I recall, the time was 3:30 a.m., so I went to sleep. I didn't know what my dad had in his mind as a plan. I went to bed, and he managed to leave the apartment quietly and head out to the police station again. He waited for my cousin outside the station all night until they dismissed him, and then he brought him home. When I woke up, I saw him at the breakfast table. I grabbed him and hugged him. I felt my prayers were answered. This was a big lesson for all of us to learn. We had to always carry our passports in our pockets from then on. And thanks to the barber because he was a great help in this matter. The next day my dad called back home to inform Pat's parents about this incident and told them not to worry because Pat decided to return to Iraq the following week.

Two weeks later and on a weekend morning we had a knock on our door. There he was, my cousin Jack along with his female cousin named Mary. We hugged each other. I was very happy to see him around us. We sat down to have breakfast together, and we remembered the good old days a few years back when we came to Beirut with his dad for a three-month summer vacation. The furniture we were using in our apartment belonged to Jack's family. His dad authorized us to use it for the time being and sitting on them brought back some old memories like we were on vacation again. Then I asked Jack, "How long are you planning to stay in Beirut?" He said, "As long as it takes this time, and until all of you fly away to your final destination." Wow! No one would know for sure when, but I told him I had heard from other refugees that it would take no more than four to five months until we go. Jack was not happy to hear that. Then he changed the subject and asked, "What are we doing after breakfast? We could go to pick up my other cousins and head out to the mountain area to the villages." These were places where in the past we all had stayed and spent good times together.

Jack asked, "How about it? Like the good old days." I said, "Well, that sounds good."

We took a ride in his cousin's car to their house I knew most of her sisters from back home. Jack had seven female cousins; all sisters in one family. Some of them went with us to the mountains, and the rest stayed behind. We went hiking in the woods having talks about the future and marriage. The girls said they would like to get married as soon as possible. Jack and I disagreed. We told them for us life has more in it then just marriage. Some of Jack's cousins who were with us on this trip were a few years older than Jack and me. Neither Jack nor I were going to marry them because they were relatives. But the girls' worries were to settle down soon in the future. They were typical old-fashioned girls, but then we were all old-fashioned too compared to today's lifestyle. The whole day had passed by, and we came back to their home, which was in an area called "Sin al Feel". It means elephant tooth (translated from Arabic). We went up to their apartment and had some tea and cookies. The name of the older cousin who stayed behind was Anna. She asked me where I work. I told her I work in a company making air conditioning vent grills. She said she knew of another factory owner, if I was interested to change my work. She said she would call and ask the owners to hire me and Jack, and we could work in the same place together. It happened that both owners were also living in the same apartment complex where she was living. Anna said, "As a matter of fact, they both live next door to me on the same floor."

In the beginning, I didn't know what job and where she was referring us to. I had to find out by asking her, "What kind of job or place do your friends own?" She replied, "A junkyard", and my heart started pounding again. I asked myself if it was possible that this was the same junkyard which Gemela had directed me to go to before. At my surprise, sure enough it was the same place. I didn't make a sign, but my cousin Jack knew the owners through his cousin Anna while he was staying at her place. I said, "Well, I'm working right now, and I'll think about it in the future." Then I said to Anna, "Thank you for your concern and in trying to help me." A few minutes later I left their place and took a cab home. All along the way the junkyard place was on my mind. I was telling myself that I was glad didn't make any signs to alert them. I don't want Jack's cousin, Anna, to know that I had already met the owners through others. I didn't want them to find out that Gemela directed me there before and about the relation that

I had with her; otherwise, the news would spread around, and then everyone would know what happened in my private life. Well, I got home early that evening. I really enjoyed the entire day and the trip. It was just like the old days spending quality time with Jack and his female cousins.

CHAPTER

11

Facing Death - Count One

Working for the aluminum company named Yuma was a big challenge for me. It was a lot of hard work for peanut pay. I can't complain. I made some good friends there. One of them was a Syrian born Armenian individual named Koko; a short cut from the original name of Krikor. We used to spend time earing lunch together daily and going on fishing trips on the weekends. He knew Beirut more than I did because he had lived there for some time with his family when they moved from Damascus, Syria to Beirut, Lebanon. He was permitted to work in Beirut on a temporary work visa where he had to renew it every now and then. But because the relationship among Syrians and Lebanese at that time was fragile in a sense, he avoided renewing his work permit due to his fear that the Lebanese authorities may not renew his work permit, and they could deport him back to Syria. This had transformed his existing status to work illegally like us. He mentioned to me on a fishing trip that he was a Syrian born citizen, and he had served the armed forces there for a period of two years. There were a lot of people just like Koko who were living in Beirut on better terms compared to their own country of Syria back in 1975. As I mentioned, the relations among the two countries were not at its best as the TV news was reporting, all due to the Israeli-Arab war and the Palestinian population who were living near the Beirut International Airport area on the west side and at the southern border towns of Lebanon.

The Palestinians were backed by the Syrians, Iraqis, Libyans, and other Arab country governments to aid them in fighting against Israel. I learned all this information from the local people in our neighborhood between 1973 and 1975. A Palestinian worker who was working with me as a laborer at the factory had informed me with a word of caution that being a radical in thought was not the wish of every Palestinian family, but they had no choice but to participate in their struggle for freeing their proclaimed lands from Israeli occupation as he had explained it to me during a lunch break. Well, none of this concerned me at that time because I was not involved in any politics or any groups, nor could I hate anyone for that matter. After all, we were all God's children.

All of us illegal co-workers at this factory had developed a habit to eat lunch in the same room every day. We all worked together as well, including me with my uncle Armo, his brother-in-law, who was our supervisor, my friend Koko and others. This pattern of all of us eating lunch together developed to be habitual. The lunch time conversation was almost about the same subjects every day. Also, my uncle was very protective of me in a sense that he was trying to prevent me from listening in on the adult conversations at times by always changing the subject of the conversation toward another direction. He thought I wasn't old enough yet to know everything because he was very conservative in his nature, and he wouldn't allow me to express myself freely and openly; acting just like a second father. He was somewhat of a controlling individual. I respected my uncle very much, and I never wanted to cross him, and I accepted his facts due to his wisdom. The age difference among those that worked in that room was obvious because some of the conversations among the workers were not suitable for me to listen to according to the living standard values of the Middle Eastern lifestyle in the old days specifically conversations about their wives or women in general. I had no privacy to openly express my thoughts to my friends about my lifestyle of going out and dating girls, etc. According to my uncle's opinion, for example, talking about dating a girl or possibly sleeping with a girl at my age was considered a sin and was not appropriate. I was nineteen years of age at the time and taking care of family, bills, and rent. So why was it not suitable yet for me to sleep with a girl? It beats me.

One day as I finished my lunch, I had another thirty minutes to kill. I asked my friend Koko to accompany me to visit this small hillside, which was located at the back side of the factory because the view from that hillside was very calming and nice. On the top of this hill there was this small twelve feet by twelve feet stone building that was standing alone without any windows, and it had an entry doorway only at the front porch. This stone building was built in the old days. I don't know how far back, but my presumption would be in the 1940's. I asked my friend if we could go back there and sit down on the front porch of this building and watch the factory from a distance along with the partial city view, which this porch was offering. The idea was to get away from all the other co-workers so that my friend Koko and I could have some privacy to talk about whatever we wanted to talk about, regardless what the topics were, and just to be away from all the elderly people. My friend agreed and off we went and walked up the dirt hill before sitting down on the front porch. At first, we went in the back of this stone building and pointed out with our arms extended out toward certain points of interest. We did point toward all directions behind this stone building before we went back to sit on the front porch to rest and continue to eat lunch and enjoy the breeze. We decided to make it a habit to eat our lunch at this porch from then on because it was very relaxing. Well, it only lasted for a few days, and on the fourth day we saw a magazine that was published and written in Arabic and was put or left on the porch representing the voice of Palestine, at least that's what the title read. This magazine was a radical magazine of its nature, which all of its views was based on hate toward the Jews and their wrongdoings. It was written and explained with colorful pictures about war, abused people and tortured people. We had no interest to explore it, and we didn't care about these kinds of subject matters. We were two young men who wanted to relax at lunch time and eat our lunch while we talked about our future and other matters, and we didn't have any interest to see and read about war and its impact on people. But, nevertheless, we did pick up the publication and read some pages in a hurry. Then we ended up throwing it in the air in disagreement with its contents. As we were having lunch and laughing, we noticed everyone from our department in the factory, including my own uncle, had started to walk toward where we were sitting on the concrete steps of this stone building porch. I turned to my friend Koko and said, "Hey, so much for privacy." Then everyone came and joined us. We were about seven people in total including my uncle. Koko and I considered ourselves expert tour guides since we had been there for the last three days enjoying the view and eating our lunch. Also, we knew the entire diagram of this spot. After the short tour that Koko and I gave the rest of the co-workers by walking around the stone building, we all came back to the front porch and sat down killing time before the factory's lunch bell rings again to go back to work. While we sat on the front porch for about ten minutes, I heard some noises coming from behind the building walls. I turned left and saw a few young men who were, at most, in their prime at fourteen to sixteen years of age carrying loaded Russian-made military AK-47 machine guns in their hands. They were waving and making signs to each other, which I gathered could be to attack us on the front porch, and before I could warn everyone, we just got closed in by three young boys with loaded machine guns in their hands. I started to yell out to the others "Hey boys! Be alert! We're getting attacked!" Sure enough, these young soldiers ran up to the front of the building and started to point their machine guns in our faces. Two young workers from our group didn't want to stay and wait. They were Syrian citizens. They took a big chance and out of their confusion and panic got up impulsively and ran down the hill passing through these gun-carrying soldiers and ignoring their endangerment. Now the two out of the three Palestinian young soldiers with the machine guns turned around toward the path of the runaways, and they aimed their machine guns in the air and started firing like no yesterday and emptied their first magazines. Without any guns in our possession to defend ourselves, I felt I was in the middle of a war and hopeless and helpless. The picture was not very pleasant and was very scary. After firing their guns, these two foolish young men reloaded their weapons and turned back, cussed at us and forced us with their guns pointing toward our faces to go with them down to their headquarters that was located on the opposite direction behind the hill about one to two hundred yards downhill. Well, folks, I couldn't believe myself. I don't know what power had gotten into me when I saw everyone, including my uncle, was all speechless and frozen and willing to follow them down to their headquarters. I got up and walked toward this one young soldier, ignoring the danger at task, and then I started yelling at the top of my lungs in Arabic on these kids, saying, "I refuse to go with you anywhere! If you're going to kill me, do it now!" I don't know how or who was giving me the courage, but I insisted firmly on my demand and stood still. My action had planted some hope in the others, and they started to do the same. They started to scream on these kids. The kids' hands started to shake, and one of them pulled up his machine gun and put the hot smoking barrel right into my chest. I could feel the heat of the gun barrel on my skin. Without thinking I pushed the kid with my chest. I started yelling and cussing more into his face saying bad words about his mom as much as he was saying the same to me. What I did was really stupid, but I didn't know or care about it at the time. Maybe all of it was due to fear, which made me act this way at that moment. Folks, on that day I believe I was very lucky again, or maybe someone up there had better plans for me. God's plan was to protect me from dying or getting killed. The reality is, what this kid soldier could have done, if he ever wanted to, was to pull the trigger and kill me since his gun barrel was pointed and rested against my chest. There, I would have been gone in a flash. As this little boy soldier and I were arguing and yelling at each other, I heard a single gun firing shots. It was the sound of a semi-automatic gun. These single shots were being fired in the air, and the sound of it was getting closer and closer to us. By now the rest of the factory workers who were with me that day, including my uncle, were in a great deal of fear standing on the sidelines with two other machine guns pointed at them as well. All six workers were watching my drama with this young soldier. When the single gunfire shots came closer to the hill, I saw this adult soldier pointing and waving his gun toward all of us as well and telling us to follow him down the hill. At this point I also noticed the entire factory workers, along with the owners, were watching the whole thing unfold in front of their eyes. They were standing on the top floor of the factory. Then in few seconds time I had to collect myself and my thoughts while the kid who was resting his machine gun on my chest started diverting his attention toward his superior officer. I reached into my back pocket and pulled my Iraqi passport. At this point, I realized we didn't have any other choice but to follow these people and go down the hill with them. I made a desperate move hoping it would work. Then I said to the adult soldier, "Sir, I'm an Iraqi citizen, I'm not Lebanese." In the meantime, I knew by living in this country that most, and not all, of the Lebanese had their share of disagreeing with the Palestinians and had not accepted the Palestinians to live on their soil permanently. Anyhow, I continued saying out of my desperation, "My country, Iraq, is one of the countries that has been helping your cause against Israel. I don't want to go down the hill to your camp with you and get tortured or killed." I was speaking with an Iraqi Arabic accent so far with this officer. I said, "That goes for all these people who are with me also."

Folks, this was my last effort to save all of us if I could from direct gun point. Wow! Sure enough, the Palestinian officer stopped and turned back, walked toward me and grabbed my passport from my hand. Then he said, "If I let you go today, would you promise me one thing?"

I said, "What's that?"

He said, "I don't want to see you or your friends on this hill again. Do you understand? We've been watching your movements for the past three days on this hill, and you've been pointing toward that direction." He pointed and showed us where we were pointing at, and according to him, he pointed to and said in a hurry, "That is our Palestinian camp, and this hill is called Tel el-Zaater. You're not welcome here because this is a military zone." In confusion and anger, I turned around and told the officer, "Screw you! This is Lebanon! You have a military zone in the middle of it? How is that possible?" I think I was a big mouth at the time. The officer was smarter than me, and he didn't get very angry. He warned me to shut my mouth and said, "Don't dirty your mouth anymore," and called me an asshole. "I could change my mind and take you all down the hill", he said. Out of his fear, my uncle yelled in Armenian for me to shut up and take the deal. Well, my passport was given back to me, and one after the other all seven of us followed each other's trail and returned to the factory. We heard a lot of cheering and clapping coming from the workers who worked with us and were watching us from the factory rooftop. When we reached the front door, everybody was patting our backs and welcoming us back to the factory like heroes of war. I was still angry about what had happened, but we were saved, and it was a big lesson for me to learn. What I had learned from it all, and what I'm saying here is that courage is not only something we learn in life, but some of us are born with it as a trait. Only life circumstances can and will trigger it at a time of need for each individual who is filled with courage. And everyone of us has a different way to react toward situations that require courage. It's also equally true for circumstances that trigger fear, which, of course, is an opposite trait.

I got home that evening, and I didn't talk to anyone. I was very quiet trying to decide for myself what had happened and why. After a few hours, my uncle and his wife stopped by our apartment. My uncle told my parents how brave I was and explained the reason. Then my uncle requested that I should tell the entire story to my parents to eventually make me vent out and not keep it to myself. At least that's what I could understand from his request. Well, I didn't want to do that in the beginning, and then I decided to speak my mind and tell my parents the whole ordeal. While I was standing up and telling them, I didn't know that my uncle and his wife had another agenda for me that evening. As I was talking about the ordeal, my uncle's wife went behind my back with a lit cigarette in her hand and without any warning, she dipped the lit cigarette's fiery end into the right side of my neck. The sudden burn shocked me a great deal and made me speechless for a moment. This was their home remedy for treatment according to her mother's methods and according to their methodology for curing fear with a sudden shock. According to them, it resets ones disrupted nervous system due to fear and eases up the emotional pain from the shock of facing the gun barrel that day. Well, it didn't work. It got me sick and lying in bed and not being able to go to work or eat properly for the next fifteen days due to the sudden burn of the cigarette and the sudden unknown shock I had received. My uncle's wife was stupid enough to do this, and it made matters worse for me. Well, my parents had to take me to a local doctor the next day, and the doctor said there was nothing better to overcome such a thing other than constantly talking about the same subject as often as possible in order to get it out of one's system, which may help. He advised me to start taking a low dose of valium pills, so I could numb myself and get it over with. Well, folks, nothing helped me to overcome it more than my prayers. I prayed while alone, while walking around our neighborhood or while sitting at the front balcony of our apartment.

My cousin Jack had heard about this, and he came to visit me several times with his female cousins. It was the best medicine for me to talk about what had happened. Shutting off the subject with a cigarette burn was a stupid and uncivilized action by my aunt. I can't believe she had done such a thing, and it wasn't a cure. Three weeks of being home and being bored, I felt useless some of the days. The effects of the valium pills were noticeable. I was like a drunken person. One weekend my cousin called me and said he would stop by and would be willing to take me out.

I said, "Let's go to the beach. I love to see the ocean." He said, "That's fine."

He came by cab during the day time and picked me up. We went to downtown Beirut and visited the same beach next to Hotel Lux where I had stayed during my first entry to Beirut and right after the time when the border ordeal had ended. The sound of the waves, the color of the water and the cool breeze along with the brightness of the sun was life at its fullest for me that day. It was very enjoyable, and it relaxed me very much. For the first time in three weeks I was very hungry. I asked my cousin Jack where we could go to eat. He knew my situation and my condition. I had not been eating well, and he was happy to hear that I was hungry. He said he would take me to The Red Street (Shaare el Hamara) of Beirut. I smiled when I heard the name of the street because I knew the area. I had my first encounter with the blonde girl, Gemela, on that street. It was another happy note in my heart that needed to renew itself. I said, "Let's do it! Let's go!" We went to the same restaurant where Gemela and I had eaten before. I didn't want to tell my cousin Jack about my encounters with this woman because Jack had a loose mouth, and he could inform everyone.

We both sat down at curb side, and I knew like an expert what to order for dinner along with some arak (an alcoholic drink). I got excited and forgot that I was taking valium pills on an as needed basis, and I had taken my pill one hour earlier. The time was early evening around 6:30 to 7:00 p.m. We ate our dinner and drank the alcohol. Well, the evening was young, and my cousin asked me if I wanted to catch a movie with him, and I agreed. He said there was this Hollywood movie called the Sound of Music playing in the theaters in down-town Beirut (the year was 1974).

I asked, "What kind of movie is it?"

He said, "It's a very famous American movie that was released in 1965, and it's a musical. It's a fun movie to watch, and you'll like it too."

Since I had been involved with music and dance with a group before, I told him I wouldn't mind it if he was paying for the whole thing as well as dinner. I had no money due to being home and out of work. I told him when I go back to work, I would reimburse him. He said not to worry as he would take care of it, and that I was his guest that day. We went to the movies and sat down watching some previews. The theater lights dimmed, it got dark so that everyone could watch the show, and the movie started. About fifteen minutes into the movie, I felt my chest getting heavy. I couldn't breathe, my left arm was getting numb, my back started to get hot and cold, and the fingers in both of my hands were closing in. I was in no condition to continue watching the movie, and I could hardly pull Jack's hand and tell him to take me home. When Jack turned and saw me like that, he panicked. He called the attendant, the lights came on, and the movie was stopped. All I know was my eyes started to get blurry, and Jack, along with the attendant, helped me out of the theater. Jack called a taxicab and pulled me into the back seat of the cab. He paid the driver and asked him to take me home while he was sitting with me in the cab. I was partially lying down on the back seat. I asked Jack to hurry, and he panicked even more and yelled to the driver to drive faster. We got home in ten minutes thanks to Jack and the taxi driver. I rushed into the bathroom and stuck my finger into my mouth, and I vomited. My body started to shake like hell, and I felt cold. My mom covered me with a blanket and gave me some 7-Up. A short time later, I was back in the bathroom vomiting again. It took several times that night until my stomach was emptied. My dad asked my cousin Jack to stay over since it was late. Jack said he was going to do just that anyway out of his concern about my well-being. I was tired, and I went to sleep afterwards. The next morning my dad and I went to the doctor once more. I had to admit to the doctor that I had an alcoholic drink the night before. He said I shouldn't mix alcoholic drinks with valium pills. He said when both were mixed together, it created a bad stomach reaction that might have caused the numbness in my body, or it could've been a mild case of food poisoning. He asked me a few questions as well, and after a short talk with him, he said the reaction last night was not just from the bad mixture, but he believed I was also experiencing some anxiety attacks. He said, "To overcome them, you have to face your fears and not drink alcohol but eat well and rest well. Keep yourself occupied with reading or work and don't think too much about what's going to hap-pen tomorrow. Don't try to foretell the future. Also, try to let go of some control you have by trying to find peace within yourself. Try to be happy with your surroundings by finding constructive activities, etc." These were the exact words of the doctor. We went home, and I noticed that our financial situation was not at its best. I hadn't worked for over a month, so my dad started to look for work the following week. He never looked for work since we had arrived in Beirut for about a year. All of this had put extra anxiety on both me and my family to take care of bills due to various reasons, which I would like to keep private.

CHAPTER

12

Accident at the Chemical Factory

My father, in an effort to find a job, spoke to his sister Sonia and asked her if any of her clients were business owners, and if they were hiring anyone. Sonia was living with her husband, Eddy, and their four children in the same neighborhood where we were in the Beirut suburbs, but they were in another building, one street north from us, and it was walking distance. They left Iraq a few months before we did; fleeing for freedom as well. She was an excellent dress maker, and due to her dress making skills and working with a variety of lady clients, she had a broad audience to appeal to for help. One day, Eddy asked his wife's client if her husband needed any help at his chemical factory because it happened that her husband was the owner of that chemical factory. Eddy was looking for work for both himself and for my dad at the same time. I liked my aunt's husband, Eddy, very much. He was a very calm and quiet person. The work at the chemical factory was physical in its nature, circulating around receiving chemicals in barrels and dividing them into smaller quantities by putting these powder formed chemicals into plastic bags, then weighted and shipped to the public marketplace. Nevertheless, all barrels were handled by lifting the entire weight by the labor force or individuals, regardless if they were fifty pounds or more in weight. This factory was located in the city of Beirut and several floors underground of a commercial building. To get a better picture of this factory's internal condition, there were no radio signals that you could receive at this site. That was how much this place was isolated from the outside world. After a few phone calls by this lady client to her husband who owned the chemical factory, she managed to get some good news for Eddy and my dad. She got them both hired by her husband regardless of their illegal status. My dad was very happy that he got some type of job where he could also be a bread winner and, once more, contribute to the family table easing the pressure that I had since we entered Lebanon.

My family's life was not short of accidents and surprises. Several months later, on a Monday morning at work, when my father was trying to open one of the chemical barrels, a small chip of chemical material flew off the lid and went into his right eye. The chip started to irritate and burn his eye lid. Luckily that morning, the owner was on the job site, and after an unsuccessful attempt to treat him, the owner escorted my father to his car and rushed him to the nearest hospital. After several hours of appropriate eye treatment, he was released to go home with a big cap and a white bandage covering his right eye. We were all horrified when we saw him. The owner of the business was a very good man. He tried to comfort us by telling us not to worry much and that he'll be fine in no time. Sure enough, my dad got well after one week's time by staying home to rest and by using the eye medication given. Then the factory owner did something very honorable. He didn't cut my dad's weekly paycheck short. He paid him in full and for the entire period missed. His boss came to our home to visit my dad one evening and handed him his pay for the lost time and made sure that his condition was improving. And, if for any reason my father needed further treatments, his boss was going to provide it and pay for it fully. Before he left, he told my father, "You are always welcome to continue working with us later when you feel better. Get well, Mike."

Good luck, and so much for my father to work anywhere or at the chemical factory anymore. He quit his job after this incident. His fears were like his friendly tokens, which took over his mental condition and shut down his physical abilities to continue working for some reason and for a long time. He decided not to work and stay around the house and around his family. This had taken away his enthusiasm to work anywhere anymore, and it was sad to see him in this condition. Well, at that time I was home for almost a month on an unpaid sick leave myself due to my condition of encountering threats from gunmen, and I was trying to overcome my fears, which I had experienced a few weeks before. Now someone needed to step up and go to work so we could survive financially and move on.

One Sunday, I was sitting down on the edge of the rooftop of our apartment building. (Can you imagine? But not to jump; it was not like that. I was just sitting and thinking.) While I was watching the panoramic mountain view and breathing the clean air, I decided to make a change and quit my job at the Yuma factory. I wanted to pay a visit to the junk- yard once more where Gemela had told me about a few months before. The next day on a Monday morning, I went to the Yuma factory where everyone was so happy to see me back to work as their young hero. I went directly to the boss's office and told him about quitting my job. My boss was not very happy to hear the news. He said that I was a very dedicated and honest employee, and he hated to see me go. Right away, he said he would go and talk to the owners of the factory and asked me to wait in his office. I didn't know why I had to wait in his office, especially since they didn't pay me for sick leave while I was at home and because I was an illegal. I didn't have any responsibility or loyalty toward them to stay and work there. All these thoughts were going around in circles in my mind while I was waiting in his office with the good habits which I had developed; that is, I always respected other's people wishes. I stayed around at the boss's office as he requested and waited to see what this whole thing was all about. After twenty to thirty minutes, my boss came back and closed his door. Well, he refused to accept my resignation and said, "I have good news for you." I was surprised, and I asked him what it was about. He said that he spoke to his bosses (the factory owners), and they were willing to pay me more money daily, so I could stay and work for them.

I said, "Sorry, boss. How much are we talking about?" He said, "Two more liras per day."

I was to make ten liras (Lebanese currency) a day, but he said I had to promise him that I shouldn't tell my uncle about my pay increase. Well, folks, I paused for a moment, thinking while we got distracted by a phone call. While my boss was answering the phone call in his office, I asked myself is this for real? It's nonsense! My uncle is a hardworking man, and he's the one who got me my job at this factory. I had to keep this news a secret from him. I had been on this route before, and soon enough, they would load me up with more work, and they would lay off my uncle because he's an old man. This kind of incident had happened before in this factory. They didn't care about anyone. We were just numbers for them. I knew my uncle needed this job more than I did because he had no one else to help him survive. He had no kids because his wife couldn't have children.

After my boss finished his phone conversation, I turned and said to him, "Listen, thank you very much for your offer, but I have a better offer from someone else." I knew even with the raise I was offered, I was underpaid about 5 to 6 liras per day compared to their local labor wages.

My boss asked, "Can I ask you where you are going to work?" I asked, "Why?"

He answered, "Well, I have to get back to my bosses and tell them about it."

I told him, "There's this home appliance repair factory on the other side of the street across from this factory, and they offered me 12 liras per day to start with them." I then gave him the name of the factory.

He was puzzled, and he looked at me and said, "I'll tell you what. I'm not going to tell my bosses where you're going." Again, he said, "I hate to see you go, but I'd like to help you with your new workplace."

I asked, "How so?"

He asked, "Your new boss's name is Ahmed, right?"

I was stunned. I said, "I think so." My boss said that Ahmed was not a very fair man and to just be careful, and he wished me luck.

I asked, "How do you know that?"

He said he knew Ahmed because he was working for Yuma factory before, and my boss said that he was hired as Ahmed's replacement. He wished me luck again saying, "Remember this kid. If you change your mind whenever and for whatever reason, come back and see me, and I'll find something for you to do around here". Wow! The man meant well, and all

I could do was to thank him from the bottom of my heart. I said good-bye and moved on. Unfortunately, I had to lie to my boss about the appliance factory place because I wanted to be free and look for something new with more pay, and I was also in fear of getting caught one day as an illegal working with no work permit. These steps were taken for precautionary reasons, and I couldn't trust anyone to tell them the truth. There were no job offers at the appliance factory. I had to make that one up. I decided to pay a visit to the appliance factory before I went to the junkyard place looking for work. All I knew was that two of my neighborhood friends were working at this appliance factory as well as my cousin named John, and Ahmed, who was their boss and who my previous boss, Mr. James, at the Yuma factory was referring to as the unfair individual.

Fortunately, all the factories were lined up on one street in that area and where every factory needed the cheap labor regardless of their working status to compete and stay in business in the marketplace.

CHAPTER

13

A Baptism and a Fight in My Apartment

It was March 1974, and we received a phone call from my aunt Noyemi saying that she just settled into the Bourj Hammoud (Hammoud's tower) area where my uncle Armo's mother-in- law was also located. It was a big surprise for my dad to see that another one of his sisters had the right idea like him to leave everything behind and to relocate and live in Beirut, Lebanon. Naturally, we rushed to go to see her and her son, my cousin John, who I was very happy to see. It was a flash from my past remembering the sports life we both shared and experienced during our high school days in Baghdad and having him as a friend around in this part of town was exciting.

My cousin John had changed his life and had gotten married. We all congratulated him, and then I asked him, "How come you got married this fast and at a young age?" He told me I should know very well that no young man over seventeen years of age could flee Iraq or travel abroad without first having served the Iraqi armed forces. I said, "Yes, I do know that." Then he pointed out to me that after my own family (John's uncle's family) had left Iraq and about seven months later things had gotten worse, especially for men. He said he was one of those young men over eighteen years old and was due to serve the Iraqi armed forces. The Baath regime had new rules placed that most men in his age group couldn't leave the country unless they had very valid reasons, so he thought of getting married and leaving for a honeymoon in order to escape Iraq, which would do the trick. Then he told me the only time period which was available to accomplish fleeing out of the country without suspicion or red flags was during the spring break period.

I said, "It must have been painful for you to go through all of this process."

My cousin John replied and said, "No, the only pain I went through was to get my passport signed by the passport authorities because as you know, Lebanon was not one of the countries we could travel to easily, and it was not permitted by Saddam's Baath regime."

I asked him how he did it then.

"Let me tell you," John said. "First, I got married not to flee Iraq, but because I love my wife. Her name is Carmen, and if you remember, she was a volleyball player with the Armenian Athletic Club of Baghdad, and I knew her for some time."

I said, "That's great! And then?"

He added by explaining the passport obtaining process, which was accomplished by bribing authorities at the Iraqi passport agency in Baghdad. John had to lie on his, his wife's (Carmen), and his mom's applications and falsely state that they'll be returning to Baghdad in fifteen days. Then he added, "So, as you can see here in my passport, our visas were permitted for only two weeks of stay out of the country." Then he pulled his passport and showed it to me.

I said, "Wow!"

"But now since we're here," he said, "we're not going back, and I'm going to register our names with the World Council of Churches where all of you are registered already to go to America."

I asked John, "What about your brothers?"

He told me one of his brothers along with his sister were going to come soon, but they were waiting to see how they were going to manage the entire process of immigrating to the west before they could move on. He said, "My sister is going to get married soon, and she's waiting for it to happen."

I said, "But she had a hairstyle salon for women. How is she going to sell it?"

He told me he didn't know, but it was his sister's problem to deal with it. While John was telling me all this, my entire family including my parents were listening to the conversation that took place. Then my dad, who was John's uncle (his mom's brother), said he would help them get started with the registration; that is, if they decided on the big decision of travelling to America. Their decision was based on another factor, and that is John's older brother, who was already a citizen of Australia, was also in touch with them to get them going to Sydney instead of America. It was a great deal of joy for me to see a cousin and a sports friend living or staying in the same town where we were living.

John's father had sold his lumber yard and followed them to Lebanon. A few weeks later as soon as their father had settled in, John's family made their decision, and they were registered with the World Council of Churches as well as with the government of Australia. All along, John's dad was not in favor of immigrating to the United States of America, and he was more in line with liking the British lifestyle, or possibly that he wanted to be among his older son's family. Every time I was at their apartment, he was trying to persuade me by explaining that the British way of life was far better than the American way of life. He was so sure of it that he tried to change my mind and make me go with them to Sydney. Well, to be honest, I was not aware of either country's lifestyle because I was not living in any of them yet. Then I got the idea that maybe he was right, and after listening to him several times, I got the message. I asked my dad why we weren't going to Australia instead of America. And right away he responded with a question. "Who told you that?"

I said, "John's father."

My dad said with a harsh voice, "I would advise you not listen to him. Is that understood?" I didn't know what happened and why my father was acting that way. My grandmother overheard this, pulled me aside and told me not to be angry because my father was right.

Some months had passed, and I was a usual visitor to my aunt Noyemi's home. I saw that John's wife was expecting a child, and I was happy for them.

In August 1974, John's wife, Carmen, was due to deliver the baby. A beautiful baby daughter was born, and by our Armenian Christian customs you must christen the baby, usually around 40 days after birth, where a godfather and godmother must be present. I was asked by John's father first, and then from John himself, if I was willing to be their daughter's godfather.

I said, "John, you do know that this will be my first time being a godfather for any child, and you have to help me know how the whole process works." I told him that I was very honored to do it, and I would be there for him in time of need.

Then I asked him who the godmother would be. He laughed and said, "You've been talking and joking with her all this time at my apartment. Who do you think it'll be?"

I said, "No! Don't tell me the landlord's daughter is the one?" He said, "Exactly."

"Hey John, we're both not fit for this. She's a foot taller than me."

John laughed and said not to worry; it'll get done. I had to break the good news to my parents first. They were happy for me and told me it was a blessing, and I should be honored. Well, at this point, there was not much I could say, so I accepted the idea. A week later we all went to the local church in the same area, and the christening ceremony took place. We had a very small gathering to celebrate the christening at John's home, but I was very shy that everyone was shaking my hand and congratulating me as well.

Three months later in November 1974, John and I had changed several jobs together, and since he resided in Beirut, we formed an amateur basketball team to compete with the locals. We traveled together to several towns in Lebanon playing and winning some games making some extra money by bidding on the games with the rival team, as well as accepting some losses at times. It was fun. We always took Carmen with us while John's mom babysat their baby on occasion. Carmen was an athlete as well but couldn't join our men's team to play basketball.

November 1974 was not a good time for us because the results of the immigration visas were out, and my family received a refusal to immigrate to America. We were all upset and angry. The facts were that some rotten apples had gotten inside the church organization from our own Iraqi community and started to infect the honest system. The World Council of Churches was formed to serve refugees around the world. The infection of the system was accomplished by bribing and selling American visas to Iraqis who had a lot of money with them and ignored the fact that this was not permissible. These visas were to be given on first come, first served basis to refugees and their families who were successful in passing the screening process. The person who was involved in getting bribe money from the refu-gees and was feeding the Lebanese officials was working inside the WCOC office and who was from our own community and our own neighborhood. The WCOC did not have any knowledge of this happening for a while. The individual who had managed the bribing pro-cess was my father's so-called good friend who got my dad and I in trouble months ago when we were encouraged by him to cross the Lebanese border on foot and were busted doing it in the late morning hours. I told my dad, "At this point, you have to go talk to your stupid friend because we're not going to follow his wishes. I hope you didn't pay him any money for this because you don't need to do so. We're all registered legally and lawfully with this church organization." My father looked at me like what do I know about anything. I asked, "What's wrong, Dad?"

He pulled me aside and said, "Listen, I agreed to pay him, so now I owe him the money. We can't escape him; he's dangerous."

I asked, "What money? And what did you do?"

Wow! Sure enough, that same night I saw his friend had sent his brother to escort my dad to their apartment because his brother wanted to talk to him about the money that my father had promised to pay him. I said, "Dad" with a loud voice. "You're not going anywhere!" Then my dad's friend's younger brother cussed and threw fists at me. We fought in my living room. Then my mom ran and called her brother Armo who was a real boxer to come to the rescue. Meanwhile, my dad's friend, who was very drunk, had walked from his home on foot, reached our apartment building and stood below it. He started yelling and cussing from the street at my dad that he wants his money. The whole neighborhood was looking at this new show in town, and we were so embarrassed. To be honest with you, I was not up to the task of fist fighting with his brother because he was powerful and bigger than me in size. I got kicked in the face and in the stomach with his foot, and I was thrown on the ground. You could see the whole family was in panic by then. The women were crying. Then I saw my uncle Armo come into our apartment, and when he saw me on the floor, he didn't care who he was going to punch. He kicked this young man's rear end and pulled him down to the street with him. Then he started to kick his older brother who happened to be the one that was yelling in the streets and had asked my uncle for bribe money as well last week. Well folks, I watched the fight from the balcony, and the two men were badly beaten and laying on the ground. The show was over and about ten minutes later, the two brothers got up in pain and went on their way home.

My stomach was hurt, and the pain was not going away. Luckily, my face was okay. My dad felt sorry about what he had done. I told him it was okay, and that I was fine, but that we had to go to the church office and report this incident the next day. He agreed.

The next day, and in approximately two years of staying abroad in Lebanon, my father went to the World Council of Churches' office, and for the first time got to meet with the head boss. He blew the whistle to help everyone that was affected with all these bribes. A few days later, John's father got bad news of his application refusal to immigrate to the U.S. after six months of being registered with the WCOC. Waiting and living in Lebanon for them, and for all refugees in the 1970's, were very costly. John's father got angry and cut off communication with us and sent a message to us that we were not welcomed in his home. I was puzzled for some time, and his assumptions were that my father Mike was the cause of his refusal from the WCOC's office. A week later and in reaction to his wrong assumptions, he caused my father some harm and pain by beating him up in the street while they were coincidently visiting the WCOC's office. We tried to look the other way because he was my father's brother-in-law and part of the family. This had ended my visitations and communication with his household, and I couldn't see them or my goddaughter again.

It was December 1974. Some time had passed, and the New Year celebration was just around the corner. Soon it was going to be January 1, 1975. The last incident of being refused and denied of going to America had taught us a tough enough lesson, and now we had to find another option in order to travel to the west. I had another aunt whose older son, Kirk, was living in Sydney as well. We wrote a letter to Kirk regarding how it would be possible to immigrate to Australia instead of going to America since it was not possible for us anymore to immigrate to the US. We stated in the letter if he could help us fast in order to achieve this new goal. My dad asked him to sponsor us to go to Sydney, Australia instead. My cousin Kirk did just that. He contacted some employers and got us sponsorships, and they were willing to employ us when we arrived in Sydney. Kirk had man- aged to get us work certificates from employers in Sydney based on our work experience, but the final sponsoring cost process responsibility relied on him. In mid-January of 1975, we received some work certificates; one for my dad and one for me. It was sent to our address in Lebanon. We were told by my cousin Kirk to present these certificates to the interviewer at the Australian Embassy in Beirut stating that we had sponsors in Sydney who would hire us when we arrive there, and that we wouldn't be a burden on the Australian government's welfare system. Two weeks later in February 1975, we went to the Australian Embassy in Beirut and applied for immigration visa status to travel to Australia, and we didn't know what the Australian immigration laws were at the time. In the 1970's, they were leaner towards getting more immigrants to their country than the Americans.

A month later and in March 1975, my dad was called by the World Council of Churches' head boss and the main office personnel for an interview and an investigation about these bribe issues. Somehow, I was proud at last for what my father was going to do. It seemed he had learned his lesson. He went and blew the whistle on everyone he knew who was involved in the scam and taking bribes from the refugees. His detailed information was greatly appreciated by the WCOC. Then my father told the office that when he registered his family with them in the beginning, they promised him that the entire process to immigrate to America would take three to four months. It had been two difficult years for him and his family, and their promise had not been fulfilled. He demanded that he and his family get their visas quickly; otherwise, he was going to write a letter to the New York office where the headquarters of the WCOC to tell them about this entire issue. Apparently, they thanked him for his courage for stepping up and doing the right thing. Later on that day when my father got home, he explained to us what had gone on inside the office with them after the meeting. He said he didn't tell them that we were also applying to get visas as refugees with the Australian Embassy and was going to keep it that way so we could be successful with one or the other in order to choose a new home for all of us to stay in forever.

CHAPTER

14

The New Job and a Gunfight

My cousin John moved to Beirut, Lebanon after he got married to one of the girls from the Athletic Union Club in Baghdad. His marriage was not only due to love, but it was a must for him in order to flee Iraq. He used the Spring break to get married since both he and his wife were still going to high school, and the schools were closed around Spring break for a two-week period in Baghdad. The Spring break was used as an excuse to travel to Lebanon for his honeymoon. He had to use bribes at the passport office or with some government agents. Bribes were a must for any young Iraqi male in order to travel out of the country, specifically for those who hadn't served the Iraqi armed forces. There was no escape from serving the Iraqi armed forces, regardless of your educational background or achievements. It was by force and not by choice for all males eighteen years of age and older.

In the end, my cousin John got out of the country with his wife, Carmen, and his mom who was my dad's older sister named Noyemi. They all traveled to Beirut, Lebanon along the same route which we had traveled two years ago, passing by Damascus, the capitol of Syria. After reaching Beirut, my aunt's family rented an apartment in an area populated by mostly Armenians called Bourj Hammoud, which was a fifteen-minute taxi ride from where we were residing.

Originally, John's family's destination was not the United States of America, but Sydney, Australia instead where his older brother had immigrated earlier and was living there for many years along with his wife. John's older brother, Manny, graduated the Institute of Carpenters in London, England with an A+ majoring in Carpentry. Part of his life's goals and wishes was to get all his brothers and sisters to move, through chain migration, from Iraq to Australia to provide them a better life and a better future for all. Manny's wife, Melisa, was a very good woman. Her wishes were like her husband's in terms of helping all of them to relocate to Australia. Both were a good match for each other. God bless Manny's and Melisa's efforts in this matter. My aunt Noyemi's older son, Manny, is a person who will give his shirt to help others in time of need, but mutual trust and respect were needed to receive his help.

My cousin John didn't hold anything against me after the incident that took place between his father and mine, and he kept his connection and communication open between us, and, likewise, I was doing the same. He was working at a home appliance restoration company and was employed illegally like me in Beirut. One day he asked me to pay a visit to his workplace. He said they paid better wages than the Yuma factory; the place where I once worked. He told me we could work together as cousins in the same company.

In Iraq, John and I had spent a great deal of our earlier, young athletic days together in the track and field sport where each of us was representing our high schools as their only champions in an individual sport. We were both part of the Baghdad high schools' competitions in the track and field sports. He won first place among his school competitors in the sport of discus and shot put. I was the champ of my school in high jump and two hundred-meter free run, so we got to meet at the "El Keshafa" stadium for the competition annually. We were also basketball teammates playing for the Armenian Athletic Club in Baghdad. As you can see, we had a lot in common to share. Why not? If I was hired, the idea of working at his work place as he had suggested was very exciting and promising.

The following week on Monday, I went and paid a visit to this home appliance factory, which was located across from the old Yuma factory. This was the same factory that I had lied about concerning the job offer to my previous boss, Mr. James. I went in and asked to see Mr. Ahmed who was the head supervisor of the factory back then and in charge of employment. My cousin John saw me waiting outside the gate, and he left his work station to come and say hello and introduce me to his boss. As we were standing together, I saw this white haired, dark skinned man with sharp black eyes who was dressed in his white doctor-like robe and started to approach me and my cousin John. Both of my hands were in my pants side pockets due to the cold weather that morning. The man came close, and John started to introduce us. I pulled my right hand out of my pocket, and I shook his hand. Then I put my hand back in my pocket again. I didn't know this was not the right thing to do, and it meant disrespecting this new boss. We talked for a short five minutes outside the factory at the side of the gate. Then this man named Ahmed said that I was hired, and he would start paying me 11 Lebanese liras per day. He told me I could start work for him the next morning, if I wanted to, and then he mentioned that he was hiring an employee and not a boss. I didn't know what he meant by that, and at the same time while he was telling me this, he got paged by others to go to his office. You could hear the paging on the factory's loudspeakers. Ahmed, the new boss, asked me to wait next to the gate and said he would be back. I turned around and asked John what he meant by saying he's hiring an employee and not a boss. My cousin told me not to worry much because his boss, Ahmed, has a big ego, and he doesn't like to see anyone making it obvious that they know more than he does. According to him, his vision of a good employee is that everyone should listen to his instructions only. He wanted to act like a master over everyone. No one should look him in the eyes directly. Then my cousin said, "Maybe when he saw you talking to him with both your hands in your pockets, he got offended." I said, "But, John, you know better than that. I didn't mean anything. It's November and it's cold. My hands are cold." After pointing this out to my cousin John, I don't know why I got a little insecure about this subject. I waited another twenty minutes for this new egomaniac boss to show up, and when I saw him coming, I was already standing there like a soldier with both of my hands out of my pockets this time. The only thing missing from the whole picture was to salute him. My understanding of human behavior is that we are all born to work and help each other because we all need each other to survive in this world. For me no one is better than anyone else. We are all God's children. I was thinking to myself, wow, what a nonsense issue! If it wasn't for my desperation to work, I was really going to say something and refuse the offer. But, apparently, the world wasn't going to see it my way after all. After a twenty-minute wait in the cold next to the factory's gates, Mr. Ahmed, the new boss, arrived and right away without any warning and by observing the way I looked, said, "See, now that's much better." He was referring to my hands being out of my pockets. Well, I had to swallow my pride and explain to him that my hands were cold, and I didn't mean to offend him in any way. Then I thanked him for his trust in me and hiring me to start working for him. I thanked my cousin John for his referral, and then I left to go home and break the news to everyone.

Everyone was happy to hear the news about my new job, the security of having a job, and my being able to work again after being sick and at home. We could all survive better now. I got up the next morning and happily went to work in the same area where my old work place was. After all the lies I fed my previous boss about this factory offering me a job, it got translated into reality. I finally got a job at this place, and I shouldn't have felt bad about what I had done, thank God. The taxicab driver dropped me off a walking distance from this new factory. I walked in and asked to see the supervisor, Mr. Ahmed. As usual, and in the Middle East, some bosses were late coming to work in the morning. I waited in his office about a half an hour until he showed up. We both said good morning to each other, and then he said, "Let me take you to our accounting office to register your name."

I asked, "Am I going to be paid weekly or monthly?"

"We pay biweekly to our Lebanese citizens, but you should be getting your pay weekly because—"

Right before he completed his sentence, I said, "Because I'm an illegal." He looked at me and said, "Yes, you are."

I walked behind him and went to meet this short-tempered accountant. He was another Muslim accountant who hated Christians. By now I was familiar with this scenario because of the last job I worked at in the Yuma factory across the street from this one. This new accountant didn't care about anyone as well. He started to talk to me in a foul language at first. I waited and listened to his abuse with no words coming out of my mouth. That was the welcoming speech I got on my first day. Then he said, "You son of bitch illegals are always here. We can't get our own people to work for us."

I said, "Sir, your own people won't work squeezing two shifts of work into one for half the price." He looked at me and smiled, and then turned to the supervisor, Ahmed, and asked him, "Where did you get this dog from (referring to me)?" The supervisor said, "Hey, finish the work. I've got to get him started before the big boss gets in." As soon as this new drama was over, I followed the supervisor down the stairs and listened to his instructions. I was handed some loose sandpapers with different grains; some were rough, and some were soft. Then I was directed to one corner of the factory where a lot of new refrigerators were standing free, and they had external body damage. This entire work process is just like repairing car body damage after an accident. I was supposed to use the sand papers to sand out the paint by hand from these refrigerators all day long. I used my hands all day long, sanding back and forth. Each hand must have gone back and forth a thousand times every day. It was very painful to do this daily to earn a living for my family. But, nevertheless, by working I didn't have to beg or ask anyone for a dime. I depended on my physical body to work day in and day out. Afterward the refrigerators were going back and forth to my department for more sanding process before its finalized stage of being restored through a paint job. After the process, these refrigerators would turn as good as new, and later they would be shipped to the market place ready to be sold for a very good profit. Apparently, all these refrigerators were getting damaged while they were being transferred via ships from Europe to the Lebanese ports in the Middle East.

I was happy to see my cousin John every day around lunch time. We got to talk about back home and high school days, and we were both sad that we couldn't live life back in Iraq the way it should have been. We worked like dogs to earn money to feed our families. We also knew that nothing in life would last forever. Two months had gone by, and I felt this job was going to finish me sooner rather than later. It was very hard physical work, and soon I would be turning into an older man at a young age. Working with your hands like a machine and doing what machines do was not easy. I worked at this place for two whole months for a period of nine to ten hours a day without missing any days, but I was only getting paid for eight hours a day instead.

One day as I was working and sanding a refrigerator, a fight among the Lebanese work- ers broke out. It was for some nonsense political reasons. One of the workers who were involved in the fight went to his car and got something from the trunk of his car, and then went back into the factory. He had a machine gun in his hand. We all ran for cover when we saw the weapon, and we hid behind the appliances. Then I heard gunfire. This worker started to fire in the air and threatened anyone that was going to say something bad about Palestinians. He was going to shoot them down. My cousin John and I were hiding behind a heavy metal appliance to have some type of cover and protection, and just in case a stray bullet would fly in the air and come our way. This ordeal didn't last more than a half hour. The factory had called the authorities who sent their SWAT-like team over. In Lebanon they were called Group 16 (Fergot el Setaash). They came with their weapons and pagers and asked the worker to surrender his weapon. No one was going to give up the fight or the weapon. It was something called Lebanese Arabian ego, or it could have been natural human pride. Both sides were not giving in. Another gunfight started and lasted three minutes where we had to get down on the floor again and seek refuge not to get hit or killed. Three minutes later we heard the factory worker yelling out in Arabic, "I'm hit. Help me please." He laid down his machine gun and surrendered himself. Well, thank God for that. It was over. We all went back to work, but my hands were shaking from the whole thing as I was in fear once more. I went home and told everyone what had happened. My dad told me to quit and not go back. I said I had no choice. The next day I went back and started the day again hoping no more surprises would occur. Sure enough, three more weeks and nothing happened. The worker in question with the machine gun was fired on the spot by the factory owner as he was getting carried out by the paramedics.

Three weeks later, on a Tuesday, I witnessed one of our factory workers sanding one of the appliances by using the sanding machine that was given to him by the factory's super-visor; a tool I had never been familiar with to use. It was all new to me. He said he would show me how to use it and share it with me, so I don't have to work that hard with my hands. I thanked him. He was a native and a legal citizen born in Lebanon. I started to use the sanding machine more often after he trained me how to use it. I started to finish more work than usual in the days that followed. As I recall, on a Thursday of the following week in January 1975, the supervisor noticed that I was using this sanding machine. Then in a rage, he walked towards me, pulled the plug and took it away from me. He told me, "We don't pay you dogs to use any machines, so use your own hands." Wow! This was very unfair and stupid as far as I was concerned, and I was confused. Instead of using my own hands where I could finish only half of my daily work, I could finish three units of appliances a day by using the machine where they could make more money. It didn't make sense to me at all. I walked to the supervisor's office to ask him why I couldn't use the machine. When my cousin John saw me getting concerned and upset about this, he knew it was because I'm a fair-minded individual that demands answers for wrong actions, especially three weeks ago my life was in jeopardy at this place, and we were going to be killed working for this idiot supervisor called Ahmed. John tried to warn me and stop me from confronting the supervisor.

Ahmed answered my question by saying that the orders were coming from the big bosses from above, and he had nothing to do with it. And then he asked me to leave his office and go back to work. Before I went back to my station, I went to my cousin's work area to vent out, and I told John that I'm fed up with this kind of treatment. I told him it was true that I needed the money, but never in my life would I be employed like a slave to anyone, regardless who or what they are. I walked to the supervisor's office for the second time and asked him why he wouldn't allow me to work with the machine once again. I told him I could finish more work for him, and he repeated that I was not getting paid to use the sanding machine. I asked what that was supposed to mean in Arabic. He got mad that I was talking back and questioning him. Then he said, "You are nothing but dogs and low-class people. As illegals, you should be thankful I'm giving you a job."

Well, folks, he was right about the words, "Be thankful that I'm giving you a job." But my pride got in the way this time. I was mad and a young fool at the age of nineteen, and I said everything that crossed my mind to him; all the nasty words came out of my mouth. I had no reservations anymore. There was this big discrimination against Christians in Lebanon at the time in 1975. Then I grabbed the sanding machine from the top of his desk, and I placed it on the ground in front of his office door, so he could see it as well, and I kicked it as far as my foot could kick it, just like a soccer ball. Then I told him to run like a dog and get it himself. I slammed the door in his face and went down the stairs. I saw that I had grabbed the other illegal workers' attention. They were looking in my direction in fear. I could see the impression on their faces that someone had to do this sooner or later, and they were mad as well. I walked past them while I was going to the accounting office. I went inside the accounting office and told the accountant that I wanted my money now because I'm quitting the job. He said he needed to talk to the supervisor. I turned around and closed the door. It was only me and him in his office. I said, "You have my time card. I want my money now or else."

He reached to his cash box and pulled some money out in fear and handed it to me. I walked out and went home.

I learned the next day that my cousin John as well as three other people had walked out on the job that day as well, realizing that no matter what the day would bring their way as far as work in order to make a living, they could do the work elsewhere. They didn't want to work in this factory like a slave and be a part of it anymore. Folks, I'm not sure if I was right or wrong but it didn't matter to me at that time. I was pushed hard enough.

I ask you to be the judge!

CHAPTER

15

Sex with Gemela, Playing Sports, and Lost Hopes

Nothing I can do or say would comfort me from the pain of losing a job and being uncertain in life. I was going to look for another job soon in another place. In the following week, I went to see the owners of the junkyard place. Gemela, the girl I knew previously, had told me about this junkyard some months ago. She asked me to call her first before going there. I did just that. I called her using the phone at the grocery store below our apartment building. She sounded happy to hear from me once more after all these months. Then she said, "Can we meet again?" I said, "Sure."

We agreed to see each other the following day, so I went to her place and knocked on her apartment door. She opened the door wearing again a veil-like see-through clothing welcoming me inside her apartment. I was thrilled to see her and to see the way she was presenting herself. I offered to take her out, so we could talk. She said she had already ordered some food, and it was on its way up. She said I should wait in the living room because she had some matters to take care of in her bedroom, and she would be back. I sat down on the living room couch and as I waited for her, I started to talk to myself that life has a price for everything, and I think I knew what my price to pay was. I was going to sleep with her again in order for her to do me a favor. Then I told myself, hey, why not? I needed some of this physical attention too, but then I was not visiting her for this. Fifteen minutes later, she came out of her bedroom all freshened up and smelling good. She came and sat next to me and kissed me on my right cheek. I kissed her back, and then the doorbell rang. She said, "Do you mind getting the food for me? The food has been paid for since yesterday." My mind went, "Oh, I see." So, when I called her yesterday, she already had all this planned for today?

Well, I did just that while she went away from the door into her kitchen because she didn't want to expose herself to others. I opened her apartment's door, got the bags from the delivery boy, closed the door and went to the kitchen to set the bags on the table. Gemela didn't wait.

She grabbed me and pulled me to the living room sofa and started to take my clothes and hers off at the same time. She said, "It's been a long time since I've done anything with you."

I said, "But I'm not here for that. I came to ask you for a favor. I need to work—"

Before I could finish my sentence, she closed her mouth on mine. I didn't have any other choice but to engage in the whole operation. I called it, "Operation Wanting Me". Well, an hour later we had to put the cold food in the oven to be heated, and then we sat down to eat. She told me how lucky she was to see me, and she had not dated anyone after we had broken up. There was no way we could end up with each other as companions. Among the reasons were that my destiny was not to stay in Lebanon, but to leave for the US. I told her that I do care about her very much, but we could only stay as friends and meet each other once in a great while and that we couldn't have a serious relationship. She agreed on this one. Then I said, "We come from two different cultures, and that was the reason I walked away the last time. Plus, my parents are very conservative in nature, they would never allow for all this to happen in the first place, and that's not fair to you. I hope you understand, and I'm sorry for all that has happened." She took my hand and said no several times. "Don't apologize. It's my fault that I got you involved with me."

I had to change the subject right away by asking, "How is your work and how are you doing with your parents?" I noticed that I touched a soft nerve in her. Then I saw her tears well up in her eyes and just about to stream down. She looked at me at first, and then said, "Let me call Pierre, the owner of the junkyard, for you now." She got hold of Pierre, and she talked to him over the phone. She asked me if I was going to be free to visit the junkyard next Monday. I said, "Sure, no problem." She confirmed it with Pierre, and then we chatted more about several things including what had happened at the appliance factory and about the madness that went on there. She agreed to the way I had acted and to the reasons behind leaving the factory, and she said I was right about some of the Lebanese people and their outlook toward others. I said I didn't mean to offend anyone. She said, "Don't worry. You did it for the right reasons." She encouraged me to act tough and to be macho in her country and not to be fearful of others. She said, "Because if you are soft, everyone will use you here, especially because you don't have a work permit." I listened from the native how I was supposed to act toward others in the workplace despite the fact that my parents had told me to do the opposite. I think it was a growing moment for me in how to face life in a man's world. We finished eating and relaxed a bit. Several hours later, Gemela asked me if I'd like to drink any alcohol. I said, "A little; not too much." She poured a glass of wine for her and for me. I was not used to drinking wine. Halfway down the glass, I felt I was getting numb. I laid back on the sofa watching TV and fell asleep. She went to the bathroom and came out walking toward me and once more she needed to have sex. Well, I was halfway asleep on her couch. She took over the show. It was another pleasant day for me for sure this time. It was 9:00 p.m., and I told her that I had to go home. She said I should stay, but I told her I don't want to worry my parents and besides I couldn't stay out all night, and that was my house rules. I knew right away she wanted to keep me there to have more sex later. I don't know for sure, but I think she was aiming in that direction because she had gotten drunk. I knew what was going on in her mind because I saw it in her eyes. I kissed Gemela goodbye that evening, and I thanked her for helping me. Gemela told me I should see her once a week at least. I told her I would try and then left her place.

I got home around 10:30 p.m. and right away went to the shower and cleaned up. My whole family was asleep in the living room. Our living room was divided with curtains into three sections. Two of the sections were used like bedrooms, and the third one was used as a TV room, and my parents had their own separate bedroom.

I woke up the next morning, and I was already feeling like a million bucks. I went to get some bread and milk from the store located below our apartment building. I got the breakfast items from the store. I saw our roommates, a couple who were sharing the apartment with us, and said good morning to them. The wife was already in the kitchen and was putting the tea pot on preparing breakfast for her and her husband. I told her the milk I had just gotten for us was available for her to use, and I handed her the bottle.

She thanked me for it and then said, "Wow, you're in a very up mood this morning, young man. May I ask what's going on?"

Well, I was not expecting to get any questions from her because she was not my mother, but I respected her as an older sister. I didn't want to expose my personal relationship with Gemela, so I came out with a fast answer for her and told her that I had a new job coming my way soon, and that's why I was happy. She nodded her head in agreement and said, "Very well, young man," then continued working. A few minutes later, my mom joined her in the kitchen and started to make breakfast for us.

She asked me, "Aren't you late for work?"

"No, Mom. I quit that job. I'm going to see someone on Monday at another place for a new job."

She agreed that I should have listened to my father's advice weeks ago when he told me to quit and not go back to the factory. I said, "But mom, how can we afford it when there is rent due the following week?" She agreed with me and kissed my forehead and thanked me in her own way for taking our family's responsibilities and burdens to bear on my shoulders at an early age.

An hour later after breakfast, I went down to walk to the soccer field, which was a block away behind our apartment building. I went there and watched some young adults playing soccer as early as 8:00 a.m. I found out they were a local group from our neighborhood getting ready for the upcoming local competitions for that area. The ball went out of the field, and I kicked it back in. After a short while as I was watching one of the players practicing how to tackle the ball, he stopped and approached me and asked if I wanted to join them and play with them on their team. After all, I was only nineteen years old at the time, and right away the blood rushed into my veins and my hopes were renewed that I could play soccer once more, especially because I was too busy to pursue my dreams for some time. Now someone was calling me to be on their team in a sport that I adore. I was almost going to say yes when my mind started to plant some fears in me about what if I got injured and how was I going to go to work. Again, work was more important to me than playing at the time. I said no at first to the player, but my heart was saying yes. He ignored my no answer and asked me again. He told me they needed a center field player, and could I be the one. Well, I couldn't refuse the offer the second time around because that was exactly where my position was back in Iraq, and I gave him a yes answer, but I told him I didn't have any sports gear for soccer with me. They told me not to worry and handed me a jersey, shorts and soccer shoes. You can't imagine the joy that took over me, and I felt a dream was coming true. I didn't care at that moment, and I got selfish for the first time in my life to say yes to something that I wanted for myself. But I didn't know what I was getting myself into. I thought playing soccer with this team was going to be exactly the way it was back home in Iraq. I started to practice with them. I knew the trick of the trade, and I was a fast runner at the same time. I was faster than the other players possibly because I took after my dad who was a champion in the 100-meter race and after my uncle, my mom's younger brother, who was a professional soccer player back home in Iraq. He played in the mid 1960's for the Iraqi national team as a professional. I guess soccer was and still is in my DNA.

Okay, now this new team, which I had just joined, had a game coming up on that Sunday. I told myself it was okay because I had some time on my hands to play. Before I went back to look for work the following Monday, I practiced with the team the Friday and Saturday before that Sunday game. I had very little time to know everyone's style at first. The Sunday game took place in the field just behind our apartment building. The game started around 3:00 p.m., and the scores were going in our favor. I managed to score a goal from the penalty box by tackling the defense line of two players and shooting the ball into the opponent's net. It was an equalizer goal, and we ended up with a 1–1 score at the end of the first half. The second half started, and more people parked their cars along the street to step out and watch the game. In the twentieth minute of the second half, our forward player managed to score the second goal, but the referee called it as offside; meaning it was not a goal. Here was where I saw two gunmen with pistols shoot in the air and run toward the center field toward the referee. Right away, when I saw these gunmen shooting, I ran out from the soccer field and up to my apartment, leaving the game and the field behind. I went to the back balcony to watch what was going to happen from a distance. The two men held the referee, and they started to kick him with their feet and punch him in the nose. I said to myself, "Wow, what a country! Everyone has a gun in their trunks. It seems no laws are getting enforced, and no one dares to do it." In Lebanon the society was divided amongst itself in groups, and most of these groups hated each other because of religion or politics for that matter in the 1970's. Well, so much for playing soccer in this neighborhood. We didn't have any situation exist like this back home in Baghdad in sports, but things changed dramatically when Saddam's regime took charge of everything. The regime had made everything worse compared to Lebanon. No one other than the police had guns in their possession in Iraq. It was not allowed and was forbidden for the public to have guns back then, but some tribes did have their own guns.

On Monday morning, I woke up and got ready to go to the junkyard to meet Mr. Pierre, the owner. I went to the other side of the town and walked into the junkyard and saw that the owner was in his office waiting for me. I knocked on his office door, and he motioned to me to come into his office. At first, he took a good look at me through his glasses and said, "Good morning."

I replied, "Good morning, Mr. Pierre."

He looked at me from top to bottom. It made me wonder why he was looking at me like that and said, "Have you ever worked in a metal junkyard before, son?"

"No, sir," I answered. I was wondering if Gemela had told him about me yet. I thought this job was ready for me to start right away. As I was thinking these thoughts in my head, he said, "I'm not sure if you are a good fit for this job."

"Sir, may I ask you why? I'm a very dependable and hard worker, and I can work as long as is needed to finish the task, sir."

He didn't know that I was very desperate for a job and money that day.

"Well," he said, "first you are not strong enough physically to do this kind of a work, and most of the men I have here working for me know what they are doing. Then I have no time to train anyone, especially someone like you who will leave this job in the end and fly away to his final destination as an immigrant. It's a waste of time for me to hire you."

I said, "I am sorry, sir. I don't understand why you're telling me all this. I was told that you needed some laborers around here, and Gemela told me she talked to you about me! And according to Gemela, you agreed to meet me and offer me this job today."

When he heard Gemela's name, he got up from his chair and said, "I don't want to hear her name again. Do you understand, young man?"

I was confused and puzzled. I said, "Thank you for your time." As I was going out of the door, he said, "Come back here."

He opened his desk drawer and said, "Grab as much as you want." I looked in the drawer. It was falling apart from being full of Lebanese quarter of a lira coin currency.

I said, "Sir, but I'm not a homeless person."

He said, "No, I know that. But please take some for your trouble for coming here."

Well, sure enough, I needed some money to go back; otherwise, I was going to walk all the way home. I took as much as it would cost to pay the cab with quarters. I said thank you, and I left and went directly to Gemela's house without thinking that I had limited funds with me in my pocket. She was not there, and the building doorman told me she would be back in one hour. I waited for a good hour and half. When Gemela pulled to the front of the building and she saw me waiting there for her, she was puzzled. I said, "Can I talk to you for a minute?"

"Let's go upstairs," she said

We took the elevator and went up to her apartment. She asked me what was wrong. I told her what had happened at the junkyard office.

She said, "Well, I'm going to tell you a secret, but I don't want you to get mad and leave me."

I asked, "What is that?"

She said, "Mr. Pierre was my old boyfriend before I met you, and he was coming to my place often. We had relations and he was paying my rent all that time. Then after I met you, things changed in me where I found that an honest person like you was more important for me in life to associate with instead of a person like Pierre who had used me all along."

The blood started to rush into my head once more, and I was getting angry inside, but I hid my anger somewhat for the moment. I said, "Go on."

She said she found a job two days ago and called Pierre and told him she didn't want to see him anymore. But she also said that she didn't have a way to contact me because she had neither a phone number, nor knew where I lived in order to warn me not to go to the junkyard that same morning. I listened, but I couldn't believe a word she was telling me. I said in a harsh voice, "Well, thanks, but no thanks for your late warning. All this time you've been with me, were you also seeing him?"

She hugged me again and said, "No, I was not. Listen I still care about you. Please don't go. I'm very sorry. I didn't mean to hurt you. I didn't mean it."

I said, "I'm sick to my stomach of hearing about this, but I will contact you later. I'm not in the mood for you now." She cried and said sorry again as I was walking out.

I walked out of her apartment, and the whole world was closing in on me with mixed emotions: anger, hate, plus the fear of not having a job promise. This situation was causing a great deal of stress in me. I had to think fast about what was going to be my next move.

CHAPTER

16

Facing Death - Count Two

After I left Gemela's place, I walked some miles in the direction of my home, and just about two miles before getting home, I noticed an industrial complex located on the right side of the road. It was an aluminum fabrication shop. I saw workers loading the truck with aluminum made windows and doors. I heard conversation among some of the laborers being spoken in the Armenian language while they were loading the truck. I got my courage back and walked toward them and noticed my friend, Art, and his older brother were working at this place. I knew them both from back home; they were our neighbors in Baghdad. They, along with their families, were also registered like us with World Council of Churches organization to immigrate to the United States of America. Art saw me walking toward the factory and asked what I was doing there. I said, "You don't want to know." He asked what was wrong. I told him that I was looking for work like yesterday and things were not looking very good financially for me. He said, "Just a minute. Wait here." Then he went inside the factory and came out and said the owner wanted to see me.

I said, "Are you sure? But how?"

He said not to worry. I was in the right place at the right time because that morning the boss had just fired one of his employees due to some misconduct, and they were shorthanded that day. The boss didn't have any plans to fire anyone, but it happened, and they needed people, and he didn't know what to do about it until I showed up. Art added by saying that they have this big project, and it must be delivered today and must be installed as well. He asked, "Are you interested to work with us today, and now?" If any of you reading this and don't believe there is a God, please think again. I didn't plan this, but it was planned for me. I was happy, very happy, and I got excited and was ready to jump in the back of the truck. I went in and met this wonderful man who knew me only through Art's and his older brother's recommendation. I was able to meet him and get hired that morning. The last name of the owner of this factory was Mr. Bald.

He asked, "Son, what is your name?" I said, "My name is Mark, sir."

He asked, "Have you worked with aluminum before?" I said, "Yes sir, at the Yuma factory."

He was happy to hear that. He said he knew Yuma because the owners of Yuma were his friends. Then he asked, "How about working for me today, can you do that?" I looked around and I saw Art's head going up and down telling me to say yes.

I said, "Yes sir, but how much are you going to pay me?"

He smiled and said, "I can pay you more than what you think. I know your situation is the same as Art and his brother, isn't it, son? Don't worry about money. You help me, and I'll help you."

Sure enough, he did just that. I started to work for Mr. Bald, also known as A/A Aluminum Company. I was thrilled that day in how God could plan the right time and the right place for you without you even knowing what good can come your way.

I started to work at this place, and my job was to get the aluminum raw bars and carry them to the second floor. Then I got trained on how to cut them, drill holes in them using the drill press machines and worked with other equipment, which were made for this type of work. I started to use some diagram plans. I learned how to put together all these cuts and formed aluminum materials to finalize them as window and door assembly products for commercial buildings. In the end, along with the other co-workers, we had to load them on the delivery truck. They were all ready to be delivered to the job site. At the job site we had to install them on the building's exterior wall openings. I was not alone doing the work. There were five other employees, including myself and Art, as well as one supervisor. The good part was we all spoke the same language, and we were Christians. We got along very well for some reason. On Fridays before the weekend and since this place was open for five days a week only, I was free on the weekends. It was the best job with the best hours that I ever had to work with. I had a chance finally to visit and explore Lebanon as a country by traveling all over the tourist attraction places and be at the beach on some weekends. We were all called to the owner's office on Fridays before the weekend. Mr. Bald, the boss, was the only person who was authorized to pay us directly. In other words, he didn't have any nasty accountants like I had encountered at the other factories who were partial in their acts and thinking. The A/A Aluminum Company was not a big company back in 1975, but it was big enough to pay eight employees in total including the owner. We got paid weekly and in cash, of course. I was told by Art that on paydays if the owner asked how much money I needed, I was to respond to him with, "Whatever your heart desires." I asked Art, "Why should I say this?"

He told me the owner was a very kind man and was a very fair one as well. He said, "If you leave it to him, he will pay you more than what you want."

I said, "How will he know how much I need and how many hours I have worked every week?"

Art said, "Don't worry. My older brother and I have been working for Mr. Bald for several months now, and we haven't been disappointed yet. Plus, the man has been in this business for a long time and he knows the pay rates."

Art also said that Mr. Bald had been paying them according to the labor board rates regardless of their illegal status. Well, this sounded very good to me. My turn came to be asked the question about how much I needed. I replied with, "Sir, I'll be happy to receive whatever your heart is set on to pay me." Then I remembered that my grandmother was sick at home, and we couldn't manage to pay to get a doctor for her that week. I told the owner about it at the same time as I was to get paid that week. Honestly, I don't know why I had to tell the owner about my grandmother too. It just slipped out, but it was the truth. The owner looked into my eyes and then said, "Listen. Stand here beside me until I finish paying everyone else." I did whatever he asked me to do and waited after the last person had been paid and gone. The owner asked me and asked his seventy-five-year-old friend, who had been working with him from the inception of this business as a store keeper and a guard, to help him close the shop that day. Well, I got worried that maybe I shouldn't have mentioned my grandmother's issue, and maybe he was going to let me go.

His old friend, who was acting as a guard and as an informer for the boss at the same time, and I helped to do the closing of the shop. I pulled the roll up gate or the shop door down to the ground, and I locked it. The roll up gate was too heavy for the old man to bear. This old man was safeguarding the shop when all employees were in the field. He took upon himself to act as an undercover informer for the boss without the boss's knowledge should anyone bad mouth the big boss or think to take action to harm the business. After closing, his old friend went home and the owner and I remained behind in the parking lot. We walked to reach the boss's car, and the boss stopped and reached into his pocket and pulled 175 Lebanese liras and handed it to me. Fifty extra liras were included in my first week's pay. The boss said, "Son, take your grandmother to a doctor right away and next week please let me know about her condition. If she still doesn't feel well yet, I can help you more financially, so she can get well. But do me a favor. Please don't say anything to the other employees that I'm doing this for you. And if you have any other issues, come to me directly and talk to me alone, and not in front of anyone else." He thanked me for my work for that week. I was speechless. I don't know why I hadn't found a shop like that to work for all along, but things really do happen for a reason. I thanked Mr. Bald and told him I would see him Monday morning and to have a nice weekend.

Folks, do you know what 175 liras could buy in Lebanon in 1975? I was getting paid like everyone else; meaning like the Lebanese citizens. The monthly rent for my apartment, the one we were all living in was only 250 liras. We were just paying 125 liras, which was our portion of the rent each month, and the rest was paid by others who shared the apartment with us. I alone was getting paid almost that much in a week's time. Wow! I was extremely happy. And I was very happy that I could do more for my entire family. I was also happy that I could go anywhere and any place, and I could pay for my food at restaurants and elsewhere due to this new 500 liras per month pay at this factory.

Well thank you, Lord, for this kind of working arrangement. I went home that day and told my mom and dad about this job, the pay rate, and how I found this place by accident. My whole family was happy to know we could live a little bit better than before. On that same day and right away, I called a doctor to come and visit our home to examine my grandmother. A few hours later the doctor was at our doorstep since this was not an emergency. In Lebanon they did have doctors who made house calls in those days. He examined her and said she needed a shot because she had a very bad cold and it could get worse, if we didn't take care of it. I said, "What kind of shot are you talking about, doctor?" The doctor reached into his bag and pulled a tiny bottle of medicine and pulled out a glass made syringe from inside a small metal box that was in his bag as well. He asked my mom if she could pour some water into the metal box and boil it over the stove and told her he would handle it from there. I was happy to see my grandmother was going to be well, and I could pay for it. After the shot the doctor wrote a prescription for her, and my dad took it from the doctor and said he would take care of it. Well for some reason there was some hardship between my dad and his mom all along. My grandmother put on an act at times, so her only born son could pay extra attention toward her needs. She wanted to be treated like my mom. This was the case with all three of them living together. I couldn't blame my grandmother because her husband died when she was young and in her thirties. When my mom got married with my dad, she realized she had to take care of her mother-in-law as well. This was part of the package in the old days. And every now and then her mother-in-law was acting up, and my mom had to learn to deal with it all her life, but, at times, unwillingly. It was not an easy task, and I don't know how she did it. My mom and my grandmother had gotten very close with each other relation-wise. When my dad was in prison back home, both women knew what to do, as well as when and how to take care of the family. In a modern society in today's world, no wife would like to live with her in- laws in the same household forever, but my mom did it without a choice in the matter and out of love and respect for my father.

Going back to my grandmother's sickness, this time it was not a false alarm. She was sick, so we all took turns taking care of her. For one, we knew some of her sickness was an emotional one due to her relocation out of Iraq; and two, it was for being away from all her daughters and their families. I took the prescription from my dad and told him I would take care of it. I had to wait until Monday for it because most of my weekly pay, including the extra pay, all went to pay for the doctor visit and the shot he gave her. On Monday I went to work and around lunch time I asked the old man to see the owner. At first, the old man got upset at the reason I gave him as to why I had to see the boss early in the morning even before I started work. I didn't understand why he acted like that. I guess he was being protective of the boss because he was his lifetime friend. My insistence had made him agree to go and alert the boss that I needed to talk to him. Then I noticed the old man was coughing very badly that morning. I asked, "Are you okay?" Because of his age, I used to call him father the way everyone else did in the factory. He responded with an angry voice and said, "I'm okay" in a short and brief manner, which was his communication style on a normal base. The old man asked me to wait outside the boss's office. He knocked on the boss's door and went in. The boss was on the phone, and then the old man came out of the office and notified me that the boss would see me soon. A few moments later the office door opened, and I was called in by the boss.

I said, "Good morning, Mr. Bald."

He said, "What's wrong, son? Did anything happen upstairs in the factory?" I said, "No, sir, but you did ask me to come to you if I needed help." "That's right."

"Sir, thank you for your help with the extra money to pay for the doctor, but I need to get medicine for my grandmother, and I can't wait until payday. Can I get an advance from you and go buy the medicine around lunch time?"

He said, "Sure, no problem." Then he called his old friend into the office. The old man said he heard the conversation, and at that moment Mr. Bald and the old man got into an argument. Mr. Bald told him, "When are you going to stop listening through the office doors? I don't want anyone to spy on my office, but I'm keeping you here to protect you as we agreed a long time ago." I was just standing there and listening to their argument. Then I confirmed that the old man was spying on all of us. Well, it was not my business to be a mediator between them. I waited until they finished arguing. Then Mr. Bald handed his car keys to the old man. He said, "Take him," meaning me, "to the pharmacy that we deal with and let him get what he wants for his family." He added he will call the pharmacist himself and will tell him that we are on our way to his pharmacy. The pharmacist was going to charge the cost of the medicine to the factory's account where Mr. Bald was going to pay the bill later.

The old man was not too happy, and he yelled at me at first saying, "Let's go now." I had to ride with him in the boss's car, and we went to this pharmacy. I gave the Pharmacist the doctor's prescription, and I got the medicine. I asked the pharmacist "Sir, while you are at it, can you give something to the old man. He sounds sick." It seems I got the old man off guard, and he got angry. He started talking back to me in an anger manner while he was coughing and said, "If I need any medicine, I'll get it myself, you little stupid son of a bitch." Well, the pharmacist knew him for a long time and had dealt with him previously. He came out from behind the counter and said to the old man, "Hey, the kid is right. Please sit down and let me see how bad your cough is." The old man didn't have a choice. He was weak physically, but very stubborn at the same time, and I heard him say to the pharmacist, "I don't want any pity from anyone, especially from Mr. Bald." Well, it must have been something bad that had happened in the past between the old man and Mr. Bald. I don't know for sure. The pharmacist examined his cough and gave him some medicine to take with him. The old man insisted that he didn't want any free favors. Then the pharmacist told him not to worry, and that he would put it on Mr. Bald's tab. Nothing was satisfying to this old man. My main concern that day was to get the medicine and give it to my grand- mother as soon as possible. We walked away from the pharmacy and got into the boss's car and went back to the factory. While the old man was driving back, I had to ask a question to the old man because it was a nature of mine to try and resolve unhappy situations, if I could. I asked the old man why he is so angry all the time and doesn't want people to help him. He said it wasn't my damn business.

I said, "Okay, but it's obvious that you need help, and you can't help yourself as far as I can see from the way you are dressed, or the way you talk and eat."

He looked at me with an angry look and said, "Okay, kid, we're just about to get to the factory, and if any word comes out of your mouth about this medicine, which I got for me, I'll be sure that you get fired."

I said, "But I only mean well, and I want to help you."

He said, "No one can help me. Even God himself can't help me, so don't try to be a hero here."

I told myself to stop asking him questions because I realized that he wasn't ready to talk about his problems. We reached the factory site, and I went to work. Mr. Bald was on the second floor of the factory where we all worked.

I thanked him for his efforts, and then I said, "I will pay you the cost of the medicine on payday."

He said, "Kid, let's get back to work." He needed to get a big load of windows delivered by Friday to this new project site in downtown Beirut.

I said, "Very well, sir, I'll do my part and my best.

On a Thursday afternoon during that same week we were at a new high-rise building construction site in downtown Beirut to work and finish the window installations, but we were short of raw materials to make the rest of the windows. There were only four large windows missing to complete the job. Mr. Bald had paid for the materials some time ago, and the raw materials were to come from Europe via ships to Beirut's port. But due to some type of civil unrest a few days earlier, the city was at a halt. No one could get near the ports to get anything out, and the word on the street was that the shipyard was on strike. This delayed the process for our factory, as we discovered. Mr. Bald said that he had already spoken with the project contractors and owners in the morning regarding a solution of some sort. He was going to deliver the finished windows and install them on time, but they had to wait for the rest of the window installations as soon as the port situation changed. This had created a delay in completing the work schedule.

That Thursday afternoon I worked to load up the finished windows we had on the truck with Art and his older brother. Helping this process also involved the old man. We all worked hard and got the delivery to the building site that afternoon. It was really an exhausting day for all of us. The next day, Friday, was a pay day. Everyone got paid first, and then at the very end it was my turn. I got my 125 liras again, and I asked the owner what the cost for the medicine was.

He laughed and said, "It's a gift from the pharmacy."

I was puzzled, as usual. He said, "Son, the work you are doing for me is enough assurance for me to know that you are doing it from the bottom of your heart." Then he added, "This is my factory and my business, and I've been watching all of you work and do your best for me so far. I like what I see in all of you, and in terms of how all of you collectively have been working hard to make me look good, which is something very valuable that money can't buy, I will fulfill my promise to pay you on time. I know all of you by now." He meant this for me, Art, his brother, and all our families. "You all had comfortable lives back home, and you had to flee your country and give up your life savings and homes to live here and work illegally to survive. I can lose little and invest in all of you by paying you more to help you all live life a bit easier in my country. Go home now, and I'll see you Monday. I don't want you to worry about the small token of medicine that you just got for your grandmother."

Wow! Again, this man was a superb man at heart. It seemed it was a good match for me to be working for him.

On Monday morning, February 3, 1975, I didn't need to go to the factory. We were to meet at the job site in downtown Beirut to install the windows on the high-rise commercial building. I got there very early around 7:00 a.m., and it was a little foggy. The building was located half a block from Beirut's port and sea shores. I went up to the fourth floor at this empty and harsh cement skeleton building. I was standing on the back balcony while eating my breakfast and drinking my hot tea that morning. You could see the blue Mediterranean Sea from the back balcony, and it was breathtaking scenery. The view of the sea felt like a million bucks. While I was enjoying the view, I heard Art in the background walking up the stairs. As he was walking up, I remembered that just that last Thursday we worked hard loading the windows inside this building by carrying them one-by-one up the stairs and set-ting them on each floor because the building's elevators were not installed yet, and now I am taking a break for breakfast before I start the day working on the installation of the windows.

Art came up and said, "Wow, what a view!"

I said, "Yep, and we're going to be here for about a month to install all of these windows. It'll be good to get some kind of mini-burner, so we can warm up here in these cold February days, and, in the meantime, we could heat up our lunches using this mini-burner."

He asked, "What for?"

I said, "Art, think. I know you're busy watching the view, but I'm going to say it again. We need a portable mini-burner to warm and heat our lunches, okay?"

He realized this a few moments later and turned around and said, "For lunch, right?" I knew he wasn't listening very well.

We went back to start work at the site, and as the day progressed, we realized we had to set up a lunch room for us somewhere on the fourth floor, and then gradually move the set up to the other floors as we finish installation on each level. I suggested the fourth-floor balcony since we were standing on it.

He said, "How are we going to keep this mini-burner safe from being stolen?"

I said, "What happened, Art? Did you lose your common sense by looking at the sea too much?"

He said, "You know we don't have such a view back home because Iraq is not located beside the ocean."

I said, "Listen, we'll hide the mini-burner with the tools inside the metal tool box." He said it was a good idea. Then I said, "The only thing we'll have to carry with us from now on is the gas fuel cylinder for the mini-burner so no one else will use it, if they ever find it while we're gone. Art agreed and said it was a good idea.

It was around 8:30 a.m. that morning and our supervisor arrived late at the job site. We didn't have any direction or any idea about where to start the work with the window installations on the fourth floor. It was my first time being a window installer on a commercial building. Jake, the supervisor, had the plans with him because he needed to study them the night before in order to put the work schedule together for the next day for us. When Jake arrived that morning, he apologized that he was late. We didn't say anything, especially because it was a good one-hour break for me and Art to enjoy the morning view of the sea. Then after getting our instructions, we started to get our tools together. Jake trained us onsite how to do the window installation. We learned that this building contractor who had done the cement work for the building window openings had done them wrong. He had made a big mistake. His crew had left out the calculation of the cement thickness from the entire opening equation. We measured the rough window openings, and they weren't corresponding with our window measurements. "Houston, we have a problem." To cut a long story short and to avoid a lengthy explanation of the technical aspects of the work, we couldn't fit the windows, which we had delivered, in the openings for each floor. They had supplied our factory with their correct plans, but with the wrong window sizes. The factory had followed the wrong measurements to make the window sizes accordingly. This was going to create a big schedule delay problem for us. One of the building engineers had come to the job site that morning to inform us about the mistakes. Jake told him that he knew about the problem already and was seeking a solution. Eventually, you could fix a problem like this by cutting out the extra cement from each window opening. Modifications of this magnitude require the availability of special equipment. In order to fix this problem, we needed to bring some other machinery to the job site from the factory. This task was not possible to achieve due to the unavailability of elevators in this building. During the communication period between the engineer and Jake, the latter had informed the engineer about an extra cost that must be associated and added to the final job cost by Mr. Bald since this was a design mistake and not a mistake in the making of the product by our factory. Well, so far, our first day on the job site didn't go as expected. All three of us had to go back to the factory and tell the owner about the bad news. Jake had informed Mr. Bald about the problem, and he was mad to hear about this unnecessary delay. First, he was mad at the building engineers for not monitoring the process, and second, at the personnel who had planned the work for this building which was totally unsupervised.

A new decision was made that afternoon as we stood and watched. We had to go back to the job site and manually load all the delivered windows, one floor at a time, on our truck and take them back to the factory. It was an extremely difficult work carrying these windows down to the truck manually due to the unavailability of elevators. There was no quality control in those years or safety measures when working on commercial buildings in Beirut Lebanon; at least I hadn't seen or witnessed any such thing. All the new modification work was charged back to the owners of the building for their errors at an extra cost. Mr. Bald, the owner of A/A Aluminum Factory, was a very happy man for getting paid twice for the same job and making more money without utilizing any new materials. His profit margin rose to two and a half times what he was expecting to get from this job in the first place, and we learned this information from our supervisor. The owner had the right to be happy, and we were happy for him as well because he was the one man that deserved to have the entire world. At least that's how we all felt about him. I was a bit disappointed because it was going to take a little bit longer for us to work inside the factory again, and we wouldn't be able to enjoy the sea view around lunch time as was planned. The days I worked at the A/A Aluminum Factory were very pleasant and rewarding, and it was full of experiences for me to learn skills with this new trade.

After work in the evenings and around the weekends, I had to get myself busy with some sort of social life. The first time I entered Beirut, Lebanon, I remember how everything was new to me, and I was not fearful to endure life's challenges. So I met this native Lebanese friend while I was working at my previous job at the Yuma Air Conditioning Grills factory. He was very funny, but he believed in magic and fortune telling though. I followed him one day to this shop, which was semi-dark and smelled bad for some reason. At that shop they read your palm and supposedly could tell you about your future's unfolded events. They were fortune tellers. I was not satisfied or happy with the idea because I was more into believing in God and Christianity then to settle with the thoughts of a palm reader. But I took it as a joke because we were young and didn't know any better. It was an adventure for us to be in. We went into this shop and sat down and paid the lady to read our palms. The old lady looked at my right palm and said, "You're going to be a great person in life and people are going to admire you and somewhat follow your judgments because you're a born leader." I was trying very hard to hold my laugh within me. I didn't want to offend this old lady. She noticed me doing that and said, "Go ahead and let it out and laugh about what I'm telling you now." Folks, I couldn't hold it in anymore. I really had to let my laugh out, and they were loud laughs. She waited for me to finish laughing. Then she continued, "As I was saying, you're a born leader, but you're going to face death three times in life." Well, here I started to get a little bit uncomfortable. We're talking about facing death. Wow! This must be a serious matter! But I forgot that I shouldn't be listening to this nonsense because my faith is in God, not in palm readers. Usually they don't mention the word God themselves, but she said, "God loves you and your family, and you'll be escaping death to live more for everyone around you." When she said the word "God", my whole body went numb, and I wanted to leave that place. I thanked the lady in a hurry. I didn't want to wait for my friend's turn for his palm reading, so I left the shop and waited outside for my friend to finish. Finally, my friend came out, and we went to have a drink together at one of Beirut's downtown restaurants. I felt better after I was out of that place. It was a tense moment for me to face unknown events in the future, and it created some confusion in me not knowing if I should believe her or not.

I told my friend she wasn't a truthful lady with what she had said. It didn't make any sense to me. It was nothing but crap to me. My friend asked, "Do you remember the first incident that happened to you and how you escaped death?"

"What are you talking about?" I asked.

He added, "Do you remember the first time and behind the Yuma factory when a Palestinian kid held a machine gun to your chest and you came out of that situation clean and alive?"

I said, "Yes, I remember that."

Then he said, "You should count that as one." I asked, "Why?"

He said, "Because as far as I remember, that kind of an incident happened to another worker from our factory many years ago, and he ended up dead. The Palestinian kids with the machine guns ended up shooting him down on the spot. He didn't have a chance to talk to them in order to save his life, like you did, or walk away unharmed. So, consider yourself lucky and count that as one."

Folks, I was speechless. Wow! Was this really happening to me, and I didn't know it? My heart started to fill with fear at this point because I began to think about when and where my second time was going to be. Where am I going to face death and escape from it again and is that being counted as number two and then three. It's creepy.

The weekend was over, and on Monday morning I took the taxicab and was on my way to the A/A Aluminum Factory. I arrived there, and we started our day to work on modify-ing the window sizes, which were wrong. We all started to work hard so we could make the changes in a week's time. After all, the view of the Mediterranean Sea was stuck in my mind as well as into Art's mind. We wanted to be there sooner than later to install these windows on that building. The entire building was twelve floors high. Sure enough, we got some of the upper floor windows done first and ready to be delivered that week. Then we continued working on the lower floor windows during the coming weeks to get them ready as well. The factory was running out of space in order to store the finished products at nights. The own-er's decision was to deliver the modified windows for the upper floors first and install them in order to save space for the new products that were going to be made. We all agreed on this. It was another Thursday afternoon when we loaded the trucks to make them ready for the next morning's delivery, and we were excited. The next morning, we delivered the windows to the project site, and we started to unload and distribute them starting from the top floors to the bottom. We managed to unload the windows on five floors from the twelfth through the seventh. It took us three weeks to do all the modifications for all of the top five floors. We were to come back the next Monday to start installing them again.

On a cold Monday morning in February 1975, I went to work. I had a slow start to work, and there was something in the air that was getting to me. I didn't want to be there and work that day. There was a strange feeling that was overpowering my thoughts. I went to the top floor balcony before anyone else arrived there, so I could have a free moment to look at the sea. Around 7:00 a.m. while I was eating my breakfast and sipping the hot tea down, the other co-workers had gotten there to start their day. As usual, our supervisor arrived late at the job site and gave us instructions on how to do the work and where to start from, including some safety tips regarding how to deal with drilling holes in the concrete and fastening the screws on the top portion of the windows. This required some special physical effort in order to do the job of fastening and securing the window frames to the exterior window openings of the building. Drilling holes into the top frames using an electrical drill machine was not an easy task, and this entire operation required a great deal of force with one hand holding a heavy two-pound electric drill machine in the air in those days, and we used our other hand to hold the inside wall of the building. We had no step ladder to stand on since our factory didn't have any step ladders or any safety lines for us to use on the job site. I had to be squatting on my toes on the exterior bottom window sills as I was drilling the concrete, but at the same time, we were without any safety lines tied to our bodies while were exposed to the outside bare space of the building.

The wind was blowing very hard on the twelfth floor that day and had caused more endangerment to do the installation. Try to imagine the difficulty of doing this job and the danger that I and others were exposed to. Our supervisor had repeatedly told us to watch out for our safety. He said, "When you start to drill holes, always lean inward with your body into the building space rather than toward the street space. Furthermore, he said, don't look down at the street below where all the cars are moving rapidly because looking down will make you very dizzy, and you could lose your balance and fall down into the street from this high elevation." I remember he made a joke about it saying, "If you fall down from the twelfth floor, don't call me, but call me only if you fall from the second floor." How could you call him after a fall from twelfth floor? You would probably be dead. But a fall from the second floor will possibly give you a chance to survive. Well, everyone laughed hard, but I took it very seriously. It was not a joke, and I especially had a lot of fear being at certain heights. In an environment like a commercial construction job site and among men, you cannot show your fear. They may think you're not up to the task, and you could lose their respect toward you. This was the old school macho man ego mentality, which is a bunch of crap and nonsense.

The plan was to start installation from the twelfth floor down. Art and I worked as a team with each window. We tried not to climb and squat on our toes to do the job. Instead, we found an old wooden Pepsi Cola case. Yes, Pepsi Cola's wooden case in the 1970's, and we used it as a step ladder. It worked for us for hours, but after drilling too many holes and with the force that our feet had been pushing down against the wooden Pepsi case, the wooden box cracked and broke, and we couldn't use it anymore. Anyhow, we didn't work on the eleventh floor that day because the windows were not made ready to be installed yet. by that afternoon we were working on the tenth floor. Art and I were installing only five windows per floor in total facing the unsafe street side of the building. The other co-workers had to finish the rest of the windows per floor, which were located at the back-balcony side of the building without any endangerment. It was almost the end of our shift that day. Only two hours left before we could go home. We were very tired. Then Art and I lifted this big window. Luckily, it was made of aluminum and not very heavy to hold up for a short while. Then while it was held upward in the air, Art hammered the concrete from the edges of the window sill, so we can fit the window frame into the opening. Then we managed to slide the big window into the opening. We worked as a team. While Art started drilling holes in the bottom and the side of the window frame, I was fastening the anchors and the screws into the holes. Art's hands got tired, and I told him don't worry about the top frame. I said, "I'll squat on my toes and continue to fasten the rest of the anchor and the screws." There were only four holes left to finish the job. Art agreed, and I got up and sat on the bottom frame, balancing myself first. Then at one point while I was working on the window and out of the corner of my eye, I slowly looked down and caught the moving cars below us from the tenth floor, which sidetracked my concentration from the job. I managed to get a hold of myself and started to drill the first hole following all the advice which my supervisor had mentioned this morning. Great! I did one. I moved to take another position to drill the second hole while still holding the inside wall of the building with my left hand. Somehow, as I started to drill the second hole, the drill bit (the iron piece mounted to the end of the drill which does the drilling), broke, and I lost my sitting position balance. The drill machine went inward while my body started to go outward. I was now facing a fall from the tenth floor onto the street. Suddenly, my left hand slipped, and I was just about to fall down onto the street. I barely grabbed the top window frame with my left index finger, which kept me sitting still. My whole body was leaning out of the window held by one finger. Moments earlier when I moved to drill the second hole, one thing I didn't notice due to the sound of the drill and the moving traffic noise from below was that my supervisor had just entered the room and stood behind me next to the same wall I was working on and talking to Art while I was doing the work. Folks, God was there for me again. Apparently, my supervisor and Art saw when I slipped, and they reacted fast and rushed toward the window. Each of them got a hold of one of my legs as I was falling, so now half of my body from the hips down rested and was lying on the bottom of the window frame inside the building, and the upper portion of my body was hanging off the tenth floor.

Wow! It was another close call!

My supervisor and Art laid me down on the floor. I remember that I was awake, and, at one point, I also remember that all the workers on the floor rushed into the room to observe. Due to my fear, I went into shock, my hands and my feet were shaking, and I was cold and numb. Someone got me a bottle of water and someone put a blanket under me and under my head. Art got another jacket along with his to cover my body. I stayed laying down there for at least a half hour. In the meantime, my supervisor went out and got me some hot tea and said, "Drink it." When I took a sip, I felt there was something else that was put into the tea. He said again, "Drink it. It will help you get up." After I drank the whole thing, I knew later that he had mixed some whiskey into the tea, so I could calm down a bit and gain my strength back. I got up on my feet and, luckily, there was nothing broken in my body as far as my bones and all. That evening Art took the cab with me to accompany me home because I was a little bit out of it emotionally. I guess the alcohol drink was a bit of a strong mix for me that day. I told Art to please not tell my parents about the incident because they would make me quit my job. This job had been paying well, and my family had been living comfortably because of it. I never told them about the danger that this job had after everything that happened. Art agreed. We got home, and I thanked Art for his friendship and for saving my life. "Of course, don't mention it. See you tomorrow," he said and went home. I went up to my apartment using the building elevator. When I entered my unit, I rushed to the bathroom and right away I started vomiting. My stomach got cleared out. My mom was standing at the bathroom door and asked me what happened. I told her that I ate something bad for lunch and didn't feel well and added, "That's why Art had to bring me home."

I want to remember here and mention my supervisor, Jake. He was a good and kind person in nature, as well as Art, and I remember all the good times that I had at the A/A Aluminum Factory working together. Jake was always a joker, and he was a very wise person. I learned a great deal about life from him. His experiences and advice for me were like a piece of gold.

At home, and several hours later when I was more settled and comfortable, I went to sit down on my balcony off the living room. The palm reader's advice crossed my mind, and I prayed silently and thanked God for sparing me again. I said to myself, "Wow, Mark, this was your number two incident. What's next?"

CHAPTER
17

Facing Death - Count Three

Several months back in the summer of July 1974, I was contacted by my friend Koko from the Yuma Factory where I had worked in the past. Koko called me and said he would like to visit me since we hadn't seen each other or gotten in touch with each other for a long time, and if I would like to hang out with him. He was willing to come and pick me up, and we could go fishing. I asked him which part of town we would be going fishing. He said around the northern part of Beirut's seaside across from Casino Du Liban.

Folks, I'd like to give you some information about Casino Du Liban:

"Casino Du Liban is located in Beirut, Lebanon and is 22 km north of Beirut with an area of about 35,000 square meters in space. This casino was first opened in 1959. It closed in 1989 and reopened in 1996 after a $50 mil-lion reconstruction and refurbishment project. Peter j. Venison wrote in his memoir, "The International Hotel Business, Shadow of the Sun: Travel and Adventures in the World of Hotel", that Casino Du Liban was elegant, yet the cabaret was spectacular and rivaled anything that Las Vegas could offer. He also described it as a backdrop of a James Bond novel where clientele from the richest elite of European and Arabian societies ventured into the casino in formal black-tie attire." (Venison, 2013)

Gambling, of course, was part of this casino. It was a playground for the rich in the Middle East and Europe, but it was not a place for refugees like us. We couldn't afford it nor were we allowed in it. With that being said, I asked Koko why not go to a local area where it could be more enjoyable rather than this side of town. But that day Koko insisted going to that specific seaside saying, "Listen, if we can't do fishing at all, we could enter the casino." Then he told me he had a connection to get us into the casino, just to explore it. My thought was, "Oh boy, this is a double feature." I asked Koko, "This is only going to happen if we don't fish, right?"

Koko asked, "What do you mean?"

I said, "Think about it. How in the world would it be possible to go into the casino with the dirty clothing we have on us after fishing and with all the fish blood and odor?"

He laughed and said, "You worry too much. I just told you either the casino or fishing. Of course, we can't do both."

Well, I just wanted to have my facts all sorted out before we go. We decided to take this trip in two weeks' time and when we both had gotten paid. You see, Koko was a very good guy. He was hoping he could go to America as well. But as a Syrian citizen living in Beirut, Lebanon illegally, he was not allowed to register with the World Council of Churches because they were only accepting Christians from Iraq at the time. As a refugee, I had tried to ask the same church office regarding Koko's fate several times in the past, but a "no" answer was given by them every time. I was trying to find a way to help him out and get him registered the same way my family did, but it was beyond my reach to make it happen for him. The only possibility that existed was for him to find an Armenian or Christian Iraqi girl to wed, and then she could have a chance to enroll him with her on her refugee application. The chances for Koko to find a single woman to marry who had been registered with the church office were very slim. I kept building his hopes up with positivity about going to America, so he wouldn't lose focus of his life objectives. Koko had escaped from the harsh Syrian unjust life too, even though he had served in the Syrian armed forces as a young man in the past. He loved Lebanon more because Lebanon for the Christians was more of a balanced life to live in Beirut than in Syria or Iraq in the 1970s, but, of course, to a certain degree. His dreams were always to live in a Christian and free country like the west. We shared the same views all along about the future.

Two weeks later, on a Saturday, I met Koko at the taxi station in downtown Beirut. I didn't have any fishing gear with me; Koko had them all. I took with me my battery-operated tape recorder, a plastic bucket and some cassette tapes, which I liked to listen to, and I'm talking about the 1970s. My audio cassette tapes were all mixes: Armenian, English, Greek and Arabic. I packed lunch for both of us and put it in a backpack. Koko's taxi arrived about a half hour late that morning. I was worried if we were ever going to make our trip that day. He had two tall fishing poles in his hand and sticking out of the cab window. I asked him what took him so long. He told me not every cab driver would want him to ride with them with the two long fishing poles.

I asked, "How did you manage then to get into this one?"

He added that he paid for an extra passenger seat, so he could ride that taxicab. I told him we were going to face the same trouble again all day today with the poles. Then I said, "To avoid all this trouble on the way back, let's reserve this cab for us for the entire day. The driver can drop us off, come back and pick us up at later in the afternoon when we're finished with fishing and ready to go home. This way we'll put the poles in the back seat and both of us can ride with the driver in the front seat. What do you think?"

Koko scratched his head for a moment and then said, "Only if we both can afford to do this."

I said, "I will share the cost with you, don't worry."

I asked Koko this question to set his mind at ease with my calculations. I said, "Koko, hear me out. The cab driver can only take five people at a time in his cab, right?" He agreed. "We don't have to pay more than five people's worth of fee each way. This way he will get to our destination faster because we're going and coming one way. Plus, he won't have to stop and go for anyone. In return, we'll save him time and gas."

Again, Koko scratched his head once more, and before he asked me any other questions, I was already talking to the cab driver about this idea. I don't know why the cab driver scratched his head as well. By the way, I wasn't asking anyone to do rocket science math. The driver asked, "Can we start going and make the decision later?"

I said, "No, you have to make a decision now, or I'll have to talk to another cab driver about this deal."

Well, the man agreed. He didn't want to lose any time. "Get in the cab with your friend." He told us twice, "Let's go, let's go."

We got to our destination about a half hour later. I watched the dark blue beautiful Mediterranean Sea waves, which were splashing heavily on the rocky shore across from the Casino Du Liban. We were going to stand at a distance from the edge of the sea on the rocks and try to fish from that spot. The taxi driver said, "Boys, today is not a good day for fishing. You should consider what I'm telling you."

I said, "Please pick us up around 5:00 p.m., if you can, and don't forget about us." The cab driver said, "Don't worry. I'll be back."

My friend Koko and I picked up the fishing poles and bucket from the cab, and we went to find a place where we could set up our equipment. We set up everything on the flat rocky shore. There was no beach sand around that area. We were about a good thirty to forty feet away from the edge of the deep-sea waves that was hitting the rocks. I put down my bucket next to this big rock, and then I emptied the backpack contents, which were the homemade sandwiches, my tape recorder and a bunch of audio cassettes tapes. I had placed all these items elevated on a nearby rock to try to avoid any water damage to my stuff including the food, just in case a strong wave would hit the shore and wash them away. Our trip would have been much easier if we had an ice chest with us in those days. The food would have been stored in a cooler place than being under the direct sun. Since we were refugees, we couldn't afford fancy items like ice chests. It was far more out of reach to own one. Anyhow, after I set everything out from the backpack down on the rocks, I saw that my friend Koko was preparing the fishing pole lines. He had one line thrown in the water already. I went to his side and took one of the poles from his hand and threw my fishing line in the deep ocean water as well. We got splashed many times with some waves at four to five feet high as we were chatting. Then the winds started to pick up more speed while we were standing at ten feet from the edge of these rocky cliffs, and we were fishing, which was a dangerous situation. We didn't get any bites on our lines, if you know what I mean. We stood there and fished for about three hours. No fish came around in that area that day, or at least we thought they didn't exist. There were no public restrooms available at this sea shore. Koko asked me to hold the fishing pole he had for a moment because nature was calling, and he wanted to go behind one of the rocks and pee.

I said, "Hurry up. I can't manage holding two poles in this wind."

While Koko was gone, somehow the waves started to calm down for a couple of minutes. I could hear my tape recorder at thirty feet behind me. It was playing a Tom Jones song from his early 1970s albums. I turned my back to the ocean, and I secured the poles by placing them in some holes inside the rocks on the ground. My face was toward Koko who had just finished doing what he was supposed to be doing and was just about to come out from behind the rock. As he was walking toward me and facing the sea, he yelled, "Run! Don't stand there, run!" Then all I could hear him say was "The water, the wave." I couldn't understand what he meant, but folks, sure enough, as I turned back to look at the ocean and what was going on, I saw a buildup of a wave of approximately twenty five feet in height behind me, and it was above my head. There was a tremendous water noise that had developed behind me, and that was why I couldn't hear Koko's voice clearly. I witnessed the biggest threat in my life, more than the fear of the Palestinian holding a machine gun on my chest in the past, and more than the possible fall from a ten-story building while I was working in construction. This wave was designed by nature to swallow me into the dark blue ocean waters by having its twenty-five-foot wave come down and hit me on my head as I was standing on solid ground ten feet away from being sucked into the ocean. The ocean waves struck down on my head and forced me to fall on the rocky ground. Then it started to pull everything, including my body, towards the end of the rocky cliff. The water was pulling me into its stomach, sort of like a hungry monster wanting to swallow me inside. Well, you want to know what happened next, right? Again, if you remember what I had told you about God, please believe me that he always loves all of us.

Folks, as I was getting pulled back into the ocean waters, possibly to drown, and as I was sliding at the speed of two to three miles backwards on my stomach toward the sea, my head was trying to stay above the water grasping for air. At one point, I felt my body and legs got stuck and held back by the two fishing poles that I had placed inside the holes in the ground earlier that day while waiting for Koko. I was speechless and in fear again lying wet on the rocks. Both poles were in between my legs as my legs clamped onto them when I was sliding backward on these rocks. The poles were holding me tight to the ground and my body settled for a short moment. My friend ran and helped me get out of the twisted fishing pole lines. Then in two minutes' time I was off the lines and the poles, but all wet to the core. One of my shoes was missing, but my tape recorder was saved. It was knocked around onto one of the corners of another rock, but the bucket and the food were all gone. Then, in a hurry, we picked up the fishing poles and ran carefully but fast enough toward the street where we got dropped off by the cab driver that morning. Here I learned that even man can and should cry to comfort himself. After all we, as humans, are not made from rocks; we are fragile. But I believe we all react differently from one another in the event we face fear.

I learned that everything happens for a reason. No one has control of their own lives. God, the Almighty, is always there for us and He's in control of our destiny and decisions. But we still don't know how to receive God or accept God. It has nothing to do with being religious or going to church every Sunday. It has to do with a personal connection that you should create within your heart to know your creator. We communicate to Him through our prayers daily. I have developed my communication with Him as a daily habit through prayer, thanking him every day for being there for me, for his will and the gifts that we ask and receive from Him in every moment of our lives as well as for his forgiveness. Well I sound like a preacher here, but I'm not. I'm only telling you about the three times I was saved by Him from death where my life was spared by the Almighty. It made me ask him this question. God, why me? It was not up to me to know why, I guess. That's the way it was. I considered myself a very lucky person in what God had done for me, and I am very grateful. I want to emphasis that no material or money in this world can replace a human life.

I turned to my friend Koko, and I hugged him thanking him for letting me have the fishing poles while he was gone. They saved my life. I don't know if it was meant to be, or was it a plan by the upper authority. Then I cried hard from my anger and the fear that I had to face again that afternoon. My friend was kind. He tried to calm me down, and I did calm down after a short while. Now the question was where to go and get my clothes dried? It was almost 4:40 p.m., and I told my friend we'd better wait for the taxicab driver. He would be coming in twenty minutes to pick us up. If we missed him, we would be stuck in that area. He agreed, but he was worried about me getting sick. I said, "Don't worry about me. I'll be just fine."

Sure enough, the man in the black taxicab arrived. He looked at me and said, "What the heck happened to you, son?"

I said, "Let's get in the cab. I'm cold. I'll tell you on the way."

As we were going toward downtown Beirut, I explained to him what had happened that afternoon. He told me that God was there for me for sure. Then he added that last year he knew of a troubled young man who had lost his wife in a car accident, and he couldn't cope with his wife's death and the pain. This young man killed himself by jumping in the water here at the exact spot where we were fishing, and no one had found his body yet.

Wow! That says it all. There was someone's unrested soul who was trying to get me to go with him into the water. I didn't know for sure or didn't know if I should believe in such karma. Then I got even more chilled and scared just hearing the subject itself from the driver. Then in an angry voice, I said to the driver, "Why didn't you tell us this story this morning?" He said he tried to warn us only about the waves, and he didn't know how we would react toward the story if he had told us about it earlier that morning. Then he said most people don't care about this story, that's why he said he avoided telling us about it.

Now we were almost in downtown Beirut where the taxicab was stationed. The man was kind enough and asked, "Listen, boys, where are you going?" We told him about our town called Sed al Boosheria, which was the same location that he had picked us up at that morning. He said he was going home in that direction as well and was going to give us a ride at no charge and help us to get home faster. We both thanked him for his kindness and for his offer, and we took the ride home with him.

When I got home, I said goodbye to my friend Koko and then took the elevator to the fifth floor where my apartment was located because I was walking unevenly due to having one shoe on my right foot only. After I got into my place, I got into a hot shower and cleaned up. I told my parents about what had happened that day. Then I saw the fear on both of my parents' faces. I knew they would be scared, but I had to let it out. I was going to be sick from fear if I didn't. They both hugged me and tried to calm me down as well, and we all broke out in tears that night. We all thanked God for everything that he had done for us so far in our lives. This was my third time facing death in my young life. It was not my choice, but every time it happened, I learned something new from each incident. It made me a better, more mature and stronger person at a young age.

CHAPTER

18

New Year's Eve 1974, and the Street Fight

Time was flying, and many months had gone by. The year was ending, and the Christmas holiday and New Year's Eve celebration into 1975 was around the corner once more.

We were thinking the New Year celebration in Beirut, Lebanon was going to be much like the celebration back home in Baghdad. As a matter of fact, we thought it would be better than the celebrations in Baghdad. It was our belief that because Lebanon's government, which was half Christian and half Muslim in power in terms of ruling the country, could lean more toward the spirit of the holidays compared to the way we had been celebrating Christmas back home. We had celebrated the New Year's Eve holiday back home very quietly. We had gathered with all our relatives and had a private and conservative party until midnight. Then after midnight, most of the women were getting things done around the kitchen, and, in the meantime, they were complaining about their age saying, "There goes another year and we're getting older." They were also complaining about how their husbands had been contributing to making them older and not younger because of all the demands that they had to put up with in their lives and to raise a family. The men already had their plans set to a gathering around the dinner table and playing a game of poker, but with real money, of course. Gambling was a forbidden game in a Muslim society like Iraq, and, unlike Lebanon, there were no casinos anywhere. The men were cautiously playing inside the house on the formal dining room table with all the curtains closed that faced the street traffic. Oh, I forgot about the best part of it all, which is that all our gift exchanges were done on New Year's Eve, and Santa visited that night as well because as Armenians we go by the old Gregorian calendar to celebrate Christmas, which is celebrated on the sixth of January and not on the twenty-fifth of December like the rest of the world.

On New Year's Eve gatherings like ours, it's customary for all the children to say a poem or sing a song before they can get their gifts from Santa. Usually, it's whatever they learned that year in school, or by their parents. Parents take a great deal of pride in their children, because they preserve their native heritage and language. It was important to know some songs or poems; otherwise, Santa was not going to reward you that night with a gift. I used to call it extortion. But, most likely, you would get your gift the next morning when you wake up. We were all, somewhat, forced to follow our parents' rules. Generally speaking, the pride and the ego-driven individuals like some of our parents in those days were a contributing factor, which had developed to have events in this fashion to take place on New Year's Eve.

We were residing temporarily in Beirut, Lebanon, and this was our first time experiencing the celebration of New Year's Eve abroad. The New Year celebration for the previous year of 1973 didn't mean much for us to celebrate because we were just newcomers to Beirut, and it went without any celebration due to many unexplained reasons. But we were not totally alone or totally away from our relatives for that year's celebration. There was my father's sister, Sonia, and her family; my mother's sister, Veronica, and her family and also my uncle, my mother's brother, and his wife; the latter didn't have any children. We were encircled by some of our relatives and other families who also made it and took Lebanon as refuge to reside in next to us in the same neighborhood. Most of them, like us, had left their homes and their country by selling all their belongings just to get to Beirut, Lebanon and in order to register with the World Council of Churches to get to America, the land of the free, as I have said in the previous chapters.

New Year's Eve 1974 had approached. We had a small Christmas tree with hardly any lights or ornaments on it, and it was placed in the living room in one corner. My mom and the other ladies cooked for the party. It was a very joyful and happy night for all of us to begin with; especially, since I knew we were living a better life emotionally infused with freedom as refugees, and we didn't have to fear anyone spying on all our movements. The moment had arrived, and everyone was getting settled in in our living room on the fifth floor. Our building faced the street with a balcony, which had a sliding glass door. My father had already shopped for hard and soft drinks. The alcohol was only for the adults, of course. Unlike back home in Iraq, there were only a few liquor stores which were open to the public legally due to it being a Muslim country. All the liquor stores were owned by mostly Christians as far as I can remember.

Then a lot of Muslims, especially men, who didn't care about their own religious beliefs, consumed alcoholic beverages.

It is New Year's Eve 1974, around 9:00 p.m., and our home was full of people. We welcomed everyone with some refreshments, and then with the first toast we remembered our relatives who hadn't made the choice to flee the country and be with us to celebrate an event like this and wished them well and good health. They claimed that we were all crazy to sell everything and leave Iraq. For one reason or another, they didn't want to be a part of the choice that we imposed on ourselves. They had ignored the opportunity to take the chance to save their own children from the tyrannical regime and unjust rulings. The next toast was for "America, here we come." Then the following toast was "Down with Saddam's regime," but this latter toast was mentioned in a low tone of voice, of course, due to fears that were planted in everyone's heart which, couldn't be erased or extinguished with overnight celebrations yet. These fears were still fresh in everyone's minds regarding arrests, torture, false accusations, and death (Most of these fears were being planted in the public's minds through the television showing their brutality at work if an individual did not comply with the regime's rules during the time Saddam was in charge of the internal security department of Iraq.) Another toast was for all the men in the family for being so brave in making such a decision to flee the country. The last toast was unique where we all had a kick out of it as a joke and that was for anyone who said a sentence in plain English. As a matter of fact, none of us knew English very well; only those who had the education. But some of us who knew English were shy to come forward and say a sentence.

The music began to play. It was a very small juke box and not like the big stereo unit that we had back home. This small juke box was loud enough to be heard and enjoyed. Unsurprisingly, I was pulled out of my seat by my uncle and pushed to the middle of the living room to dance. The setup for our living room furniture in a three hundred square foot area for that night was not bad. It was like an I-shape almost where we all had enough room to move around and dance. The next thing was to play a simple Middle Eastern game called Luck with two groups (A and B) consisting of five to six adults in each group sitting down and facing each other with one of the individuals from the opponent group trying to find a hidden ring inside a closed fist of the challenging group and vice versa. After one hour of playing, group A had won with two games out of three, and one player from that group kept the ring.

The game was over, and everyone was back to eating and drinking again. The time was 11:58 p.m. on December 31st, 1974, and it was two minutes before the New Year. We learned there was no Santa this year because we were all in the same boat financially. No one could afford to buy gifts for anyone. After all, as I mentioned previously, all of us were working at very low wages to survive as refugees and just being around each other was a gift itself for that year. The moment had arrived, and everyone yelled, "Happy New Year!" Then we heard this loud noise coming from outside of our apartment. It was like a war going on outside. Most Lebanese citizens who had a gun or a machine gun were shooting in the air celebrating the New Year. We were all scared. We never had such a thing happen in our country where everyone can have a gun and shoot it freely in the air. The only people who possessed guns were the police, some government's employees of the regime, the army, and some of the Arab tribe leaders and their followers. Wow, that night the whole sky turned into dotted lights going upward. It was not a smart thing to do; it was foolish. A lot of people were injured in this process because of the fallen bullets. Let's not forget the physics of what goes up must come down. That's a fact. All eighteen of us ran and took refuge in the hallways in the middle of our apartment building. The hallway was small, and we were like sardines in a can piled up next to each other and away from any windows or sliding doors. Our happy hours were over, and ten to fifteen minutes later everything was calm again, and the nonstop gun firing in the air had come to a halt. When things were calm again, we went back to the living room. We found several fallen bullets inside our balcony area. Luckily, the bullets didn't reach or go through the sliding glass doors. Wow, it was some New Year's Eve we witnessed, but we had to get used to it. I guess that's living in Lebanon. After the party some of our relatives started to go home trying to get to their comfort zones without getting hurt, and I couldn't blame them. But my uncle George was a brave man. He asked his brother-in-law, who is also my Uncle Armo, how about taking his mother-in-law home with his new VW Bug that he had purchased lately. He asked my dad as well to accompany them, but my dad was hesitant to join them. I repeatedly said I would like to go and insisted on it because I wanted to explore the outside world on New Year's Eve. I was young and restless. My dad got upset and said, "Enough! You can't go with them. What if something happens to you?" Then my Uncle George, my dad's brother-in-law, interfered and told my father, "Hey Mike, don't worry. I'll protect him," and pulled a small pistol from his jacket pocket and said, "I have this." We were all surprised that he had a gun with him all that time in our home without our knowledge. Then the entire subject of fear had changed. Now the interest of the men went toward the gun because no one had a gun before in Baghdad. Twenty minutes later, and while all the men were still gathered around George exploring his pistol, I asked, "Are we going, Uncle?" He answered back saying, "In a moment, son."

Well, I wanted to go and see what had happened around the city with all the commo-tion that went on earlier that night. I was not scared at all. Sure enough, both of my uncles, Uncle George and Uncle Armo, and I along with Armo's mother-in-law went toward a town heavily populated by Armenians called Bourj Hammod where my Uncle Armo's mother-in-law lived with her son and his family. On the way there, the street we were driving on was jammed because of the New Year's Eve traffic. It was moving very slow, and, as I remember, no one had any respect for traffic laws in Beirut that night. You couldn't afford to insult anyone in Beirut or direct them to doing things your way because most people had guns or machine guns in their trunks or in the glove compartments of their cars. I said most and not all.

We got stuck in street traffic after a short drive, but after ten minutes the traffic ahead of us had cleared and gotten lighter. Uncle George moved forward very carefully but got stopped again. This time we witnessed a black car, an expensive Jaguar, which was stopped and was blocking the street, and a young man who was heavily drunk had his arm inside the driver's side window, which was half closed, was holding the driver's throat with his hand and trying to choke him. He was cussing him out so bad in both Armenian and Arabic. The driver couldn't drive, which had caused the blocking of the traffic lane on our side of the road. At first, we, meaning my uncles, didn't want to get involved until my Uncle Armo started to lower our car window on his side and started shouting to the drunken man, "Hey! Move on! Get your problems solved elsewhere! We need to pass!" When the drunken man saw our car was stopped next to him in traffic, and with one of his hands still holding the Jaguar driver's neck, he turned around and started to cuss at my uncle telling him your mother is this, and your mother is that. I was sitting in the back seat of the VW Bug with my uncle's mother-in-law beside me. At first, my Uncle George told his brother-in-law not to listen to the drunken man because he didn't know what he was saying. My Uncle Armo was hot-blooded, but then he calmed down a bit until the driver of the Jaguar started yelling for help and that he couldn't breathe. Here's where all hell broke loose. Just like my Uncle Armo and his temper, he was waiting for an excuse to get out of the car. He got out of the car and ran toward the drunken man. At first, he used his left hand to grab this man's 1970s style long hair, and then he used his right hand to punch the man right in his nose and face. The punches were very strong, and it made the drunken man let go of the driver's neck. Also, the punches had made this drunken man kneel in front of my uncle. Now my uncle took advantage of the situation by punching the man in his face several times while asking him, "What did you say about my mother?" He was really going crazy and was going to kill this drunken man with his punches. I witnessed this whole thing, and it looked funny because now the drunken man started to ask for help for himself and calling others to rescue him from my uncle's punches and grips. Well, my Uncle George and I got out of the car and ran towards my Uncle Armo trying to end the fight. Uncle George and I reached Uncle Armo, and we held one of his arms to stop him from punching this young man more. The entire street was still blocked, and by now everyone was enjoying the show without paying for a boxing match ticket, if you know what I mean. It was like an open street boxing match. Then we asked the driver of the Jaguar if he was okay, and we asked him to pull his car to the side, so traffic could move. We placed the beaten drunken man on the curb away from the street traffic, and I saw one of his eyes was swollen from my uncle's punches and was bleeding. It was not something I would be proud of my uncle for doing. Then Uncle George also had to move his VW Bug from the middle of the street as well so that the traffic could flow again. I heard my Uncle George asking the driver of the Jaguar a question as to why this young man was choking him in the first place. Well, at everyone's surprise, the driver of the Jaguar said that the young man was very much in love with his daughter, and he was against their marriage. Wow, all this for a marriage approval. We were living in a crazy town with some crazy lifestyles, and that's for sure!

Someone must have called the police because police cars had just passed by us to park their vehicles. We had to flee from that location as fast as we could so no one would go to jail that night by driving out of that area, turning around and driving on the opposite direction of the street so we couldn't be detected that we were there in the first place. After all, we couldn't afford to go to jail and have an arrest record. We were advised not to fight because that would damage our relations with the refugee office (WCOC).

Wow! After all that, I learned one thing from this incident, and that is never get involved in something when it's not your issue or if you don't know the details. Plus, someone choking someone else's throat might seem bad, but we shouldn't judge too fast just by looking at the picture, but it was only humanly right to get involved and save a life. Instead, we should call the police and not take matters in our hands unless we we're allowed to interfere. My uncle was lucky that night because the young drunken man didn't have a gun with him, or maybe he did, and it was in his car, but because he was drunk, he couldn't focus to go and get it to protect himself from my Uncle Armo's punches. It was not the best approach to solve problems. As the saying goes, "Don't fight fire with fire."

It was January 1st, 1975, and it just got started two hours ago with a fist fight and gun shots. What an experience that was! I had just witnessed and learned from it. I didn't want to see all that violence, but maybe it was time for me to grow up. I have always been a peace-seeking person and a peaceful person, but I always believed and said that "There's much to gain from peace than losing in a war". This is what I had always agreed to accomplish in life and with the world that I had lived in back in the '70s. Unfortunately, it was different, and it was in another country and another lifestyle, but ultimately it was similar because at the end they were all people.

CHAPTER
19

A Civil War, and Rushing to the Airport

I t was still January 1975. We had been turned down in July 1974 by the World Council of Churches to obtain visas to travel to America, or, in another words, our refugee case had been declined to go to America. Then in November of 1974 we applied with the Australian Embassy to immigrate there instead. Three months after applying to the Australian Embassy, we were called for an interview and a date was scheduled for our family to appear. This was great news that the Aussies, "down under", were working much faster than the Americans, but, again, and to be realistic, America was a big country with big demands for immigrants. That's why it took a longer time in order to get refugee cases settled to travel to the United States of America. Or, did it? Then, again, for us not to get our plans exposed, we used a great deal of discretion in order to keep it a secret from others, even from our own relatives except Uncle Armo, just in case they unknowingly spoke to others about it.

We got up one morning in late February 1975, and we all dressed well and went into downtown Beirut for an interview with the Australian Embassy. I can tell you this, all went well, and we did well. The ambassador at the time was very funny in nature and in a joking mood. He had an enjoyable personality; a type that you wish to see around more often and at all the times. We hadn't experienced this kind of welcoming attitude anywhere else.

Unfortunately, I can't recall his name. The ambassador said that he would let us know in thirty days about his decision regarding our case. We all thanked him and walked out. When we came home, Uncle Armo and his wife had paid us a visit. We told them about the morning interview, and Uncle Armo was surprised and very happy that we wouldn't be left behind, and there was new hope for us to be settled elsewhere. Approximately two weeks later, around March 14, we received a letter of approval from the Australian Embassy to immigrate to Sydney, Australia. Wow! It was a big relief for all of us after living almost one year and ten months in Lebanon and after all we went through together in this journey. Now we had renewed hopes, and we were very happy once more. But my dad's heart was still set to go to the United States of America, a place where he had dreams and hopes for himself.

Well folks, at the beginning of this book I told you how God and his will had never been apart and away from our home and my family and how he always looked upon us and saved us from troubles and wrongdoings. Two weeks later around March 28, 1975, we were called for a final interview with the World Council of Churches' (WCOC) office. We had already lost all our hopes to go to America. To our surprise and after the interview with the WCOC office, they asked us to go and get our physical checkups and chest x-rays done right away, which was normal procedure for refugees to follow. This could only indicate that we had approval by the WCOC's office as well to leave for America pending good physical and healthy body conditions for all of us in the family.

All of us, including my grandmother, went to proceed with our medical examinations as we were asked to comply with. Our results were negative, and we all passed the medical exams that afternoon. On April 7, 1975, sure enough, it was "America, here we come!" We got our visas, and we were ready to immigrate to the U.S. Wow and, again, a big wow! How lucky can you get? We were holding multiple visas in our hands, and we had a choice of immigrating to the U.S. or to Australia. Both of my parents said that they should never make a fast decision on this one, and it didn't matter to them because both countries were very fine places to live in and start a new life. But since we had no clue of either country's lifestyles yet, we had to think and ask around to gather information regarding life values of each country which would help us decide where to go from here. Discussion was a must among the adults of our family and our relatives' families, and since we had visas, then the matter was no longer a secret and it was okay for our relatives to know the issue and help my parents make a choice for all of us in the family. Well, to be honest and regardless what went on between my dad and John's dad, my heart was leaning toward Sydney knowing that we had relatives living there. But I also loved America as well because all along as I was growing up in Baghdad, I was listening to songs on the American radio program, which was called the Sound of America. It was broadcasted on the FM radio frequency, which had inspired me very much as a young adult.

Let's divert for a moment and let me tell you what was going on with the FM radio frequency in Iraq. Back in the 1970's, all FM radios in Iraq were forbidden for the public to have and listen to. This was ordered by the Iraqi government regime at that time for several reasons. First, Sound of America was American propaganda against the Baath regime as it was explained to me when I was young. How much of this was fact is uncertain, and whoever got caught listening to this station was going to be imprisoned. Second, there was another reason why the FM radios were forbidden for the public to have. It was because most police car radios were using the FM frequency to communicate with, and whoever had FM reception on their radio, they could listen to the police conversations as well. That is if you knew how to tune the frequency to the police station. I was given this information by my father, and, again, how much of this is fact I don't know. I believe my father was possibly over reacting at times to protect us due to his fears after he had left the harsh Iraqi prison because listening to any American subject or radio program will put him and his family in danger, if we get caught. This was the case with the FM radios in Iraq, or maybe it was my dad's imagination. Possibly, out of his overprotecting nature, he was trying to keep me from using that FM frequency on the radio to avoid any complications with the local authorities back home. I must admit that we had an FM radio device in our household at the time, but I managed to keep the radio on low volume every time I had to use it, and I was using it at nights only and before we went to sleep in the open rooftop of our home in Baghdad. Iraqi homes have a different architectural design than American homes. The rooftops were built flat with walls as perimeters around the roof where you could set up your beds in the summer season only in the open air watching the stars and enjoying the cool breeze of the Arabian nights while you slept.

By listening to the Sound of America station constantly every night, it created some motive within me to want to travel to America more than Sydney. I wanted to see Tom Jones, Engelbert Humperdinck, The Temptations, Barry White, Frank Sinatra, Dean Martin, and many other soul, jazz, and classical singers in person. I always loved to be in the land of the free as the Sound of America station did an excellent job in advertising and promoting songs about the American culture. I knew very little about Australia myself, but having relatives in a new country to live in verses knowing no one in America was the topic of discussion for the adults for days to come in trying to decide our travel destination. Three days had past, and it was April 10, 1975. My parents' discussions with the others were completed. Again, there was no more fear about telling anyone about our plans, but everyone started to envy us again. Now we held visas for two different countries in our possession. The final choice was made, and the final decision was to travel to America. The United States of America had won the contest. There was an important reason why my dad's heart was set for America. He loved Hollywood since he was a teenager, and he always wanted to be an actor.

The World Council of Churches informed us about the date and time that was planned for us, along with other refugee families totaling 120 people; men, women, and children, to travel to New York with a stopover to transit through London, England. The travel date was set for April 28, 1975. It was a glorious day for all of us. Now all the furniture that we had in our apartment had to be out and stored away, but we had to lend it to my Aunt Veronica's family (my mother's sister). The deal was that since we were moving out of the apartment by end of the month, they were to occupy our apartment as a new tenant. We had to speak to the landlord about this and arrange for them to take over everything that we had left behind. They had fled Iraq as well, and now they were newcomers to Lebanon to receive refugee status just like we had for approximately the past two years.

Finally, after almost two years of waiting and suffering as refugees, the travel date had arrived, and just two days earlier on April 26, 1975, we noticed that signs of civil war and civil unrest were obviously going to take place in Beirut. The city was getting tense. We could hear machine guns at nights and some army tanks and vehicles which were moving around Beirut and the surrounding towns. We didn't know why, but it created some anxiety and fear in all of us since we had seen this kind of event in the past in Baghdad, the capital of Iraq, which had revolutions happening to take over the government every three to five years.

The ruling government was getting thrown out and was getting replaced with a new one. This was before the Baath regime had come to power for the second and permanent time in 1968. For almost the past two years since we settled in Beirut, the fear of any kind of revolution were defused from our minds, and for something like that to happen again, it might possibly be bad karma for us to accept at the eleventh hour. The little we knew about Lebanon's internal affairs, we had to ask ourselves, "What had just gotten into this beautiful city?" But there were no answers to make us understand their situation.

On the contrary, on the morning of April 28, 1975, we were all tired from lack of sleep and worries because on the night of April 27, a fight between Palestinians and the Lebanese army and others had started. All night long our prayers were for every soul and for all the other refugees who were going to be left behind in Beirut because their time hadn't come to travel because they hadn't gotten their visas yet. Our prayers were for our relatives as well as for those who were going to be left behind in Lebanon, waiting for their fate to be decided by the World Council of Churches. This was, again, God's will for all of this to happen.

We got up that morning and ate a fast breakfast. Most of our relatives, aunts, and uncles with their families were at our doorstep in the early morning hours to say goodbye to us. Everyone was worried about our safe trip to the airport. A lot of tears were shed by everyone already. I loved everyone, and I encouraged them not to be too late to meet up with us in the U.S. Some of them started laughing, but I was trying to ease the tension. We found a local taxi driver who was a Muslim fellow and a brave man to take us to the airport on that fearful morning. We packed the cab with six of our luggage and said good-bye to everyone for the last time. This was the second time in the past two years of our lives where we had to travel and change countries. We had to start another life from zero again in America as it was now our final destination.

We had one and half hours to reach the airport and meet our flight. The cab was moving very fast, but the city was in the middle of a civil war. There were bombshells all over, and you could hear machine gun shots in the open as well as single shots from handguns. It was a very scary and fearful moment for us to witness and experience throughout the taxi ride. We moved and stopped several times because you could see some rockets were going from one point to another across town and damaging structures. We were about twenty minutes closer to Beirut's airport. The cab driver said he couldn't go any further because the war was getting very tense, and he was worried about our safety as well as his. My father begged the taxi driver saying,

"Listen, we will pay whatever money you want. Please don't go back. This is what we've been waiting for two years to happen, and that is to get to our freedom." Our taxi driver noticed the pain in my father's eyes and on his face. The driver was a very smart man, and he saw the need of doing good regardless of the danger and fear of the situation. He understood the sacrifices that we all went through to get here and not to be able to make it. He came up with a fast idea. He said he was going to move some of our luggage from the trunk and put them on the top rails of his cab. Then he asked if we had any white shirts that we didn't need. Right away my mom opened one of the bags, and she pulled my white shirt and gave it to the cab driver. Then the driver reached and grabbed a piece of wood from the street to use it as a stick. He wrapped the white shirt on the wooden stick and used it as a flag for surrender and peace and held it in his hand high enough for others to notice. He said he couldn't guarantee our bags from being saved or not getting damaged on the top of his cab because he was going to drive fast without stopping to reach to the airport. He moved our travel bags and placed them on the top rails of the taxicab. Then he tied them to the cab railings in a hurry. All this happened within five to seven minutes. He said we were using the bags on his top rails as protection from the fallen bullets and that would protect us from getting hurt too, hopefully. Then he said, "I hope you don't mind that."

My dad thanked him for his efforts and told him he didn't care if he went to America without the bags, but that we must get to the airport at any cost in order to take the flight. This was the travel schedule we were given by the World Council of Churches. If we lost the flight, then we would have had to wait again for the next flight on a different day and time. Only God could tell when or how many months more we would have to be delayed from travelling again. We had to do this, and we had every good reason to try and catch our flight that day at any cost.

The cab driver's idea was great; it worked. He drove very fast and in a zigzag pattern at times to avoid rocket-propelled grenades (RPG) that were fired on us. Finally, we got to the airport, and we rushed in. We were late ten minutes for our flight. You can imagine the pain we went through. The cab driver only got his promised fee from us, and not one penny more; that was his wish. He wished us good luck. He was going to stay at the airport terminal until the fight decreased, and then he was going to go home. My dad told him he didn't know how to thank him enough as a human being. Although he was a Muslim fellow, but just like us Christians, he loved to help people in time of need as well.

Now some of the church authorities were at the airport terminal to check and process us into the flight. We were scheduled to fly by Swiss Air, which was going to pick us up and fly us to London first.

Let me tell you how this all ended. The moment we were dropped off by the taxicab at the airport, we had to run inside for cover; then our luggage was hand- delivered later by airport security.

After settling in, I had to run to one of the airport's glass windows which were over-looking the runway. I wanted to see the plane that was to deliver us to our freedom and saw the Swiss Air plane was parked and waiting for us to depart from Beirut Lebanon. The war got very tense and the sound of gunfire and bombs were non-stop. Fear was a visiting factor in everyone's hearts and minds, and we all wanted to depart after two years of living a harsh refugee life and working in Lebanon.

Forty-five minutes later we had a break and were directed to go out and walk hastily towards the runway in order to board the plane as fast as we could because the airport's buses were not in operation that day. I had to help my grandmother and accompanied her and asked the rest of my family to run ahead of us to board the Swiss Air plane. I walked with my grandmother, and we made it and boarded the plane.

It was so hot and muggy inside the plane since the engines were not in motion yet. We were asked by the captain to sit tight as it was going to be a risky flight, hoping that no one would try to shoot any rocket grenades to bring the plane down while we wanted to take off. Our only friend accompanying us was silence. Then suddenly, peace and quiet took over the airport runway…no gunfire, no rockets and our plane engines started to operate, and we waited on the runway for another half hour. There were two other refugee planes taking off ahead of us in a hurry, and we were the third in line. Our plane took off next, and after 20 minutes in the air we heard the captain's voice once more saying, "I would like you to shout and cheer as loud as you can because we are safe now and on our way to London." None of us could speak English, but earlier at the airport's desk one individual was designated by the church authorities to lead us through the trip because he spoke English. He had translated the captain's message to us.

You can imagine everyone's joy and happiness when we all realized that finally we were flying to our freedom!

APPENDIX

I

Facts about Iraq

The Republic of Iraq, SW (southwest) Asia, bounded on the N (north) by Turkey; on the E (east) by Iran; on the S (south) by Saudi Arabia, Kuwait, and the Persian Gulf; and on the W (west) by Jordan and Syria. The country has an area of 434,924 sq. km (167,925 sq. miles). Some of the world's greatest ancient civilizations were developed in the area that makes up modern Iraq.

Land and Resources

The N portion of Iraq, known as Al-Jazira, is mountainous. Elevations of nearly 2,135 m (nearly 7,000 ft) above sea level are reached near the Turkish border, and in the NE part of the country are peaks ranging to 3,600 m (11,811 ft), atop Haji Ibrahim, the highest point in Iraq.

Farther S the country slopes downward to form a broad central alluvial plain, which is occupied by the valley of the Tigris and Euphrates rivers. The extreme SE portion of Iraq is a low-lying, marshy area adjacent to the Persian Gulf on which Iraq fronts for a distance of about 40 km (about 25 mi). West of the Euphrates, the land rises gradually to meet the Syrian Desert.

Present-day Iraq occupies the greater part of the ancient land of Mesopotamia, the plain between the Tigris and Euphrates rivers. The two rivers flow through Iraq from NW to SE. They meet about 160 km (about 100 mi) N of the Persian Gulf to form the Shatt Al-Arab, which drains into the gulf. The chief tributaries of the Tigris are the Great Zab, the Little Zab, and the Diyala Rivers. Level terrain separates the Tigris and Euphrates rivers in their lower courses. In ancient times the Tigris and the Euphrates were joined by a network of canals and irrigation ditches, which directed the water of the higher-lying and more westerly Euphrates across the valley into the Tigris.

Climate

Most of Iraq has a continental climate with extremes of heat and cold. The mountainous N portion of the country has cool summers and cold winters, often accompanied by snow. In central Iraq the summers are long and hot and the winters short and cool. The mean January temperature in Baghdad is 9.4° C (49° F); for the months of July and August it's 33.3°C (92° F) and temperatures as high as 50.6°C (123° F) have been recorded. In the S area around the Persian Gulf some of the highest atmospheric temperatures in the world have been recorded, and humidity is high. In the NE highlands rainfall is considerable during October to May, but farther S on the central alluvial plain, precipitation is slight, averaging approximately 152 mm (approximately 6 in) annually. The Syrian Desert gets little precipitation or none. (historychannel.com, 2006)

Overview of Governments and Regime Changes in Iraq (1953–1979)

I.   May 2, 1953

King Faisal II formally assumed the throne on his eighteenth birthday (I was told by my father about this event. I was not born yet).

II.   July 14, 1958

The country was proclaimed a republic. King Faisal II, who assumed the throne, was killed by a sudden coup d'état led by the Iraqi general, Karim Abdul Kassem (I was told by my father about this event as well. I was three years old at the time).

III.   February 8, 1963

Gen. Kareem Abdul Kassem was overthrown by a group of officers from the Baath party, General Kassem was assassinated the next day, February 9, 1963, and Abdul Salam Arif became the president (I was only eight years old when my father turned on the black and white TV set in 1963).

IV.   April 13, 1966

Abdul Salam Arif, the new president, was killed in a helicopter crash, and his brother Gen. Abdul Rahman Arif was named his successor as president (I can only see and hear for the second time in my young life that people are cheering again for another downfall of another so-called bad man. I was ten and a half years old then).

V.   July 17, 1968

General Arif's government was overthrown, and Maj. Gen. Ahmed Hassan al Baker was appointed head of the revolutionary command council of the Baath Party ruling Iraq (all Iraqis were cheering again, as I remember).

VI.   July 16, 1979

President Baker stepped down for presumably a health reason, and so-called General Saddam Hussein replaced him from his own Baath party to rule Iraq (the black chapter for humanity was just about to begin).

Important Facts - Iraq Mentioned in the Bible

1. The Garden of Eden was in Iraq.

2. Mesopotamia, which is now Iraq, was the cradle of civilization!

3. Noah built the ark in Iraq.

4. The tower of Babel was in Iraq.

5. Abraham was from Ur, which is in southern Iraq.

6. Isaac's wife Rebekah is from Nahor, which is in Iraq.

7. Jacob met Rachel in Iraq.

8. Jonah preached in Nineveh, which is in Iraq.

9. Assyria, which is in Iraq, conquered the ten tribes of Israel.

10. Amos cried out in Iraq.

11. Babylon, which is in Iraq, destroyed Jerusalem.

12. Daniel was in the lion's den in Iraq.

13. The three Hebrew children were in the fire in Iraq (the lord Jesus has been in Iraq too, as the fourth person in the fiery furnace).

14. Belshazzar, the king of Babylon, saw the "writing on the wall" in Iraq.

15. Nebuchadnezzar, king of Babylon, carried the Jews captive into Iraq.

16. Ezekiel preached in Iraq.

17. The wise men were from Iraq.

18. Peter preached in Iraq.

19. The "empire of man" described in revelation is called Babylon which was a city in Iraq.

20. Israel is the nation most often mentioned in the Bible. But do you know which nation is second? It is Iraq! However, that is not the name that is used in the Bible. The names used in the Bible are Babylon, Land of Shinar, and Mesopotamia. The word Mesopotamia means between the two rivers, more exactly between the Tigris and Euphrates Rivers. The name Iraq means country with deep roots. Indeed, Iraq is a country with deep roots and is a very significant country in the Bible. No other nation, except Israel, has more history and prophecy associated with it than Iraq.

(Ciniraj, 2005)

APPENDIX

II

Pictures and Documents

My grandfather (1901-1948). Passed away in Iraq due to Leukemia.

My grandmother (1902-1988). Lived in America for ten years
and passed away in Iraq due to kidney failure.

My great grandmother an Armenian Genocide survivor (1859-1962).
She lived to be 103 years old.

My parents in 1954 during their engagement party.

My parents in December 1999. A New Year's Eve dinner-dance celebration
in the U.S.

My father receiving his first-place trophy in 1947 from King Faisal II of Iraq.

My father during the final 100-meter race in 1948. An object was thrown at him purposely and had distracted his win for first-place to represent Iraq in the Olympics.

My father with his first-place trophy and medals in 1947.

My house in the suburbs of Baghdad, Iraq. This picture was taken in 1970.

Kindergarten graduation ceremony in 1960, and I was reciting on stage.

My Aunt Safina's wedding day. Both my parents are at her
side, and I am on the far left with a striped jacket.

My cousin Jack (on the right) and me as Boy Scouts
in 1969.

My high school teacher, Mr. Hesham in a dark jacket, during
an Iraqi Boy Scout camping trip in 1971. I am second from
Mr. Hesham on the far left.

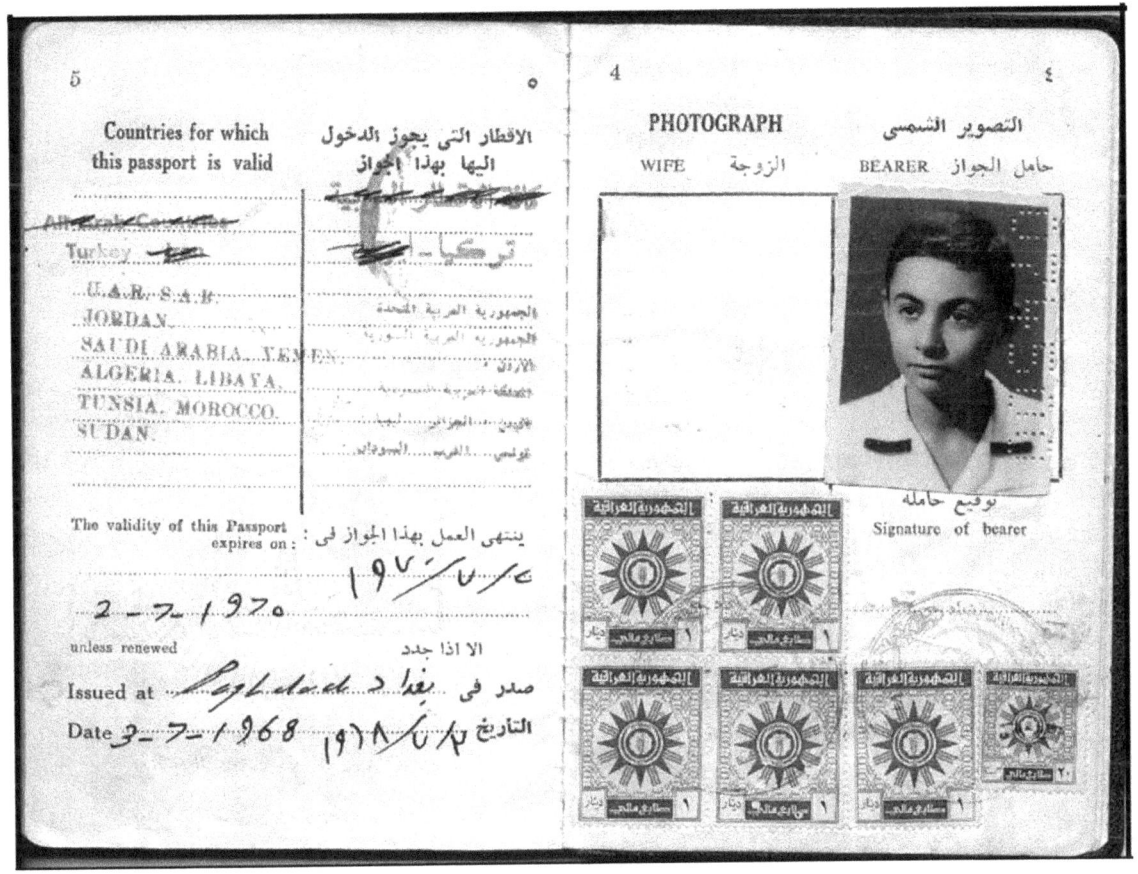

My discriminatory passport (for males) in 1970. See top left for the original
visa stamp that was altered by the passport office forbidding male individuals to
travel to Lebanon by the Iraqi regime.

My parents' passports issued in 1971 and 1975. Notice the difference between the male and female passport bearer. The same discriminatory male passport where the original visa stamp was altered by the passport office forbidding male individuals to travel to Lebanon by the Iraqi regime.

My Aunt Sofina and her husband Steve after Sunday mass in Baghdad in 1969.

My Uncle Armo, his wife on his left, and his mother-in-law on his right in 1961.

My step cousin Jack when he returned to Iraq in 1981. Standing tall at his father's vineyard before joining the Iraqi Army.

My step cousin Jack after the Iraq-Iran war. He was admitted into a psychiatric hospital after running away from the service. This picture was taken in 2004.

Baghdad's Armenian Athletic Club (AAC) basketball youth team. My number was 13. Picture was taken in 1968.

The AAC's Boy Scout's trip to northern Iraq in the Kurdish village of Zakho. This picture was taken during a sports competition in 1970. My step cousin Jack is standing at the far left, and my cousin John is 4th from the left.

WORLD COUNCIL OF CHURCHES
DIVISION OF INTER-CHURCH AID, REFUGEE AND WORLD SERVICE

IMMEUBLE JOSEPH & NOUR TAKTOUK
RUE BADARO (FORET DES PINS KFOURY)
P. O. BOX 11-5209 — BEIRUT, LEBANON

TELEPHONE: 381368 - 381369
CABLE: WORLDCOUNCIL BEIRUT

April 21, 1975

TO WHOM IT MAY CONCERN

(4)

This is to certify that the above-named
has/have applied to this Office for immigration to
the United States and that ~~his/her~~/their case is
under processing by the U.S. authorities.

~~He/She~~/They ~~is~~/are expected to leave
Lebanon for the United States ~~within the next~~
on April 28, 1975.

N. Essayan
Acting Resettlement Officer
Service to Refugees.

NE/dt.

The finalized approval letter for our departure from Lebanon sent from the World
Council of Churches (WCOC) in 1975.

Bibliography

Baker, m. (2013, October). Ehow mom. Retrieved October 27, 2013, from ehow.com: Http://www.ehow.com/list_6394786_harmful-effects-potassium-chloride.html

Ciniraj, p. P. (2005, June 16). Iraq in the bible -- interesting facts. Retrieved November 24, 2011, from free republic-salem voice ministries: http://www.freerepublic.com/ focus/f-chat/1424483/posts

Historychannel.com (2006, July), Retrieved July 14, 2006, from historychannel.com: http://www.historychannel.com/thesearch/the _resourcedetail_do?encyc_id=212866

History of telecommunications and post in Iraq. (2009, November 16). Retrieved December 13, 2013, from wikipedia: http://www.thefullwiki.org/Iraqi_ telecommunications_and_ post_company

Venison, p. J. (2013, April 30). Casino du liban. Retrieved November 24, 2013, from wiki-pedia: http://en.wikipedia.org/wiki/casino_du_liban